D0397636

UPSIDE

UP**SIDE**

Profiting from the Profound

Demographic Shifts Ahead

KENNETH W. GRONBACH

WITH M. J. MOYE

AMACOM

AMERICAN MANAGEMENT ASSOCIATION

New York • Atlanta • Brussels • Chicago • Mexico City • San Francisco
Shanghai • Tokyo • Toronto • Washington, DC

This publication is designed to provide accurate and authoritative information in re-gard to the subject matter covered. It is sold with the understanding that the publisher is not engaged in rendering legal, accounting, or other professional service. If legal advice or other expert assistance is required, the services of a competent professional person should be sought.

Library of Congress Cataloging-in-Publication Data

Names: Gronbach, Kenneth W., author. | Moye, M. J., author.
Title: Upside : profiting from the profound demographic shifts ahead / by
  Kenneth W. Gronbach, with M.J. Moye.
Description: New York, NY : AMACOM, [2017]
Identifiers: LCCN 2016044183 (print) | LCCN 2017000734 (ebook) | ISBN
  9780814434697 (hardcover) | ISBN 9780814434703 (eBook)
Subjects: LCSH: Target marketing--United States. | Consumers--United States.
  | Marketing research--United States. | Demography--United States. | United
  States--Population.
Classification: LCC HF5415.127 .G763 2017 (print) | LCC HF5415.127 (ebook) |
  DDC 658.8/3--dc23
LC record available at https://lccn.loc.gov/2016044183

10 9 8 7 6 5 4 3 2

CONTENTS

Foreword

I HAVE SPENT A good part of four decades studying and relying upon demographics. For some, the use of population trends and statistics is the stuff (or perhaps the stuffy) of cocktail parties and testy holiday dinner conversation. But for those of us who make forecasts and guide our clients through the turbulent waters of disruptive change, demographics provide the tools, the content, the baseline, and the trend lines to buttress our peek into the future.

Our capacity to collect statistical data continues to grow by leaps and bounds, and with breathtaking speed. We are well into the world of Big Data—mind-blowingly large amounts of data that can be analyzed to reveal patterns, trends, etc., about all sorts of human behavior. We even wear it in the form of Fit Bits, heat and cool our rooms in the form of smart thermostats, swipe our credit cards when we make purchases or draw from our accounts, and track it in the form of Google Analytics.

Do we need this information? Yes, resoundingly, of course. And we need the people who know how to look at it, read it, ask the right questions of it, make some good sense of it, and finally point us in the direction of that which we as humans all seek answers to—what will our future look like? Where are the opportunities to improve our lives? What are the pitfalls and obstacles to avoid? Those who can help us answer these questions can give us the edge financially, open possible doors to growth, or offer our children a better chance.

Ken Gronbach is among the best at reading and finding meaning from demographics—and seeing into the future. We once spoke at a conference in a lovely spot in Minnesota and I was mesmerized by his aplomb in discussing potential opportunities in the numbers where others less talented might see only concerns. He also has the very rare ability to entertain—demographics can indeed be fun.

Upside is a very important contribution for anyone who could benefit from a peek into the future.

John Zogby is the founder of the Zogby Poll, senior partner at John Zogby Strategies, and author of three books on the future, most recently *We Are Many, We are One: Neo-Tribes and Tribal Analytics in 21st Century America.*

Introduction

WHEREVER PEOPLE ARE, they are always making a demographic impact. Whether a population is large or small,
people always leave their mark. I believe that the science
and art of demographics is grossly underrated and unappreciated.
It is a simple science, really, that deals with live births, fertility,
immigration, migration, aging, and death. This book was written
to demonstrate the enormous power of counting people, promote
the understanding of population change through time, and show
how distinct population groups and shifts in population size significantly impact the world around them.

While the impacts of shifting and changing demography are
global, the eye of the perfect demographic storm is in the continent of North America in general and in the United States in
particular.

Immigrants will continue to pour into the country and enhance
and complement the U.S. population at a rate of about 1 million per
year. Our fertility remains above replacement level, and we are having enough children—about 4 million per year—to sustain the country for future generations. The members of the largest generation

in U.S. history, Generation Y, are moving out of their parents' homes, entering the workforce, setting up households, marrying, and having children. One-third of the U.S. population of 320 million or so—composed of about 40 million African Americans, 55 million Hispanics, and 17 million Asians—will benefit socioeconomically from a new and honest diversity. The largest generation ever to retire in the United States will do just that, as Baby Boomers will retire at the rate of about 4 million per year. This will create new markets, cause a drop in unemployment, and dramatically boost the economy of the Southern and Western "Sun Belt" states. It is all good!

There is more. While the demographic climate of the United States looks especially good, the demographic-based outlook for much of the rest of the world is bleak. The labor forces of the European Union, Eastern Europe, and all of Asia will be decimated by poor fertility. A country that does not have babies cannot expect to maintain its numbers of adult workers, consumers, and taxpayers over the course of twenty to thirty years. The net result will be a steady flow of manufacturing back to the United States to take advantage of the best labor force in U.S. history.

This book is about finding the potential "upside" opportunities borne by changing demographics. While in many cases demographic change tends to be gradual, sometimes change comes on much more quickly. In both cases, though, recognizing the potential upside can be difficult.

Generally speaking, potential upside opportunities are more prevalent with growing population shifts than they are with declining populations shifts. And, as with the above-referenced population change in general, it is also difficult to foresee the potential downside caused by population declines.

I sometimes refer to growing population shifts that represent potential upside as "tsunamis" and often refer to declining population shifts that represent potential downside as "sinkholes." The former represents a counterintuitive metaphor because I am seeking positive results from it. Nevertheless, "tsunami" perfectly describes the power of large growing shifts in population: These shifts are immensely powerful, hard to see, and incredibly challenging because the power is not really recognized until, like a tsunami, the shift actually hits. Just think of America's Baby Boomers, who, as you will read in the pages ahead, have collectively acted like a tsunami as they've aged through all the key epochs of life. And now, as they enter the retirement years, as by far the largest such cohort to ever retire, they will sweep over all things related to retirement like a tsunami—an "upside tsunami."

Interestingly, people knew that this Boomer retirement tsunami was coming, but for the most part America heard a warning siren that sounded way too early and has been looking out to sea ever since in a vain effort to mark its approach prior to making preparations. Well, the tsunami is hitting the shoreline, but we're still not ready for it.

While perhaps more apt as a metaphor for the purposes of this book, referring to demographic changes related to population decline as "sinkholes" makes perfect sense as they are also immensely powerful but difficult to perceive until the ground actually collapses. America's Generation X has caused some sinkholes as it has aged through time, one of which caught me back in the late 1980s with the collapse of the U.S. market for Japanese motorcycles.[1]

So, for the purposes of this book, when you read about a demographic tsunami it will almost always represent a potential upside, and when you read about a demographic sinkhole I am more likely than not warning you about potential downside. But remember, forewarned is forearmed, and upside opportunity can sometimes be discovered on the cusp of potential downside. Or, to put it another way, tsunamis and sinkholes both create immense challenges, but while tsunamis definitely provide more potential upside opportunity, sinkholes can provide upside opportunities as well. Read on to learn about this fascinating science—some would say "art"—called demography, understand its incredible power, and learn how to discover potential upside in demographic tsunamis and sinkholes before they strike, or bury you.

PART**ONE**

THE DEMAND SIDE OF THE EQUATION:
Generations and Regions

1

Counting People— What a Concept!

SPEAK FORTY OR fifty times a year all over the United States and Canada to very different audiences. I speak to manufacturers, distributors, importers, exporters, educators, students, funeral directors, insurance executives, marketers, human resource executives, sales executives, politicians, government employees, and retailers, to name a few. All of my audiences seem to share a similar vague notion of what demography might be. As a demographer I am often asked if I make maps. That, by the way, would be the field of cartography.

My family knows what I do.

When my daughter Libby was 15 she and a close friend were riding in the backseat of our Volvo station wagon. I heard her friend ask, "What does your dad do?"

Libby replied that I was a demographer. There was the usual pause. Then her friend asked, "What's that? Is that like an economist or an accountant?"

I could tell that Libby was searching for the right answer. Then she replied, "No. Accountants and economists count money and stuff—my dad counts people, and people are more important than money and stuff."

Good answer! That's exactly what I do—I count people. Most people don't count people, even at the most basic levels. Most people have no idea how many people there might be in the world (as of June 2016, an estimated 7.3 billion people, so now you know), or in the United States (about 320 million give or take a few million),[1] or even in their own town or city (depending on the town or city, I might be able to pull up the number). But what may be more problematic is that many marketers have no idea of how many consumers (people) there might be in their specific markets. Let me give you some examples.

I grew up with three older brothers in a single-parent household. They were considerably older than me. Chuck was eleven years my senior and the twins, Bob and Roger, were nine years older. Chuck was big and very aggressive so there was a clear pecking order. When my mother would put an apple pie on the table, a battle would erupt and often injuries would result. It was a clear dynamic of supply and demand. Chuck, of course, would get the biggest piece; the twins would get theirs; and, if I was lucky, I would get a small piece. My mother didn't interfere with the battle because she was flattered that we all loved her pie and were so enthusiastic about getting a piece. It made her feel good. Then Chuck joined the navy and left home. We kind of missed him . . . a little. Things changed around the house. There was a new pecking order. When my mother would put a pie on the table, the reaction would be measured. There was no more fighting. We didn't have to. Everyone got all he wanted. What was my mother's reaction? She was hurt. We apparently didn't like her pie anymore.

So, what was my mother's problem? She didn't understand shifting demography and shifting markets at the most basic level. My mother did not stop cooking quantities for four boys until we had all left home.

I can't explain exactly why, but I am pretty sure it has something to do with an inability to count people.

About six years ago I was speaking in Florida to a large group of municipal financial workers, and as soon as I began speaking, I discerned that this group seemed decidedly solemn and distracted. I am not the best speaker in the world, but my jokes are funny and I can normally hold a crowd pretty well. Not this one, and it was getting very painful.

Finally I just stopped my routine PowerPoint presentation, held up my hands, and said, "Whoa, time-out—what's going on here?"

I wondered whether I needed to start my presentation by doing CPR. "You guys look like someone just told you that the world was ending." What I didn't realize was that many of them might have been thinking exactly that.

Apparently an earlier speaker had filled them full of Florida's gloomy financial future. I asked the audience to volunteer what they were thinking, and there was no shortage of replies. It seems that the local economist who spoke just before me showed a lot of crash-and-burn graphs and charts that demonstrated how hard Florida had been hit by the recent housing and financial crisis. The bottom line was that many of the folks in the room were thinking they were facing the possibility of being laid off. The world was ending!

One gentleman near the front volunteered: "Things are bad in Florida and clearly they are going to get a lot worse. It looks like retirees from the North have stopped retiring to Florida and our life-blood of tourism is in steep decline. Everywhere you look you see empty storefronts, deserted condos, and houses in foreclosure."

I said, "Now I get it. So why don't we all slit our wrists and get this over with?" OK, so I was a bit harsh, but sometimes I find that necessary when you want to bring people back into reality. I told our doomsday spokesman that he was half right. Things were bad here in Florida. But they were not going to get worse. They were going to get better, a lot better, incredibly better. I had gained their interest. I needed to deliver.

I explained to my Boca Raton, Florida, audience that it is never a good idea to project the present infinitely into the future. Despite what economists might imply, things do change. I told them that the largest U.S. generation ever to retire was about to do just that, and that this generation, the aging Baby Boomers, had their retirement held hostage by the housing crisis and resultant diminished equity. I told them that the housing market was coming back, slowly at first, especially in states that had judicial foreclosure, but that once the foreclosures were cleared a vibrant housing market would reemerge. Baby Boomers would then sell their homes, recoup their equity, and descend upon Florida and other warm states like swarming locusts. I told them that they did not have sufficient infrastructure to handle the millions of Baby Boomers who were headed their way. They would need to build airports, harbors, roads, bridges, houses, condos, hotels, strip malls, office buildings, shopping centers, and parking structures to handle the volume. Before I knew it, the cheering crowd was carrying me on their shoulders and someone nominated me for mayor.

OK, so I exaggerated a bit, especially about the mayor part. The rest of it is true. Florida will blossom economically and demographically, and, as of the first half of 2016, it certainly appears that my rosy projections are starting to come true. But more on this later.

Meanwhile, I continue to believe that the folks in Florida still have no idea just how much their lives are going to change, just how much Florida is going to change. And that's because no one down there has bothered to count people. They haven't counted the massive numbers of Baby Boomers and played around with these numbers based on historic growth and migration patterns for the state of Florida. When they do decide to start counting, I am positive it will be an eye-opener.

Now if you read my 2008 book—*The Age Curve: How to Profit from the Demographic Storm*—or you've heard me speak, then you are familiar with my theories regarding the collapse of Japanese motorcycle sales in the United States in the late 1980s and early 1990s. It bears repeating here because it is the perfect example of corporate failure to count people.

In 1992 our advertising agency lost one of its biggest and most profitable accounts ever—American Honda Motorcycles. It was no real surprise because Japanese motorcycle brand sales had been plummeting during the previous six years. Between 1986 and 1992, the market for Honda, Kawasaki, Yamaha, and Suzuki sport bikes fell by about 80 percent and most of the dealers closed. No one knew why. Not the Japanese. Not the big American advertising and marketing agencies.

It didn't make any sense. Sales had been so robust throughout the late 1970s and early 1980s that we thought this would go on forever. The shift happened in 1986 when in early spring we ran the television, radio, billboard, and newspaper ads for about 180 dealers from the tip of Maine to Pittsburgh to Washington, D.C., and then waited for the usual tidal wave of customers. It never arrived. Customers trickled in. Our dealers became predatory and began seriously discounting the bikes. It was the beginning of the end. By 1992 it was over. It was the end of an era for the Japanese motorcycle sector. No one, and I mean no one, had an explanation. I remember the folks at Honda saying that they could not compete against the legendary Harley. They even started making bikes that copied the Harley style. They knew the "what" but they did not know the "why."

I discovered the "why" in 1996.

I had been troubled by the popular and growing perception that Generation X, born 1965 to 1984, was a generation of lazy slacker couch potatoes. I believe this perception gained even more credence with the popular 1991 book *Generation X* by Douglas Coupland. But I wasn't buying it. Of the forty people working at our advertising agency, thirty of them were Gen Xers and not one of them was a lazy slacker couch potato. So I had the research department of our agency dive into the real facts about Generation X by looking at data from the U.S. Census Bureau, *CIA World Factbook*, and Bureau of Labor Statistics.

The findings of this research were simple and profound. Generation X *appeared* to be underperforming compared to the Baby Boomers they followed simply because Generation X *was* smaller. We discovered that there were 9 million fewer native-born members of Generation X compared to the Baby Boomer generation. That's a lot of people. It is almost equivalent to the population of Serbia.

American Honda, Suzuki, Yamaha, and Kawasaki, along with their advertisers, did not see the end of the Japanese motorcycle sales boom because they all failed to understand that the last members of the Baby Boomer generation were marching past their places of business along the generational parade route as of 1986. By 1992 the Baby Boomers had completely exited the Japanese brands' sweet spot of 16- to 24-year-old men. The diminutive Generation X that followed the Boomers simply did not have the critical mass of 16- to 24-year-old men to satisfy the needs of the market left behind by the Boomers.

Generation X was essentially 11 percent smaller by birth than the Boomers who preceded them through those key sport motorcycle buying years. But no one ever gave any thought to counting them before they were due to arrive.

In the first months of 2016, a news story making the rounds caught my eye. After fifty-six years of Barbie sporting the same body style, toy maker Mattel Inc. introduced its new Barbie with three new body types, seven skin tones, twenty-two eye colors, and twenty-four hairstyles. I applauded the company for rolling out a more realistic version of its iconic doll for impressionable young girls, but it was a number in the news story that caught my eye. Every news byte on the issue I read pointed out that Mattel sales had been declining for two years, with the end of 2015 showing even further sales declines in all categories. None of the "news" writers tried to explain the reason behind the drop in sales, though several alluded that ennui must be at the root of the problem—"Barbie has become increasingly out of touch." None of the writers, nor Mattel apparently, gave thought to maybe looking at the population of its customer base. From what I could tell from the half-dozen or so stories I read, and from Mattel's annual report, no one seemed to even consider that just maybe there might be fewer potential customers. In fact, in his message to shareholders, Mattel CEO Christopher A. Sinclair ascribed Mattel products that "were not sufficiently compelling to consumers" as the primary reason for the year's lower sales.

So, I counted. And guess what? As of the end of 2015, the number of potential Barbie-owning children in the United States within the prime Barbie-owning year of age 5 was about 7 percent smaller than it had been at the end of 2012.[2] The number of 6-year-olds was about 3 percent smaller, while older children numbers between the two years were roughly equivalent.

Going forward, I don't care how many changes Mattel makes to Barbie in an effort to make her more compelling to consumers, because that's not going to change the fact that Mattel's core customer base is getting smaller. All someone has to do is look at the birth numbers to see that annual births declined by about 300,000 within three years of the 2007 U.S. peak birth year, likely in response to the housing market meltdown and subsequent Great Recession.

Mattel had some boom years due to the robust birth years of 2000 to 2007, but as those customers age out of the toy market there are fewer customers aging into the market. Anyone can look at the birth numbers and figure that out, but has anyone from Mattel bothered to? I doubt it.

Having given you the four examples above regarding most people's inability to count people, I suppose I should give you at least one example of someone, other than myself, who does count people.

I belong to a workingman's yacht club on the Connecticut River, just down the 154 Highway in Chester, Connecticut. We keep the expenses down by sharing a lot of the work as opposed to paying someone to have it done. Last year the club put on its annual BBQ chicken fund-raising luncheon, and my wife and I were assigned to help the experienced crew that always puts it on. On the day of the BBQ, vast quantities of chicken appeared near the BBQ pit as did many large bags of charcoal.

I thought to myself, *I hope we have enough*, but at the same time thought, *I hope we don't have too much*. If we didn't have enough, some people were going to go hungry and get irritated with us, but on the other hand, if we cooked too much chicken, it would likely go to waste and reduce the amount of money that the club would make.

The cost was $25 each, all inclusive. Phil Visintainer is "Mr. Chicken." He has been barbecuing chicken for decades, both at the club and at the Haddam Neck Fair. I asked him if we had enough chicken, and got an icy stare back. "Of course we do," he chided me.

I wondered if the BBQ pit was big enough to do all the chicken at once and if the chicken be thoroughly cooked on time. I didn't ask because I knew Phil's answer would be, "Of course." I complimented Phil on his professional confidence but couldn't resist asking him how he was so confident in his projections.

"I got an accurate count on the people who would be eating with us today," he replied.

He had done his homework. He knew his market demand and prepared his supply accordingly. We served 144 perfectly barbequed chicken quarters right on time, with four left over to account for any unexpected guests. And if there weren't any, as Phil had predicted, then he was more than happy to bring the leftovers home for his next day's lunch and dinner. Mind you, I made him share with me.

Counting people—what a concept!

Pretend you set up a hot dog stand at the state fair. It was not cheap. You had to pay thousands of dollars for a prime location, and you had to pay it up front and pray that it didn't rain. It's the morning of the opening day and business has been disappointing. You are vexed. Should you reduce payroll and send people home or should you expect an afternoon rush and order more hot dogs?

You could call your accountant and she would tell you what you did last year. That's no good.

You could call an economist and he would send you some graphs. No help there.

Or, you could call a demographer. You could call me. Here is the conversation:

You: "I don't know whether to send people home or to buy more hot dogs. Business has been very disappointing so far."

Me: "Can you see the parking lot from where your stand is located?"

You: "Yes."

Me: "Describe it to me."

You: "It is filling up with school buses."

Me: "Buy more hot dogs!"

Really, now, is that so hard?

2

The People Are Demanding

"EVERYTHING IN BUSINESS—EVERYTHING—IS affected by supply and demand."

That's the first sentence in the first chapter of my first book—*The Age Curve: How to Profit from the Coming Demographic Storm* (AMACOM).

So, why are you reprinting it here? you ask.

Because this book is all about the demand part of that quote. When I wrote *The Age Curve* in 2008, I did so in an effort to bring readers into my world, the world of counting people. It is a lonely place, really. *Demographics* is not a household word, and the science of demography often takes a backseat to the science of economics. I find this quite ironic because demographics precipitate economics, not the other way around. So while *The Age Curve* was a big-picture overview from 30,000 feet high on this relatively unknown and misunderstood science, *Upside* represents a deep dive. Readers of *The Age Curve* often asked me how the science of demography applied to them specifically. Readers of *Upside* should be able to bring demography into the world where they live, work, and play. It represents demographics up close and personal.

And what is demand?

People.

Without people, there is no demand, and without demand there's no need for supply and, of course, without the two of them there's certainly no need for business.

As noted in the previous chapter, I count people, and you should, too. Especially if you are in business. But it's not only the counting of people that's important; it's figuring them out.

And I'm not talking about figuring out their tastes, style, fashion, or anything that might be the hottest seller in a given market; I'm talking about figuring them out on a demographic basis—figuring out what their numbers mean. Counting people is the easy part; working out the implications of those numbers can prove more difficult, but it shouldn't be that way. Both the numbers and implications of those numbers are right there before our very eyes, and yet we so often remain totally blind to them.

I recently had a comprehensive eye exam. The doctor dilated my pupils with a medication that really irritated my eyes to the point that I could not open them comfortably in the sunlight. I was glad that one of my daughters was with me so she could drive home. On the walk back to her car I held her arm, and she cautioned me about approaching cars and when to step up on curbs. Trust me, I am not saying I suddenly understood what it would be like to be blind, but I certainly got a taste. When you can't see, things can hide in plain sight. In this case, where was my daughter's SUV? It is big and red and hard to miss, unless you can't see, and I couldn't see it.

On the way home, the irritation slowly subsided, but I could not stop thinking about the experience. Knowledge is all around us, the answers to big questions. Why can't we see it? Seems to me that we collectively have our eyes closed and allow ourselves to be led around by other people. So let's open our eyes and have a look at why counting people is so important.

Voltaire is quoted as saying, "Common sense is not so common." What an understatement. I am amazed at how few people really think things through, how few folks employ simple logic. I believe that a working knowledge of demographics is an enormously powerful tool, especially for marketing and advertising. But the real beauty of a working knowledge of demographics is its simplicity. Presented correctly it is very easy to understand. If you can count and comprehend how population numbers can impact just about everything, I can help you become a demographic expert in no time.

I make demographic presentations all over the United States and Canada. I get rave reviews, not because I am really smart and able to dazzle people with esoteric data. It is because I simply remove the mystery of the science of demography and present it in a way that almost everyone can understand and use. It is the use part that makes a difference. It is a way of looking at the mysteries of the world in a way that people can understand.

Is an understanding of demography the beginning of wisdom? No, but it is a perspective that will change your thinking forever, especially relative to marketing and business.

Are demographics a new science? Hardly; they have been around for as long as people have been on the planet.

Then why aren't demographics common knowledge? Good question. I believe it is because really smart demographers like to write articles and books for other really smart demographers and not for the general public.

I know, go figure. I am a marketer turned demographer. I know how to write to the public only because I am accustomed to writing advertising copy. I want everyone to know what I know. Listen, I know I make generalizations, but if you want to dive into the esoteric DNA of demographics, you won't understand anything. My simple theories stand the test of time, and that is my validation. Once you understand the principles of shifting demography, you can forecast their impacts on markets, politics, economics, commerce, and cultural change.

Can you count? Can you tell the difference between large and small? It is people who drive the world. Not systems, governments, or management styles. The most important question that anyone who markets anything must ask is: How many people are in my market and is that number getting bigger or smaller? An understanding of this simple concept will shape your success or failure. If you don't know how many people you are dealing with, you simply don't know what's driving the world.

Ever notice how the *Wall Street Journal* humanizes its stories about the stock market? The stock market can "shrug off" disappointing updates, "get jittery" about bad news, "be giddy" about good news, and even "embrace" federal reports. The stock market is not a person. People are people. And only people are people. If you understand the dynamics of the people and populations that drive a particular market, you can capitalize on this information in the stock market. People drive sales, and more people generally leads to more sales, while fewer people usually indicates declining sales. It is so simple.

So simple that back in 2008 I started a demographically based investor newsletter designed specifically on this concept. I would pick out business sectors that were likely going to be impacted by generational population shifts, and my colleagues—who were better versed in securities knowledge such as price-to-earnings ratios and other stock valuation indicators—would pick stocks in the sector that would benefit the most from the expected demographic changes. In two and a half years our demographically based model portfolio was up more than 100 percent compared to the S&P 500, which had gained just over 35 percent during that same time period.

It wasn't rocket science. America's Generation Y, composed of about 86.6 million people born between 1985 and 2004, is big, and as they aged there was little doubt that they would have a big impact on specific companies.

Which companies, you ask? Well, consumer electronics, toys, and youth apparel were definitely feeling Gen Y's impact, and played a key role in the portfolio. As did specific food and beverage companies that we felt would appeal to what we perceived as the refined taste of this generation.

For an example of this latter point, consider the Boston Beer Company. We determined that not only would the number of people reaching the legal age for drinking alcohol increase dramatically going forward with Gen Y, but also that members of this generation seemed to have higher standards with regard to their consumption habits. Thus, Boston Beer had a much greater chance of capitalizing on Gen Y than did, say, Budweiser. We recommended Boston Beer when its stock was selling for about $25 per share. Its price in the closing days of 2015 was north of $200, for an increase of about 700 percent.

One of our most bearish calls was based on the Baby Boomers. Perhaps we called it a bit too early, as the Boomers just don't want to age, but we were (and still are) convinced that demographics do not support Harley-Davidson, which is definitely a Boomer brand. I mean, Grandpa is eventually going to get too old to handle that Hog. One of these days he'll pull up to a stoplight, kilter a bit off balance, and be unable to stop the Hog from falling over on its side.

On Wall Street you are a visionary if you think out to the next quarterly report, that is, three months. In demographics the people who will shape the world fifty years from now are already born. Want to be a real visionary? Count them and figure them out.

The science of demography is nothing more than good statistical information seasoned with common sense and logic. It is the world I live in, and with a little luck I can bring you into my world. You will never read the newspaper or watch the news from the same perspective again. Demographics precipitate economics, politics, commerce, and culture. Why do so many people think it's the other way around? I'll say it without reservation: A working knowledge of demographics could be the best marketing and business tool you or your organization will ever have.

3

The Ever-So-Important Delineation of the Generations

COUNTING PEOPLE IS the easy part. Figuring them out takes work. It's one thing to say that according to U.S. Census Bureau estimates there were roughly 320 million people living in the United States as of 2015. It's a whole other thing to explain exactly who these people are. Some of the ways in which we can describe these people are by sex, age, race, ethnicity, state of residence. Or we could get into religion, employment, income levels, or even sexual preference. Essentially, any group that can constitute a distinct population can be used. But I tend to focus primarily on age, or, more specifically, the age cohorts known as generations. Thus, I am considered a "generational demographer."

On the one hand this is quite effective because people can easily relate to the different U.S. generations, especially given that "Baby Boomers" have been making news since they were first described as a "boom" by Sylvia F. Porter in a 1951 *New York Post* article, and Generation Y has been making news since researchers decided in about the early 1990s that Gen X was no longer worth talking about. Plus, generations, which tend to have distinct personalities all on their own, are fun to write and speak about.

On the other hand, the effectiveness of generational demographics is mitigated by the fact that there are no clearly established and universally accepted birth-date ranges or age spans that specifically delineate the different generations. Next time you read an article about Gen Y, take note of whether the author has bothered to delineate its members by noting their age span or birth-date range. If so, try to compare that delineation with another source from a different article. I'll bet you'll find that they are different and, more likely than not, many years apart. I've seen Generation Y described as being born between 1980 and 2000, or 1985 to 2006, and even 1977 to 1994. They usually get a twenty-year time span, and sometimes less, but rarely get more. In fact, I recently noticed that the U.S. Census Bureau has apparently given Gen Y an eighteen-year span, calling them born between 1982 and 2000. The Bureau delineates Boomers as having a twenty-year span, so why would it shortchange the Ys? I just don't get it.

When I first started examining the generations, I noticed that poor Generation X, already being maligned for all kinds of shortcomings, was usually shortchanged by researchers who granted them only a ten- to fifteen-year span. It made me want to scream then, and I still want to scream today every time I see Gen X shortchanged by a researcher who gives the generation only ten years, yet gives the other generations twenty. How can a generation span only ten or fifteen years? It's not like they started having babies at age 10. I mean, really!

I think part of the reason there is no universally accepted delineation is because researchers and marketers like it that way. It lets them move the goalposts in case they need to shift populations in order to fit a particular preconceived premise. And, actually, I must confess guilt to sometimes moving the goalposts, though not for the purposes of making population numbers fit a preconceived notion, but because it makes sense.

For example, I adopted the twenty-year time frame to delineate the generations because the traditional view of a generation holds it to be roughly twenty years—the time between the birth of the parents and the birth of their offspring. However, in my book *The Age Curve: How to Profit from the Coming Demographic Storm*, I attempted to give Generation Y a twenty-five-year span, based on the fact that North Americans are delaying childbirth and that twenty-five years is now a much more realistic time frame between the birth of parents and their offspring. However, I abandoned this delineation with its attendant oversize numbers soon after the book came out because a twenty-year Gen Y span was big enough on its own right without the additional population of five more years. Those extra years and resultant additional people just weren't fair to the earlier generations. And, as a public speaker, having to explain Gen Y's abrupt delineation change to audiences disrupted the smooth flow of my generational descriptions.

Nevertheless, I still believe that generations should now be delineated with twenty-five-year time frames going forward—maybe we can push this through with Generation Z as it continues to usher in this still new century.

TABLE 3.1

THE U.S. GENERATIONS DELINEATED

G.I. Generation	1905–1924	56.6 million births
Silent Generation	1925–1944	52.5 million births
Baby Boomers	1945–1964	78.2 million births
Generation X	1965–1984	69.5 million births
Generation Y	1985–2004	79.5 million births
Generation Z	2005–2024	40.9 million births (as of 2014)

With my standard generational delineation, as utilized for my books and speaking, I selected the most accurate generational chronology that I felt defined the Baby Boomers. The baby boom began in 1945/1946 and represents the large population boom that developed as the soldiers returned home from World War II. Among the most common delineation of the Baby Boomer years is 1945 to 1964. This being established, it was easy to align the Silent

Generation, G.I. Generation, Generation X, Generation Y, and the oncoming Generation Z into twenty-year segments.

I have also worked with the delineation based on the Baby Boomer years being 1946 to 1965—not to make the generational numbers fit a particular preconceived notion, but in order to better align the generations with the U.S. Census Bureau's five-year counts, so as to provide clients with the most accurate counts of smaller age cohorts within the specific generations. With the exception of the Boomer population, this one-year shift does not significantly change the overall birth numbers of each generation. For the Boomers, this one-year shift forward increases their birth population by 1.4 million. This shift also adds 300,000 to Generation Y, but decreases the Silent Generation by 100,000.

Numbers aside, it is important to always remember that generations are markets and these generations are always on the move because they are aging. You can't slow aging down, you can't speed it up, and you can't pretend, like Hollywood, that aging doesn't happen. Think of a parade of customers/generations marching past your business. Some have passed you by, completed the parade route, and are already disbanding. Some customers are marching in place directly in front of you and you are selling them your goods and services. They are buying your goods and services because this is the stage of their lives when they consume your particular goods and services. Most goods and services have an age-related sweet spot. For example, babies consume formula and diapers; children under 10 consume clothing, candy, and Coco-Puffs; teens consume fashion, soft drinks, and video games; people in their 20s consume entertainment, cosmetics, and more fashion because they are looking for mates; thirtysomethings consume houses, household items, insurance, baby products, and automobiles; folks in their 40s consume houses, legal services, boats, and more automobiles; 50-year-olds are at their peak earnings and consume everything, including second homes, bigger boats, bigger cars, expensive divorces, and travel; 60-year-olds consume cruises, pharmaceuticals, and retirement; 70-year-olds consume more pharmaceuticals and one-story living; 80-plus-year-olds are just happy to be alive and consume assisted living and funerals. OK, so this is a bit simplistic, but I think you get the point. Your future customers are aging toward you and the youngest are just now forming and joining the parade at the fairground. Thus, it is important that you understand the sizes of the different generations no matter how they've been delineated so that you can plan accordingly.

So now that you better understand the generations and how they are delineated, let's take a closer look at the U.S. generations, and the U.S. population as a whole.

4

Who Are These People?

HOW MANY PEOPLE are currently living in the United States? Come on, I gave you the answer on the second page of this book, and then again at the start of Chapter 3.

That's right, roughly 320 million people, and I say *roughly* because counting that many people isn't easy, and any official "big number" count you might see—say from the U.S. Census Bureau, United Nations, U.S. Central Intelligence Agency (yes, the CIA counts people), U.S. Department of Homeland Security (yep, they count people, too), etc.—is only an estimate or projection.

But wait a minute, maybe that's why nobody seems to count people—why bother if the government does it?

OK, but does anyone bother looking at their numbers?

Do you?

Anyhow, the "roughly 320 million" estimate I'm using is based on U.S. Census Bureau estimates and projections. In 2013, the Bureau projected that the U.S. population would be at 321.4 million in 2015, but in June of 2015 it estimated that the population as of 2014 was at 318.8 million, and then in December of 2015 it estimated that the population was at 321,418,820 as of July. So, I call the current population as of the end of 2016 "roughly 320 million."

But, just to confuse you more, we are now going to use the Census Bureau's 2014 estimates, because the Bureau has done us the favor of parsing those 2014 numbers out to determine who is who and how many whos there are by age, race, ethnicity, and other parameters.

Were you 50 years old in 2014? Well then, according to the Census Bureau you shared that age with 4,491,431 other people living in the United States in 2014. Sadly, the estimates suggest that more than 170,000 of your fellow 1964 birth year U.S. residents had passed away since the 2010 Census.

Interestingly, though, you folks born in 1964 still kind of rule the roost on a population basis, as only five other U.S. birth years have populations greater than yours. And the largest population by birth year/age of 4,698,584—those born in 1991 and currently (as of 2017) age 26—isn't really that much bigger, is it?

Are you Hispanic? If so, you join an estimated 55,279,452 U.S. residents who identified as such in 2014. And guess what? That represents a 56.5 percent increase from the 35 million or so residents who identified as Hispanic in 2000.

TABLE 4.1

RACIAL AND ETHNIC POPULATION CHANGE 2000–2014

RACE OR ETHNICITY	2000 POPULATION	2014 POPULATION	NUMERICAL CHANGE	PERCENTAGE CHANGE
White	211,460,626	233,963,128	22,502,502	10.6%
Non-Hispanic White	194,552,774	197,409,353	2,856,579	1.5%
Black	34,658,190	40,379,066	5,720,876	16.5%
Hispanic	35,305,818	55,279,452	19,973,634	56.5%
Asian	10,242,998	16,686,960	6,443,962	62.9%
All	281,421,906	318,857,056	37,435,150	13.3%

Do you think this is a growing market? This market has just begun to grow and is expected to almost double in size by 2050, to reach about 105.5 million, according to U.S. Census Bureau projections.

TABLE 4.2

PROJECTED RACIAL AND ETHNIC POPULATION CHANGE 2014–2050

RACE OR ETHNICITY	2014 POPULATION	2050 PROJECTED POPULATION	NUMERICAL CHANGE	PERCENTAGE CHANGE
White	233,963,128	280,503,000	46,539,872	19.9%
Non-Hispanic White	197,409,353	188,419,000	-8,990,353	-4.5%
Black	40,379,066	56,007,000	15,627,934	38.7%
Hispanic	55,279,452	105,550,000	50,270,548	90.9%
Asian	16,686,960	34,359,000	17,672,040	105.9%
All	318,857,056	398,328,000	79,470,944	24.9%

Or are you perchance Asian? If so, you join an estimated 16.7 million U.S. residents who identify as such, and a population that has grown by almost 6.5 million, or 62.9 percent, since 2000. This segment of the population also represents a growth market, and its numbers are expected to double and reach about 34.4 million by 2050, according to the Census Bureau.

Are you African American?[1] There were 40.4 million of you as of 2014. And with the population growing by only about 16 percent from the 34,658,190 recorded in the 2000 Census, growth can be considered modest when compared to the Hispanic and Asian populations. Going forward, the Black population is expected to grow about 15 million, rising to 56 million by 2050, for a gain of about 39 percent. While 39 percent certainly represents "growth," it could be considered modest when compared to that of Hispanics and Asians. To look at it in another comparative way, both the Hispanic and Black populations were roughly the same size in 2000, but the Hispanics had overtaken the Black population by more than 15 million people in fourteen short years, and within another thirty-four years will have outgrown the Black population by a 3-to-1 ratio.

How about White? Well, that all depends upon what kind of "White" you are. While the overall White population is growing, the population that the U.S. Census Bureau calls "Non-Hispanic White"[2] barely grew at all between 2000 and 2014, and is projected to decline going forward to 2050. In 2000, the non-Hispanic White population was pegged at 194.5 million, growing to 196.8 million by the 2010 Census and then to 197.4 million in the 2014 American Community Survey. By 2050 the Bureau believes that the Non-Hispanic White population will fall to less than 188.5 million.

When the Census Bureau adds in Hispanics who identify as White, though, the numbers are somewhat better, with a population of 211.4 million in the 2000 Census, rising to 233.9 million in the 2014 American Community Survey, and projected to increase another 19.9 percent to 280.5 million by 2050.

So, if you were forced by some arcane reason to market exclusively to only one of these groups, what do the above numbers mean?

Stumped? OK, let's start with an easy one. Which one is the biggest market?

That's right, Whites inclusive of those also identifying as Hispanic. And it also represents a growing market.

Here's another easy one. Which market is not growing at all?

Correct, "Non-Hispanic White." If you were exclusively selling to this market and Census projections hold true, your sales would likely decline in the coming years.

At this point you should be realizing that this demographics stuff is pretty easy, but let me give you one more: Fastest-growing market?

"Asians!" Of course. You must be a demographer!

Now, another thing to keep in the back of your mind is proportional representation.

Say what? I can hear you saying. Well, just keep in mind that Hispanics made up only 12.5 percent of the total U.S. population in 2000, but then expanded to 16.3 percent by 2010, and will likely be nearing 30 percent by 2050. Non-Hispanic Whites, meanwhile, went from 69 percent of the total population in 2000 to 63.7 percent in 2010, and are expected to fall below 50 percent before 2050, and perhaps as early as 2042. This idea of proportional representation, then, can obviously have an impact on overall marketing decisions. Think back to 1992 and the election that ushered in Bill

Clinton as president. Do you recall any mention of the "Hispanic vote" back then? Nope, it was barely a factor, but the 2016 presidential election almost hinged upon that "Hispanic vote." Amazing what a difference twenty-four years can make, and you'll see more examples of proportional representation in a later chapter.

So, where did all these people come from? How did we end up with an estimated 320 million or so people in America as of the past couple of years?

Well, most of them were born here, and for the ease of keeping track of them we can narrow them down on a generational basis. And on this basis there are currently six generations alive in the United States today.

TABLE 4.3

THE U.S. GENERATIONS TODAY*

G.I. Generation	1905–1924	2.3 million
Silent Generation	1925–1944	28.6 million
Baby Boomers	1945–1964	78.0 million
Generation X	1965–1984	82.9 million
Generation Y	1985–2004	86.6 million
Generation Z	2005–2024	40.9 million

*OK, so not today, but 2014, which marks, for the most part, Census numbers being used for this chapter.

The G.I. Generation (aka, the Greatest Generation) was born 1905-1924 and registered 56.6 million U.S. births. Currently aged 93–112, there were only about 2.3 million still alive as of 2014.

The Silent Generation (aka the Lucky Few) was born 1925–1944 and registered 52.6 million U.S. births. Currently aged 73–92, there were about 28.6 million still living in 2014.

The Baby Boomers (no other names needed) were born 1945–1964 and registered 78.2 million U.S. births. Currently trying to keep young at ages 53–72, there were still about 78 million alive in 2014.

Generation X (aka, the Slacker Generation, Baby Bust, Generation Me) was born 1965–1984 with 69.5 million registered U.S. births. This so-called "slacker" generation, currently aged 33 to 52, had grown to about 82.9 million by 2014.

Members of Generation Y (aka, the Millennials) were born 1985–2004 with 79.5 million registered U.S. births. Currently aged 13 to 32, the population of this largest U.S. generation ever stood at about 86.6 million as of 2014.

The still emerging Generation Z (aka, IGen and Post-Millennials) was and will be born 2005–2024, and had registered about 40.9 million U.S. births by 2014,[3] while the U.S. Census Bureau pegged its population at roughly 40.4 million as of this year.[4] Currently spanning the ages of 0 to 11, Gen Z produced the country's biggest one-year population by birth year in 2007, with 4,316,233 registered births; however, annual birth numbers have since dropped by almost 10 percent.

Now, at this point some of you are probably thinking, *Wait a minute, some of those numbers just aren't making sense.*

And on the face of it, they don't. Sure, the G.I. Generation makes total sense because they're so old most of them have died off. But what's up with Generation X? How did they grow from 69.5 million to 82.9 million? And what about Gen Y, up more than 7 million from their birth numbers? And what's the story with the Boomers? What, they're *really* not dying (psst, what's their secret)?

One word answers those questions: *immigration.*

About 16 percent of the adult population—or nearly one out of every six adults—immigrated to America. According to the most recent available Census Bureau data, 42.4 million immigrants live in the country. And while many people are prone to believe that this does not account for all of the "illegals," the U.S. Department of Homeland Security has determined that 90 percent of illegals are accounted for through the Census Bureau's American Community Survey (ACS). So, while those numbers might be a bit light, they are official, and they are what I work with on a demographic basis.

And these immigrant numbers account for the discrepancy between birth numbers and recent Census Bureau counts. Roughly 40 percent, or 16.9 million, of these immigrants were age 25 to 44 during that last ACS. And that cohort of immigrants is almost a direct match minus a couple of years to the age range of Gen X. So, that can certainly account for the differentiation between birth numbers and recent Census numbers.

Gen Y? Well, 12.7 percent, or about 5.3 million, of the U.S. population ages 5 to 24 are immigrants, and, yep, that cohort of immigrants matches Gen Y minus a couple of years, and undoubtedly accounts for the increase in Gen Y.

And, yes, similar accounting can be made by looking at the Boomer numbers, with 32.5 percent of the age 45–64 population, or 13.7 million, composed of immigrants, and more than 12 million of the original Baby Boomers already passing on to the next world, and well. . . .

Wait a minute, I can hear you saying, *why weren't those Gen X immigrants buying Japanese motorcycles?*

Well done! You are starting to consider the numbers of people and the relevant implications of those numbers without any prodding from me.

The easy answer to that question is that they hadn't yet arrived in significant numbers by the time Gen X hit those key motorcycle-buying years, and the bulk of those who had arrived by those years were likely not in an economically feasible position to consider the purchase of such toys.

During the Gen X birth years 1965 to 1984, America welcomed about 9 million legal immigrants, of whom the vast majority were 20 and older and helping pad the Baby Boomer population, which was already exiting the motorcycle-buying market. During the next twenty years, America welcomed another 18 million or so immigrants, but the bulk of them were also past their key motorcycle-buying years, and arriving as Gen X was also exiting those key years. Thus, immigrant Gen Xers did not flow into the country in accord with the native-born generation's early purchasing tendencies.

OK, I have given you a general picture of the U.S. population. And I mean general. I could have slapped in a lot more information and data, just using Census Bureau information alone. Such as where do the roughly 320 million Americans live? Well, I can tell you that about 3.5 million of them live in my home state of Connecticut. And we are outnumbered by a 10-to-1 ratio by the 38 million or so residents of California. But that's OK, because we outnumber the 920,000 folks who live in Delaware by a 3.5-to-1 ratio.

Or we could look at what the 320 million Americans do. Such as, roughly 2 million of them are employed as registered nurses, but only about 6,000 are employed as embalmers. About 850,000 Americans are employed as lawyers, but only about 725,000 Americans are employed as physicians and/or surgeons. "Demographer" was not on the Census Bureau's "Detailed Occupation for the Full-Time, Year-Round Civilian Employed Population 16 Years and Over," but according to the Bureau of Labor Statistics that occupation falls under the "Miscellaneous Social Scientists and Related Workers" category, of which the Census Bureau has determined that there are about 35,000.

I could go on with any number of other parameters, but would you retain any of this supplemental demographic information?

Would you find it useful going forward?

Perhaps, but more likely not, unless this information was provided along with appropriate context. What's important is to consider what any demographic numbers might mean while you're taking account of them. Let's look a bit more closely at each generation, and as I parse through their numbers, see if you can discern what these numbers might mean before I tell you.

Ready? Let's go.

5

On the Way Out with the G.I. Generation

OUR OLDEST GENERATION, the G.I. Generation, also known as the Greatest Generation, is sadly on the way out. And I'm fairly certain you can figure out the implications of their fast-dwindling numbers. But can you remember what those numbers are?

That's right, 2.3 million as of 2014 and dropping fast. The youngest ones right now are 93 years old, and there's just not that much of any market for people that age. But can you name three businesses that should still maintain interest in this generation?

That's right, healthcare, assisted living, and death care. And while numerically small, the last members of this generation are prime customers of these three businesses. And going forward, these businesses should be keeping count of who is left in the Silent Generation, and, much more important, keeping an eye on those oncoming Boomers, even though they are purportedly refusing to age.

Born between 1905 and 1924, the G.I. Generation became a large generation comprising about 56 million native borns and an immigrant contingent of about 14 million. This big, noble generation lived well below their means. They fought and nearly half a million died in World War II, thus their "G.I." moniker, as G.I. means Government Issue. They left a record $7 trillion–$10 trillion to their Baby Boomer kids, who squandered it on starter castles and SUVs and lost the rest in the stock market. The members of the G.I. Generation were crippled by bigotry and lost their connection to their Baby Boomer kids in the 1960s, 1970s, and early 1980s.

In fact, there has probably never been such a distinct generational disconnect between two generations as there was between the G.I. Generation and their Baby Boomer kids. They were from different planets. It was a battle of right wing and left wing with the G.I. Generation serving as the right-wing establishment and Baby Boomers emerging as hippie, left-wing revolutionaries.

I am a leading-edge Boomer. In the late 1960s and early 1970s we believed that there just might be a revolution in the United States. That probability faded as we aged, got married, had kids, and bought homes. It soon became very clear that our parents were not so far off the wall after all.

The G.I. Generation was a huge market that drove housing and the economy for more than three decades starting in the 1940s. The younger generation following right behind them was the Silent Generation born 1925 to 1944. The vast majority of them did not fight in WWII because they were too young. The Silent Generation lived in the shadow of the G.I. Generation. The Silent Generation was just that, diminutive and quiet because of their 50 percent or so smaller critical mass as compared to the G.I. Generation.

This is an important concept. When a small generation follows big generations, some very predictable things take place, especially in commerce. Can you name what would perhaps be the most important predictable thing with regard to commerce?

If the first thought that came into your head was "sales declines," then you get a gold star, and we will see samples of such declines in the coming chapters.

. . .

I was born on Long Island, New York. It is a real island about 150 miles long and about 50 miles wide at its widest point. I call it a "real" island because if the East River that divides Long Island from Manhattan Island were really a river, then Long Island would really be a peninsula, not an island at all. But because the East River is really not a river but just a tidal cut into the Long Island Sound from the Upper New York Bay, it is legitimately an island. So there.

The G.I. Generation developed Long Island. As first- and second-generation immigrants advanced socioeconomically, they moved east onto the island, away from Manhattan, Brooklyn, and Queens and into the wilderness of Nassau and Suffolk Counties. The famed Hamptons are in Suffolk County and so is Montauk Point at the very end of the island. Yes, the mansions of the Hamptons are famous, but the real G.I. Generation housing story is found in Levittown.

Abraham Levitt and his sons were demographic visionaries. In 1945, up to 16 million G.I.s were returning home from the Pacific, from Europe, and from military installations around the country. These 16 million young men and women were very ready to get married, start families, and set up households. There was only one problem. Because of the war, there was a shortage of building materials so housing came up about 5 million units short of what the G.I. Generation needed.

What an opportunity! The Levitts owned former potato farms in Nassau County, Long Island, and mass-produced 2,000 rental homes on the former farmlands in 1947. The homes were immediately rented and the demand was not yet met. So they built an additional 4,000 rental houses using non-union labor and their own precut lumber and nails from their own factory. In 1949 the Levitts began building the famous 800-square-foot Levittown ranch-style home for sale. The house sold for $7,990, and if you could put $90 down and make payments of $58 a month, you were golden. The Levitts went on to build a total of 17,447 homes. The last house was sold in 1951. Despite the fears of critics who railed that the houses would fall apart, they are still there today. The Levitts hold the U.S.

record for having the most houses ever built by a single builder. At the height of their production, the Levitt builders could produce thirty houses a day. On July 3, 1950, Abraham Levitt was honored by being on the cover of *Time* magazine.

In business it is one thing to meet an existing demand and it is another to anticipate a demand. Being able to anticipate a demand sets you apart and probably makes you a lot richer. As the G.I. Generation aged through the time continuum, it was a market to be reckoned with. Just think about the markets that the huge G.I. Generation influenced and expanded along its way through time: entertainment, apparel, transportation, housing, food, pharmaceuticals, education, legal, healthcare, insurance, military recruitment, home and garden, and much more.

I have heard success defined as the collision of preparation and opportunity. If you understand shifting demography, you can prepare for what's next. The opportunities to serve the G.I. Generation are past. There aren't too many products or services you can market to people in their 90s. Maybe someday.

It is a pretty simple concept, don't you think? Big populations/ generations increase and influence the size of markets. Now think of the inverse that can be created by generations with smaller populations, which is exactly what happened as the Silent Generation followed the G.I. Generation.

Sales decreased and people scratched their heads in bewilderment, because no one apparently bothered to count the customer base or consider how it might change as the generations aged through time.

6

The Still Quiet Silent Generation

THE BIGGEST STORY about the Silent Generation is its size, or lack thereof. Born 1925–1944, its members were several million smaller by birth than the G.I. Generation, and their numbers did not really experience much of any increase due to immigration. While native-born G.I. Generation numbers were bolstered by about 14 million immigrants, immigration into the ranks of the Silent Generation was muted by stricter immigration laws, the Great Depression, and then World War II. In fact, legal immigration only added about 3 million people to the U.S. population during the Silent Generation birth years, and the majority of these immigrants likely provided the most boost to the ranks of the G.I. Generation. Immigration into the United States remained somewhat muted during the Baby Boom birth years but did add a few million to the Silent Generation ranks. Overall, though, the Silent Generation has always remained diminutive when compared to the preceding G.I. Generation and, more significantly, to the successor Baby Boomer generation.

Similar to Generation X (as you will see in Chapter 8), the story of the Silent Generation revolves more around the generations that preceded and followed it than it does the actual generation itself. With regard to the former, members of the Silent Generation are essentially clones of the G.I. Generation. The only difference between them is critical mass, or lack thereof, based in large part on limited Silent Generation immigration. The Silents were about 34 percent smaller. That is a significant difference. From a marketing standpoint, a 34 percent difference in the size of a market is huge. A 34 percent increase in the size of your market will produce astronomical sales and big profits. A 34 percent decrease will put you out of business.

Now, if you have been reading carefully, at this point you should be saying something along the lines of, *Wait a minute here . . .* and then question why the Silent Generation did not put the United States out of business.

I have not researched this anomaly in any depth but believe it to be largely a matter of lucky timing, a belief shared by others. Demographer and historian Neil Howe (who is believed to have coined the term *Millennials* for Generation Y) said that the Silent Generation's "age location has been very good to them—and given them a lifetime ride on the up-escalator coming off the American High." Demographer Richard Easterlin refers to the Silents as the "Lucky" and "Fortunate" generation because of their great timing. In short, the Silents came of age as World War II ended, and benefited from a new American economy forged by the war and perhaps too bulked up on steroids to notice that the Silents' numbers were deficient. The size of the G.I. Generation may have shielded the economy from the population deficiency, and, interestingly, the Silents ended up having babies at a younger age than any other generation in American history.[1]

The vast majority of the Silent Generation was too young to fight in WWII, so no hero stories there. They looked like the G.I. Generation, wore the same clothes, liked the same music, and drove the same cars. They were culturally the same as the G.I. Generation, just a smaller group living in the shadow of the huge gallant generation it followed. It is interesting to note that the Silent Generation sided almost completely with the G.I. Generation when the great cultural divide occurred in the 1960s and the Baby Boomers set out to change the world with peace, love, and free clinics.

The difference in the size of the Silent Generation and the Baby Boomers is overwhelming. The Silent Generation is only about two-thirds the size of the Boomers. In marketing this was a bonanza. Sales of everything increased, and all the marketing geniuses took the credit. If your market size increases by one-third, you will sell more. So guess what? As the Silent Generation aged through the time continuum and was followed by a generation almost 50 percent larger, what do you think happened? The larger generation, the Baby Boomers, consumed a lot more. Ford sold more cars. Chevrolet sold more cars. Levis sold more jeans. Honda sold more motorcycles. Advertising and marketing fanned the flame and life was good. And no one really understood why—no one, it seemed, ever bothered to count who the people were who might be responsible for the economic good times . . . or bad.

Demographers in the 1980s and 1990s promised an overwhelming graying of America starting in the year 2000, but it didn't happen. Were they wrong? No, they were just twenty years too early. Go figure. The diminutive Silent Generation has proved to be a real problem for industries that geared up for the graying of America. Funeral homes and assisted living facilities have gone begging these past fifteen years, but I am positive that this is starting to change.

Today, the youngest members of the Silent Generation are currently 73, and still have a lot of life in them. The oldest members, at age 92, are fading fast. Similar to the remaining members of the G.I. Generation, the elder half of the Silent Generation represents a declining market, and a market that has few needs.

The younger half of the Silent Generation, those about 73–81 years old, still represent a declining market when compared to the G.I. Generation, but on the whole should carry a bigger population than their older Silent Generation predecessors because they were part of an expanding population—a small precursor to the massive population expansion wrought by the Baby Boomers. The years 1933 to 1936 marked the smallest U.S. birth years for the entire 20th century, with annual numbers several hundred thousand smaller on average than the thirty or so years preceding. Coincidently, these years are also marked by having among the lowest levels of incoming legal immigrants, with only between 23,000 and 36,000 arriving in each of these years.

Following the last of what were four record low birth years, with about 2.3 million births in 1936, the number of births started going up in 1937, which recorded about 70,000 births more than the previous year, and then went up by another 75,000 in 1938. There was a bit of a drop—30,000—in 1939, but then in 1940 the number of births jumped by almost 100,000, and then another 150,000 in 1941, and then 300,000 in 1942. The year 1943 served as a mini-peak with another 100,000 increase, but annual births then dropped by about 180,000 over the next two years. Perhaps it was just a brief pause before the Baby Boom liftoff.

I am a Baby Boomer. I have a brother eleven years my senior who is a Silent, and he is anything but silent. Brother Chuck is not done by a long shot. He is very conservative and takes a traditional stance. He has strong political opinions and is not afraid to write a letter or even call his representatives when he wants action. He and his wife, Adele, have over 200 country stamps each in their passports. They both love to travel, especially if they can explore a new country. Chuck is not ready to be elderly and neither is Adele. They still decorate, remodel, and buy furniture, food, and new cars. My brother bought a new 2015 high-performance Mustang last year. I wait patiently for his hand-me-downs. He is not done.

My colleague has old Silent Generation family friends approaching their 80s who are just now buying a winter home in a chichi city in Florida. This couple had the means to buy such a home back when they retired in their 60s, and then again while they were in their 70s, but it's only now, as they hit 80, that they are starting to find the long New England winters "unbearable."

Are we starting to see "80 is the new 60"?

Are my brother Chuck and his lovely wife, Adele, anomalies? Are my colleague's old family friends? Maybe. But I think we have a new market brewing here. With modern medicine, quality nutrition, and, yes, exercise, we are living longer—much longer. I almost believe it is a personal decision. My brother and his wife have decided to live longer, richer, fuller lives that will extend well past their 70s into their 80s and 90s. I believe this will be a continuing trend established by determined Silents. It is, however, only the beginning because right on the Silent Generation's heels is the largest generation ever to retire, the Baby Boomers.

Will the Boomers live long lives, similar to what seems to be happening with members of the Silent Generation who are apparently on the crest of a wave of expanding life expectancy?

Let's see. . . .

7

Those Transformative
Baby Boomers

WHAT ARE FOUR primary business sectors that perhaps experienced some disappointment with the Silent Generation in recent years, but need to keep their eyes on the younger members of this generation going forward, but also, more important, on the fast-approaching Baby Boomers? Can you guess what they might be?

That's right: retirement, healthcare, assisted living, and death care.

If you got at least two of these, you're doing pretty well. If you got all four, you are definitely thinking like me. All four of these business sectors make money off of aging populations, and (all things being equal) the bigger the population, the more money they stand to make.

And guess, what? The aging population is poised to get bigger—much, much bigger. As mentioned in Chapter 6, the years 1933 to 1936 mark the smallest U.S. birth years for the entire 20th century, which suggests that the country currently has the smallest crop of elderly folks aged 80 to 84 we've seen in a long time.

However, two factors might belie this thought: one being the incredible advances made in healthcare over the past thirty or so years, which have significantly boosted life expectancies, and the other being immigration, although data suggests that immigration did not boost the ranks of this "smallest-birth-years" cohort to any significant degree. So, even though the cohort is small, it's unclear whether it is so small that it's been causing financial hardship for the above-mentioned businesses. Perhaps a bit . . .

But these business sectors better not get complacent because there is a slow-building wave approaching, and it's turning into a tsunami. The evidence for this oncoming tsunami is all around us, but we can start at the beginning by looking at its birth.

Recall from the last chapter that I explained how the latter stage of the Silent Generation birth years was marked by increasing births, with 1943 serving as a mini-peak, followed by a two-year birth number decline of about 200,000. And what happened in 1945, the second of the two-year pause in rising birth numbers?

That's right—Game on! Hello Baby Boomers! (Though with only about 2.8 million births that first year.)

However, the 3.47 million births registered in 1946 broke 1945's birth numbers by more than 650,000, and within five years were breaking those 1945 birth numbers by over 1 million per year.

There's evidence of these expanding numbers all around us. For example, the number of retirees receiving Social Security benefits jumped by more than 5 million from 2009 to 2014.

But why not just consult the U.S. Census Bureau to see examples of this growth spurt? As of 2014, the U.S. Census Bureau counted 2,572,527 people age 68. Guess how many 67-year-olds? Almost a million more, at 3,485,502. So, if you sell something that every 70-year-old just has to buy when he or she turns 70, your sales are about to soar to the stratosphere like one of Elon Musk's experimental rockets. And those sales will likely stay up in that generational stratosphere for at least the next twenty years until the Gen Xers start hitting 70. And they might even stay up at that level given the Gen X immigration population.

. . .

There's little doubt that the Baby Boomers made an impact with their numbers alone. Never before in American history had birth numbers surged in such a dramatic fashion; never before had America's youth population expanded so quickly nor encompassed such massive numbers. And the rise of the Baby Boomer seemed to go hand in hand with the rise in America's prosperity, with the Boomers seeming to serve as both a driver of economic growth and as a benefactor from it.

By the time the boom in baby making tapered off in 1964, the Baby Boomer population represented about 40 percent of the population. This population was so big that *Time* magazine named "The Generation 25 and Under" as "Persons of the Year" in 1966.

Along with the rise of the Boomers came the rise of shopping malls, supermarkets, fast food, discount megastores, and suburbia in general. The Boomers arrived with the rise of the automobile and extensive expansion of America's road and highway system, including construction of the Interstate Highway System, the largest U.S. public works project to date. The Boomers arrived in step with technological advances such as nuclear power, antibiotics, jet propulsion, and synthetic fibers, and with a vast expansion of modern conveniences such as disposable diapers, air-conditioning, automatic washers, high-fidelity record players, and, of course, television.

These Boomer kids grew up in lockstep with the rise of American Consumerism, and while their G.I. Generation and older Silent Generation parents started to splurge on the newfangled household gadgets, the Boomer kids consumed toys such as Hula-Hoops, Barbie dolls, Frisbees, and coonskin caps by the millions. A 1958 article—"4,000,000 a Year Make Millions in Business"—in *Life* magazine asserted that the 4 million or so kids being born per year were making America recession-proof.

But when those Boomer kids started reaching adulthood, enough of them began to resist the cultural and socioeconomic norms that by the late 1960s and early 1970s America was in constant turmoil as Baby Boomers revolted against the Vietnam War and agitated on behalf of numerous other social causes. The Boomers seemed to have all but abandoned the cultural ethos of their parents and rebelled against them with a soundtrack of alien-sounding music, rampant drug use, sexual promiscuity, and outlandish clothing and hairstyles. G.I. and older Silent Generation parents across the country hardly recognized their children anymore.

But size is in the perception, and the majority of Boomers did not tune out, turn on, and abandon American society (though a fair number briefly flirted with it). If they had, America would not likely have been able to maintain its long-standing position as the world's largest economy.

Boomers have always been oversized. As a generation they proved to be equivalent to the "Supersize" or "Big Gulp" soft drink sizes introduced in the 1990s by fast-food restaurants and convenience stores. Boomers are bigger than big, and I've long noticed that their impact on markets is always far more disproportionate than their already massive size, in influencing both expanding and shrinking markets. When the Baby Boomers exited the Japanese sport motorcycle market of men ages 16 to 24, the market was not reduced by 11 percent, the difference in native-born population size between the Boomers and native-born Gen Xers. No, it fell precipitously by about 80 percent and then disappeared almost entirely. It's like markets have a mind of their own and rise and fall on demographic suggestion.

Levi's jeans were very popular with the Silent Generation. My three older brothers, all Silents, lived in them. When the Boomers aged into adult-size jeans in the 1960s, Levi's popularity took off like an Apollo moon rocket launch. The sale of Levi's didn't increase by 50 percent, the approximate difference between their numbers and those of the Silent Generation. No, sales increased geometrically. Levi's sales volume increased to $8 billion at their height in the early 1990s. Why? Because a market multiplier somehow takes over. When the Baby Boomers stopped wearing Levi's in the late 1990s, sales plummeted by 75 percent, not by the 11 percent that marks the difference between them and the native-born Xers.

Here is where I am going with this line of thought: The Silent Generation is currently consuming everything that 70- to 80-year-olds would normally consume, and they are doing it commensurate to their population size. I believe that when the Baby Boomers age into the footprint left behind by the Silent Generation, everything elderly will be put on steroids. I really do not think that we, the United States, are ready for the magnitude of marketing, political, economic, cultural, and commercial changes that are going to take place as the Baby Boomers become elderly.

America certainly wasn't ready for them when they started reaching adulthood.

8

The Unfairly Maligned Generation X

WHILE THE BABY Boomers are undoubtedly the most influential generation of the past 100 years, if not the entire history of the United States, Generation X is perhaps the most maligned generation of the past 100 years. Following in the footsteps of the massive Baby Boom generation, the Gen Xers had big shoes to fill, but it was like putting size 6 ½ feet into size 12 combat boots.

Let's look at the math again: The Baby Boomers by birth numbers added up to 78.2 million people as of the onset of Generation X in 1965. This compares to the 69.5 million native-born Gen Xers, a population 8.7 million smaller than the Boomers preceding them. That is 11 percent smaller, which, when representative of a customer-base decline, would be considered highly significant—perhaps "terrifying" would be a more apt description from a marketer's point of view.

So what problems do you see with this difference in population? Can you name some of the difficulties this presented as the generations aged through the time continuum?

Japanese sport motorcycle sales! Right on, but I already told you that one.

How about schools, toy sales, pediatric care? And then, further on in time, college and university enrollment, and then the job market? Think Gen X caused some difficulty with all of them? Well, you would be correct.

As Gen X came into the world between 1965 and 1984, toy sales nosedived, schools and maternity wards closed. When the first of them started reaching adulthood, universities and colleges were forced to lower admission standards so as to entice more potential applicants, and jobs went begging. And, in my opinion, this relative scarcity of younger workers and resultant need to raise wages to attract talent was partially responsible for the collapse and off-shoring of America's manufacturing industry.

This dearth of Gen X workers was also partly responsible for the large increase in immigration into the United States, both legal and illegal, with the annual number of legal immigrants surging dramatically starting in 1989, almost as if trying to catch up with the large decline in births that had begun some twenty-four years before. Or, to put it another way, as of 1989, there were more than 1.5 million fewer native-born job seekers ages 20 to 24 than there had been as of 1985. Thus, in 1989 legal immigration almost doubled to about 1.1 million, which was followed in 1990 by a surge to 1.5 million, and then to about 1.8 million in 1991. Not that all of these immigrants were ages 20 to 24, but I'd be willing to bet that a vast majority of them were in their 20s and 30s. And as such, these younger, Gen X–aged immigrants served as padding, so to speak, that helped the native-born Generation X fill those size 12 combat boots. Not that it became a perfect fit, more like padding the insides of the oversize boots with newspaper, but we'll explore that further later in the chapter.

So, why did the Baby Boom peter out and lead to the diminutive Generation X? Well, a variety of factors contributed to this drop in population. One such factor was certainly the popular perception that Zero Population Growth was the answer to all the earth's issues and problems. Eliminate the people, eliminate the problems.

Rings hollow to me. Yes, we had fewer kids per couple during the years of 1965 to 1984. Fertility dropped to below replacement level of 2.2 to 2.4 kids per couple to about 1.5 to 1.6 kids per couple. If you don't replace yourself, your population shrinks. It is not a good thing for marketing. Another obvious reason there are fewer Generation Xers than Baby Boomers is the fact that Generation X had fewer potential parents. Most Generation Xers had Silent Generation (born 1925 to 1944) parents. The Silent Generation was the smallest U.S. generation of the last 100 years. Baby Boomers were primarily the kids of the huge G.I. Generation born 1905 to 1924.

Perhaps a more important question is why weren't people generally aware of this population decline and taking active steps to mitigate the impacts? People became very aware of the Baby Boom and to a large degree anticipated its implications (it being the first generation to be thoroughly dissected and analyzed by marketers as it was coming into the world), but as the Gen Xers came of age few people seemed to focus on the generation's diminutive size, but instead chose to chastise them for being lazy, unmotivated couch potatoes. This despite the fact that demographers recognized and had reported on the decline in birth numbers, and that Gen X was referred to as "Baby Bust" long before being labeled Generation X. Instead of acknowledging that there just weren't enough of them to fill the job market, people seemed to assume that large numbers of Gen Xers were staying home and avoiding work. I've said it before: People just can't seem to count people, especially, it would seem, when distinct populations go into decline.

As the Baby Boom became apparent in the late 1940s, demographer P.K. Whelpton was quoted in *Newsweek* as saying, "When the number of persons is rising rapidly it is necessary to prepare for the increase. Houses and apartments must be built; streets must be paved; power, light, water, and sewer systems must be extended; existing factories, stores and other business structures must be enlarged or new ones erected; and much machinery must be manufactured." Why weren't demographers being quoted about the inverse when the Baby Bust become apparent in the late 1960s and early 1970s?

Generation X is undoubtedly also the most misunderstood American generation of the past 100 years. Heck, people can't even come close to agreeing to an approximate delineation for it. While the Boomer delineation is generally agreed to span the end of World War II until about the mid-1960s, Xer delineations are all over the map. As noted in Chapter 3, it is often delineated as spanning only ten to fifteen years, and it has wide variations in researcher-denoted year-of-birth spans.

Only ten to fifteen years, really? And how can a researcher justify starting Gen X in 1961 when the Baby Boom was still very much in full swing? Or for that matter starting the generation in 1970, long after the Baby Boom was over? No wonder Generation X is so hard to define and that researchers can't seem to agree on what distinguishes the generation.

Generation X, now aged 33 to 52, has grown to a population of 82.9 million, thanks to the addition of about 13.4 million Gen X immigrants. While those immigrants did not arrive in time to help maintain the robust Baby Boom–influenced sale of Japanese sport motorcycles or Levi's jeans, they will undoubtedly help mitigate what could be a looming catastrophe.

Say what? you ask.

Think about this: By birth numbers Gen X was 11 percent smaller in total mass than the huge footprint of the Baby Boomers. With those diminutive numbers it could not compete quantitatively at any level, whether in consumption, cultural participation, contribution to GDP, or business and political leadership. The live birth peak of the Baby Boom generation in 1957 to the trough of the X Generation in 1973 represented a 25 percent free fall.

There are stages in our lives when different things are expected of us, and understanding what is expected of us is very important. When we are born, we are totally reliant on others. We eat a lot and produce nothing. If we were left alone, we would probably die. We gradually become more and more self-reliant as we age. In theory, at least, when we are in our 20s we begin to make our own way. We can provide for ourselves. What we eat is on par with what we produce. As we age through our 30s, we begin to produce more than we eat so we provide for others who are producing less than they eat. As we age through our 40s, the dependence of others, both young and old, on our ability to produce a lot more than we eat becomes very great and peaks at age 50, when we are at the height of our productivity. Between 50 and 60 our production begins to diminish as does the reliance of others on our ability to provide. Between 60 and 80 we tend to be self-reliant, meeting our own needs. After about age 80 the total dependence starts all over again. We can no longer effectively produce, but we still eat and require care. This principle of reliance and provision can be found in families, cultures, and countries throughout the world. It is a very old principle that dates back to early man. It is a natural balance. It is so powerful that it drives economies and provides health to nations.

So how does Generation X fit in with this principle? By birth numbers Generation X had about 9 million fewer people in its ranks than the Baby Boomer Generation it followed and about 10 million fewer people than Generation Y right behind it. Generation X is taking over the role of the nation's primary provider and by birth numbers cannot possibly succeed because they don't have the critical mass. And as most first-generation immigrants do not generally became high-wage earners, it is unclear as to how much the immigrant population will be able to help Gen X carry what is a very large load.

As you will see in Chapters 19 and 20, Gen X was not able to help maintain the shared-risk insurance model and seemed unable to afford the housing that started coming online as the Boomers started retiring. Will federal, state, and local governments be able to generate tax revenues equivalent to those garnered from the Baby Boomers during their peak earnings years? All indications suggest that the answer might be no, but without the additional Gen X immigrant population, the answer would be a resounding "no way," and America would likely be facing a financial catastrophe that would cripple the country for the next twenty-five years, if not longer.

9

Coming of Age with Generation Y

WHAT IS THE biggest thing that differentiates Generation Y from the other generations living in America today?

Stumped?

The fourth word in that opening question provides a big clue: "biggest"!

Born between 1985 and 2004, and currently numbering about 86.6 million souls, Gen Y, also commonly referred to as the "Millennials," is the biggest generation in the nation's history.[1] By birth numbers alone, Gen Y, with 79.5 million native-born members, beat out the Baby Boomers by 1.3 million, and have thus far added another 7.1 million immigrants to their ranks. Currently aged 13–32, no other living American generation has boosted its ranks with such a large number of immigrants so quickly. And with legal immigration alone boosting the U.S. population by 1 million annually, and with Gen Y still a few years away from the midpoint of the 31.6-year-old average age of an immigrant arriving in the United States, it would appear that Gen Y numbers could near 100 million within the next twenty years.

Generation Y did not erupt into existence like the Baby Boom year 1946 but instead rode a slow-growing wave of increasing births that started in the mid-1970s following the Gen X 1973 low year for births. The 1985 first year Gen Y crop marked an increase of about 100,000 births from the last year of Gen X, and by 1990 annual births were more than 1 million more than those of that Gen X 1973 birth trough, which had registered only about 3.1 million births. Naturally, the number of Gen Y births varied every year, but on average Gen Y produced about a half million more people per year than had Gen X.

Needless to say, but, a half million is a "big" number . . . especially when you multiply it by 20. And as we know from previous chapters, bigger population cohorts generally lead to bigger markets. Thus, in considering the size and expected continued growth of this generation, what conclusion immediately comes to mind?

"Growing market," perhaps? If so, you would be correct, and on so many different levels, because the generation is just so massive that it should increase demand for just about everything money can buy in America and the rest of the world. By some measures Gen Y is already having an impact on particular markets, such as education, clothing, and food, but Gen Y is still relatively young and the full extent of its power yet to be realized.

As with the large Boomer generation during its ascent, Gen Y is under significant observation and study by researchers and market analysts eager to capitalize on this large generation by determining exactly what makes its members tick. The amount of study conducted on this generation will undoubtedly dwarf that which was done on the Baby Boomers; however, I believe the findings will be all over the map due to vast differences in delineation. With the Millennials, I've seen just about every variation possible, from ten-year generational spans to twenty-five, and being those people born within a range anytime between 1977 and 2010. What really gets my goat, though, is those researchers who delineate Gen Y with an ending birth date range prior to the year 2000, and yet still call the generation "Millennials."

Researchers have also had difficulty agreeing on the appropriate name for the generation. "Generation Y" reportedly first came into use by *Ad Age* magazine in 1993, in an article that referred to it being the generation following Gen X, and naming its beginning birth year as 1982. Meanwhile "Millennials" was reportedly coined for the generation in 1987 by authors William Strauss and Neil Howe in their book *Generations: The History of America's Future, 1584 to 2069*. Other researchers tagged the generation with "Echo Boomers," in reference to the generation's apparent size relative to the Baby Boomers. Other names include "Trophy Kids," "Generation Next," Generation We," "Generation Flux," "Peter Pan Generation," "Boomerang Generation," and more. One researcher has even suggested that the Millennials should be combined with the younger members of Generation X and be called "Generation Me" to account for their overwhelming sense of entitlement and narcissism.

All in all, until the growing attention in recent years on Generation Z, the newest members of the generational parade, I had never seen so much disagreement about what constitutes a specific generation as I had with Gen Y. Fortunately many researchers do delineate Gen Y similar to my twenty-year generation span, and close to my 1985 to 2004 generational birth range, and most researchers seem to be ascribing similar attributes to this generation as it ascends into adulthood.

While the Boomers essentially came of age with the optimism of the Kennedy years and subsequent assassination, the 1960s civil rights movement, the Vietnam War, and societal upheaval, among other things, Gen Y has come of age with the War on Terrorism, Great Recession, climate change, and the greatest upheaval in communications technology in history. When I was coming of age, the biggest "high-tech" consumer goods were television sets and the transistor radio, and the biggest high-tech development was "color" TV. Gen Y lives and breathes high-tech, and its members spend far more time interacting with various high-tech gadgets than doing anything else.

This might seem somewhat scary to us old Baby Boomers, and maybe it should be, given an experience I recently had in a supermarket checkout line. It wasn't the cost of food, although that was staggering enough. It was a comment by the young woman who was checking me through the line at light speed.

I estimated that she was in her late teens, born in the late-nineties, a perfect example of a Gen Yer. She looked at my wristwatch and said, "You don't see many of those anymore."

I thought that this was a really cool comment because it is rare that anyone recognizes the fact that I wear an antique Rolex. I thought to myself that this young woman was surprisingly savvy for her age. I proudly told her that it was a 1974 Stainless Rolex Precision that actually needed to be wound in order to operate. Her response was a blank stare, not what I expected, and an obvious communication disconnect. Then she said, "Most people don't wear watches anymore." It was my turn for the blank stare and then the chill. Watches are outdated. I am old.

When I got home, I relayed my experience in the checkout line to my two Generation Y daughters, one 19 and one 22. Their expressions essentially said, *"Where have you been?"*

My oldest said, "Haven't you noticed that we don't wear watches?"

I guess I hadn't.

My youngest then dropped the real bomb: "Dad, you wear an analog watch. I have friends who cannot tell time that way."

Was she kidding? No, she was not kidding. Is this what Bob Dylan meant by the lyrics "The Times They Are a Changin'"?

I'm not sure who the first self-made Baby Boomer millionaire was, but there are already three self-made Generation Y billionaires, and perhaps as many as 1 million Gen Y millionaires, though certainly not all of these are "self-made." Pretty impressive given that the oldest members of Gen Y have been in the workforce for only about ten years.

No matter how this generation finds itself defined or defines itself in the next few years, there is little doubt that Generation Y is going to be a force to be reckoned with.

By the way, have I mentioned that it's big? Really, really big?

10

The As-Yet-to-Be-Defined Generation Z

WITH MY DELINEATION marking them as being born between 2005 and 2024, and as of 2015 ages zero to 11, Generation Z remains undefined. As of 2015, about 43 million had been born, perhaps somewhere in the neighborhood of half the birth numbers that we can expect from this still-forming generation. While the generation is still too young and small to assert itself—or for that matter, make a name for itself—I believe that this generation will emerge as the most ethnically and culturally diverse ever in the United States. I also would expect that this generation will become more technically savvy than their predecessors, Gen Y. But this stands to reason, because as the technology evolves we have to evolve with it.

While I refuse to define this generation beyond its expected diversity and technological ability because it has yet to "come of age," there is no lack of pundits and generational "experts" out there willing to wax poetic about the characteristics of this still-to-emerge generation. And these characteristics are all over the map. "Least likely to believe that there is such a thing as the American Dream." "More risk adverse than the Millennials." "Have a digital bond to the Internet." "Tend to be independent." "Expect to find a job that will be an expression of their identity."

A job! Really. . . ?

The oldest are only 11 years old, and I seriously doubt that these 11-year-olds are already pondering their future employment.

Oh, and many of these pundits are also asserting that it is the largest generation currently alive in America, but I would surmise that these generational geniuses are either using an especially broad birth range, or just haven't bothered to actually count their numbers according to the delineation being used.

From what I can tell, the wide variety in opinions about characteristics and size of Gen Z is due primarily to the broad disparity in delineations given for Gen Y, which was caused in large part to the widespread mis-delineation of Generation X. In fact, I believe that this wide variation in delineations is going to make it about the most screwed-up generation with regard to perceptions about exactly how many they are, how old, and what range of ages.

You have heard me rail in previous chapters about the problems caused by the wonky delineations of Gen X and Y, and those problems are really coming home to roost with Gen Z. I have seen Gen Z's first birth year called as early as 1990 and as late as 2010, and seen the generational timeline described as as short as seven years to as many as twenty-five.

Seven years? Yeah, born between 1996 and 2003. Oh, and this narrowly defined Gen Z is "independent, stubborn, pragmatic, and always in a rush," and they also "live a life that seems a million miles removed from the hopes, dreams, and morals of previous generations."

Ludicrous, I say, about both this pundit's delineation and his description of this age group.

The nine-year Gen Z delineation I saw used the birth years 1990 and 1999, and made me wonder what happened to the Millennials.

In so many of the descriptions and delineations I've seen, the lines between Gens Y and Z seem so blurred, and yet the pundits profess to have a clear understanding about what distinguishes them from each other. And yet these experts cannot even agree on a moniker for Gen Z. Take your pick: "Post Millennials," "Net Gen," "Gen Wii," "iGeneration," "Homeland Generation," "Digitarians," "Internet Generation," "Digital Natives," and "Plurals."

Plurals? I know, *say what?*

Oh, and some pundits have tried to refer to Gen Z as Generation Me, calling them "narcissistic," self-absorbed, etc. And yes, that same name and vapid descriptions were also applied by some to Gen X and, to a greater degree, Gen Y. I would have to say that these pundits are all mixed up because of their wonky delineations.

The Baby Boomers were cut-and-dried, with just about everyone agreeing that the Boomer birth years pretty much ranged between 1945 and 1964 and consisted of the long-accepted twenty-year generational span. Because so-called experts played around with and/or short-changed the age range of Gen X so much, it naturally affected the subsequent delineations of Gens Y and Z. So much so that most people don't really know where Gen X ends and Gen Y begins, and that one person's definition of Gen Z might be another person's definition of late-year Gen Y.

This lack of consistent delineation has gotten so bad that pundits are already starting to spout off about the next generation, which is thus far being referred to as "Generation Alpha," with a few of these pundits claiming that this generation began in 2010.

Bottom line is that if you're going to pay attention to any so-called generational or demographic "expert," make sure that he or she has clearly delineated the generation in question, and that the delineation makes sense.

But I digress . . . back to Gen Z, or, more specifically, back to *my* delineation and understanding of this still-emerging generation.

Generation Z births began in 2005 at the tail end of a Generation Y slow rise in birth numbers that started in 1997, which represented Gen Y's second-lowest birth year, with about 3.8 million registered births. By 2004 the annual number had risen to just over 4.1 million, and was followed by an increase of roughly 26,000 births in Gen Z's first year. Birth numbers continued a slow increase for the next couple of years, hitting over 4.3 million in 2007, but then, in what is largely believed to be a response to the financial crisis of 2008 and subsequent Great Recession, birth numbers dropped by about 70,000 in 2008 and then dropped down just below 4 million in 2009, where they remained through 2014.[1]

My belief that this generation will be the most ethnically and racially diverse to date in the United States is being borne out by the official annual birth data. While Hispanic births represented about 12.5 percent of annual births during the first year of Generation Y, as defined in this book, was actually 1985 . . . by the first year of Gen Z in 2005, Hispanics represented about 25 percent of annual births, a figure that has held up until 2014. Asian births, meanwhile, climbed from about 3 percent of annual births in 1985 to about 7 percent as of 2014. Consider also that prior to 1980 Asian birth data wasn't even recorded as a separate entity by the nation's vital statistics system.

On a numeric basis, the number of White births and Black births has been holding consistent since the start of Gen Y, with a respective rough annual average of 3.1 million White births and 625,000 Black births. As most Hispanics tend to identify as White, this has not significantly altered the racial birth proportions; however, the ethnically based proportions have definitely shifted with the rise of Hispanic births. While Asian birth numbers reached an all-time high of more than 280,000 in 2014, the proportional increase is relatively small.

What does this portend? I believe that this will serve to continue the "colorblinding" of America that is so evident with Generation Y, which appears to be the least bigoted and racially prejudiced of any American generation in history.

Given birth numbers to date, it would appear that Gen Z could end up as large as its preceding generation, Y, and thus, will not likely cause any massive sales declines as was the case with the diminutive-by-birth Gen X. On a strictly numeric basis, Gen Z appears to be a continuation of Gen Y. Unlike the four previous generations—Silents, Boomers, X, and Y—which arrived with noticeable shifts in numbers, there is nothing numerical yet to really distinguish Z from Y. Perhaps another reason pundits are having such a hard time differentiating between the two.

11

Now That You Know Who These People Are, and How Many, Where Are They?

O**K, YOU NOW** understand the U.S. population on a generational basis. At this point you should be able to answer some
basic questions about these generations in relation to
markets.

Such as, which generation represents the largest potential
market?

Did you answer Generation Y? If so, give yourself a gold star.

Which generation is going to have the biggest impact on healthcare over the next twenty years?

I trust that you answered the Baby Boomers. While I only alluded to this potential impact, it couldn't be more obvious to anyone who understands the generations and/or has done some basic
counting.

Which generation, despite its large numbers, is likely going to
struggle as it follows its predecessor generation?

No doubt you were reading carefully and correctly answered
Generation X, and understand that this is due to its relative low
birth numbers and the lower earning power of the immigrant component of its population.

If you take these six generations and mix them together, what do you have?

The roughly 320 million people who constitute the resident population of the United States. And while counting 320 million people certainly presents difficulties, think about this: These 320 million people are interspersed across a country that covers more than 3.5 million square miles. If all things were equal, this would mean that something along the lines of ninety people lived in every square mile of the country.

But of course, it's not that easy, as the population is not evenly spread out across the country. While the overall U.S. population usually experiences steady growth, on a regional, state-wide, county, city, and even neighborhood basis, populations are often in flux in one way or another. Some places never seem to change, while other places change so fast that they're hardly recognizable twenty years after you last saw them. Populations are not static, and Americans tend to move around a lot. And even the places that never seem to change undergo population shifts that may appear subtle on the surface but may lead to any number of unexpected consequences as the years pass by. For example, the slow erosion of a school's student body ultimately leading to school closures, or the "geriatrification" of a town to the point where the town council realizes that the majority of its citizens are on fixed incomes and can't afford any more tax hikes.

Consider this hypothetical location-based demographic scenario: In 1990 two brothers, Phil and Ted, received the exclusive right to franchise McDonald's restaurants in their respective counties. Phil has the franchise rights for the fictitious Mayberry County, North Carolina, while Ted has the franchise rights for the equally made-up Moosejaw County, Maine. We'll say that both counties are an equal mix of rural and urban and include one county seat city and four small towns, with the 100,000 population of each county distributed in this mix in a similar fashion. Each county is equal distance from its respective state population center and/or state capital, and both have similar breakdowns of employment opportunities with two textile mills, 100 small-scale farms, a furniture-making factory, a pharmaceutical plant, and sixty retail establishments. Finally, we'll assume that the populations of these fictional counties will grow in approximation to the average population growth of their respective states.

Assume that Phil and Ted each opened their first McDonald's in 1990. As of 2015, how do you think each of the brothers has fared with his business and how many restaurants do you believe each brother has opened in his respective county?

Stumped?

Well, given that the state of North Carolina's population has almost doubled since 1990 and that its population's median age has been steadily declining to a recent low of about 36, I would posit that Phil has opened at least four McDonald's restaurants and is feeling fairly well off. But because the state of Maine's population has hardly grown at all, and its median age has been steadily rising to a recent high of almost 42, I would suggest that Ted is still operating just the one restaurant and perhaps struggling to get his second kid through college.

Granted, this is a very simplistic hypothetical scenario, and certainly other factors would likely play a role in the level of success for these brothers' respective businesses, but absent population growth there is usually little reason for the expansion of such businesses.

In fact, I know of several towns in North Carolina that only had one McDonald's restaurant back in 1990, but now have anywhere from three to eight. Likewise, I know of towns in Maine that today still only have the same one McDonald's restaurant that they had back in 1990.

Let me restate the premise of this chapter: Population changes can have vast and profound impacts on countries, regions, states, counties, and towns. Population increases can provide a boost to an area's economy by driving the growth of industries, services, jobs, and tax revenues. And while not the only catalyst for driving economic growth, population increases are certainly one of the linchpins needed for perpetuating economic growth, as a fall in population can put the brakes on the "perpetual" part of the growth and lead to a decline in industries, services, jobs, and tax revenues. In many cases, economic stagnation begets population decline, but in some instances population declines can presage economic downturns; no matter which comes first, these population declines are almost always indicative of current or imminent economic deterioration.

And while an increasing population is generally beneficial for economies on the local, state, regional, and national levels, a growing population also presents numerous challenges, such as the need for more government services such as schools, hospitals, and social assistance, along with whatever infrastructure may be needed to support the additional population. The composition and the rate of the increasing population brings additional challenges and potential stressors on all levels.

Consider these questions relating to population growth: Is the increase being driven primarily by

- births?
- births with a lack of elderly-related mortality?
- highly educated immigrants looking for high-tech work?
- undereducated immigrants looking for any work?
- under-30s looking for work and the good life?
- Baby Boomers seeking paradise in retirement?
- urbanites moving to the country?
- rural folks moving to the city?
- or, and most likely, some combination of all of the above?

Consider also: Is the increase looking like

- a fifty-year population double?

- o a thirty-year population double?
- o a twenty-year population double?
- o a ten-year population double?
- o indeterminable because it's coming in spurts and sputters?

All of the above composition and rate scenarios present significant challenges but also offer opportunities. And these composition and rate scenarios, along with scenarios related to population declines, play out in a wide variety of ways depending upon the city, state, and region.

So, let's take a closer look at the demographics of the country on a regional basis.

TABLE 11.1

REGIONAL RATES OF POPULATION CHANGE 1990–2015[1]

PLACE	1990 POPULATION	2015 POPULATION	NUMERIC CHANGE	PERCENTAGE CHANGE
Northeast	50,809,229	56,283,891	5,474,662	10.7%
South	85,445,930	121,182,847	35,736,317	41.8%
Midwest	59,668,632	67,907,403	8,238,771	13.8%
West	52,786,082	76,044,679	23,258,597	44.0%
United States	248,709,873	321,418,820	72,708,947	29.2%

TABLE 11.2

REGIONAL GROWTH BY DECADE—1990S VERSUS 2000S

PLACE	1990S NUMERIC GROWTH	PERCENTAGE CHANGE	2000S NUMERIC GROWTH	PERCENTAGE CHANGE
Northeast	2,785,149	5.4%	1,722,862	3.2%
South	14,790,890	17.3%	14,318,924	14.3%
Midwest	4,724,144	7.9%	2,534,225	3.9%
West	10,411,850	19.7%	8,747,621	13.8%
United States	32,712,033	13.2%	27,323,632	9.7%

TABLE 11.3
REGIONAL RATES OF POPULATION CHANGE 2010–2015

PLACE	2010 POPULATION	2015 POPULATION	NUMERIC CHANGE	PERCENTAGE CHANGE
Northeast	55,318,348	56,283,891	965,543	1.7%
South	114,562,953	121,182,847	6,619,894	5.8%
Midwest	66,929,897	67,907,403	977,506	1.4%
West	71,946,907	76,044,679	4,097,772	5.7%
United States	308,758,105	321,418,820	12,660,715	4.1%

We have three tables showing different values for varied time periods, but all telling a similar story. As a budding demographer, you should be able to look at these tables and tell me this story.

You can hardly fail to notice the phenomenal population growth of the South and West, and that growth in the Northeast and Midwest is comparatively muted. But if you look closer, you should notice that not only is the growth in the Northeast and Midwest significantly weaker than that of the South and West, but that their rates of growth are in significant decline.

While the overall greater than 10 percent population increase experienced by the Northeast and Midwest between 1990 and 2015 would suggest healthy population growth, the Northeast's growth dropped by more than 60 percent between the 1990s and 2000s, while that of the Midwest dropped by 54 percent. As can be seen, the South's growth hardly dropped at all, while that of the West fell by a relatively modest 16 percent.

Looking at the current decade, it would appear from the "2010–2015" table that the Northeast should be able to maintain, if not exceed, its 2000s growth rate, while the Midwest seems to be heading for a further decline. The South and West, meanwhile, seem to be heading for modest declines.

The overall takeaway from this is that in considering increasing population as a positive factor, the South and West are on target to be the primary economic beneficiaries of population growth, as both regions are experiencing well-above-average growth, while the Northeast and Midwest are experiencing significant below-average growth.

According to the 2010 Census, the U.S. population grew by about 27.3 million from 2000 to 2010, and, according to recent Census Bureau estimates, grew by another 12.6 million from 2010 until July of 2015, for a combined total of almost 40 million. Regionally just over 52 percent (20,946,027) of the nation's 2000 to 2015 growth occurred in the South and about 33 percent (12,846,747) in the West. The Midwest accounted for only about 9 percent (3,514,627) of the nation's growth, while the Northeast accounted for less than 6 percent (2,689,513). The natural increase—births minus deaths—was strongest in the South and West, while the Northeast and Midwest lagged considerably. In fact, in looking at the 2010 to 2015 period, the North recorded 35 percent more births than deaths, while the Midwest recorded 41 percent more births than deaths. The South recorded 52 percent more births than deaths during this period, but was far outdone by the West, which recorded 90 percent more births than deaths.

I would surmise that the relative high number of births compared to deaths in the South and West are due in part to the large Hispanic populations in each, as Hispanic families in America have historically had the highest fertility and birthrates. I would also posit that the ratio is much stronger in the West than the South because mortality rates are generally highest in the Southern states.

Perhaps more telling from an economic standpoint are the rates of net migration, and, in particular, rates of domestic migration into or out of the regions. Net migration, which accounts for both the total number of international migration into the country and domestic interstate resident migration, represented population declines in excess of 500,000 for both the Northeast and Midwest but accounted for about 50 percent of the population increases in both the South (6.2 million) and West (3.1 million) from 2000 to 2008. While 3,609,854 domestic U.S. residents moved into the South and 445,496 moved into the West, almost 2.5 million migrated out of the Northeast and about 1.6 million departed from the Midwest during this time frame.

This decline reversed to a small degree for the Northeast between 2010 and 2015 but continued in the Midwest.[2] In the Northeast, the 1,247,700 domestic residents who moved out of the Northeast between 2010 and 2015 were offset by about 1.4 million international migrants[3] for a net migration gain of about 152,000. In the Midwest, 962,626 domestic residents moved out while just under 700,000 international migrants moved in, for a net migration loss of 269,501.

Those migratory population declines for the Northeast and Midwest represented gains for the South and West, which took in about 1.8 million and 350,000 domestic migrants, respectively, along with about 1.9 million and 1.3 million respective international migrants.

TABLE 11.4

COMPONENTS OF POPULATION CHANGE 2010–2015

REGION	NATURAL INCREASE	DOMESTIC MIGRATION	INTERNATIONAL MIGRATION	NET CHANGE IN POPULATION*	2015 POPULATION
Northeast	871,276	-1,247,700	1,399,939	965,543	56,283,891
South	2,741,639	1,860,218	1,944,324	6,619,894	121,182,847
Midwest	1,279,234	-962,626	693,125	977,506	67,907,403
West	2,433,677	350,108	1,297,501	4,097,772	76,044,679
United States	7,325,826	n/a	5,334,889	12,660,715	321,418,820

*If you take the time to calculate the numbers in this table—for which I would commend you for your interest in "counting"—you will notice that the sums of the natural increases, domestic migration, and international migrations do not necessarily add up to the net changes in population. This is because the U.S. Census Bureau includes a "residual" in this number to account for "changes in the population that cannot be attributed to any specific demographic component." I toyed with using the "true" net change in population numbers according to calculating the aforementioned sums but decided that for the sake of consistency I should utilize the "official" numbers despite the odd variance and potential confusion that might ensue should a reader count my sums.

It is interesting to note that the regions with the smallest overall populations, the Northeast with almost 56.3 million and the Midwest with around 67.9 million, experienced large outflows of resident domestic migration, while the West (about 75 million) and particularly the South (just over 121 million) experienced healthy inflows. This would seem to follow the adage of "people want to go where the people are."

Also of significance within the "Components of Population Change 2010–2015" table is the large population number of international migrations. With the 5,334,889 international migrants representing just under 43 percent of the country's growth, the United States remains very much a nation of immigrants.

State population trends are far more complicated than regional trends, but in general states in the South and West experienced the healthiest population increases from 2000 to 2015. The states of Texas (plus more than 6.6 million), California (plus almost 5.3 million), and Florida (plus about 4.3 million) experienced the largest numerical population increases, followed by Georgia (plus 2 million), North Carolina (plus 2 million), and Arizona (plus 1.7 million). On the opposite end of the spectrum, Rhode Island (plus 7,615), Michigan (plus 16,357) and West Virginia (plus 43,767) recorded the smallest population increases during the 2000 to 2015 time frame.

But these large and small numbers tell only part of the story for these states, much as the numbers for the other states tell only part of their story. California's growth numbers, while certainly big, have significantly subsided from previous decades when it held the title of fastest-growing state, and domestic migration has reversed for perhaps the first time in history, with the state recording out-migration of more than a quarter million people between 2010 and 2015. Or take Michigan, which experienced a loss of about 54,000 residents between 2000 and 2010, but gained back over 38,000 between 2010 and 2015, thanks to a favorable birth-to-death ratio (net migration losses amounted to almost 100,000 during this time). Even Florida, with the second largest numerical increase, experienced a period of population decline, albeit brief, following the housing market meltdown of 2008. Or take North

Dakota, which was suffering population declines in the early 2000, only to experience significant migratory population gains in recent years due to the shale oil boom—little doubt that North Dakota will soon see signs of domestic migration reversal with the relative collapse of the price of oil.

And I'm just scratching the surface with regard to how complicated each state's demographics can be. In fact, during the various research I've conducted, I am always amazed by how different each state can be with regard to its respective demographics. Take my own state, Connecticut. Because Generations X and Y are proportionally smaller than that of the nation as a whole, and its Baby Boomer population is proportionally much bigger than that of the rest of the country, we Boomers still totally rule the roost. In fact, Generation Y, which is set to have such a big impact on the rest of the country, is, relatively speaking, a nonevent in the state of Connecticut.

And other than Fairfield County, international migration is not boosting Connecticut's population ranks, as the 104,537 domestic residents who moved out of the state between 2010 and 2015 were not supplanted by the 88,195 international migrants who moved into the state.

Hispanics? Sure, there are almost 500,000 within the state's 3.6 million population, but almost 60 percent of them are second- and third-generation Puerto Ricans. And, as these Puerto Ricans are essentially Americans and share a similar relative low fertility rate, they are unlikely to provide a population boost similar to that of the rest of the nation's Hispanic influx.

While I'm happy to be ruling the roost in Connecticut, I know that the state's demographics portend trouble ahead. Our Baby Boomer population is poised to overwhelm the state's healthcare and senior care services, with elderly populations set to rise from 44 percent to more than 125 percent by 2025 depending upon the town. My own town of Haddam is projected to see its elderly population more than double in the next ten short years. Meanwhile, we don't have a robust Generation X and Y following on our heels, and their smaller numbers might hinder their ability to carry our load. Adding insult to injury, Generation Z is also coming up quite short compared to the rest of the country. The state's youth population age 25 and under is projected to drop by almost 7 percent over the next ten years. It is clear that Connecticut towns will need to take a hard look at closing and consolidating schools. The upside is that schools are far and away the biggest local tax burden. Will taxes go down? They should. But don't get excited—diminishing populations of children don't bode well for the future of any Connecticut town. I am hoping that the remaining Generation Y young married couples have three kids each!

While people are people, demographers also keep track of the racial and ethnic composition of populations. This has become increasingly important in recent years, as the nation's population growth is no longer being driven by the majority White population. As you may recall from Chapter 4, Hispanics are experiencing the greatest rate of growth, while the White population is hardly growing at all. In fact, Whites are expected to lose their majority status by about 2045 if not sooner. Of course, there will be regional variations in the growth, or lack thereof, as you will see in the coming chapters on each region.

TABLE 11.5

RACIAL AND ETHNIC COMPOSITION OF U.S. POPULATION 2014

PLACE	2014 POPULATION	PERCENTAGE WHITE	PERCENTAGE HISPANIC	PERCENTAGE BLACK	PERCENTAGE ASIAN
Northeast	56,152,333	73.3%	13.8%	11.9%	6.2%
South	119,771,934	71.3%	16.9%	19.4%	3.1%
Midwest	67,745,108	84.2%	7.5%	10.4%	3.0%
West	75,187,681	69.5%	29.5%	4.6%	9.9%
United States	318,857,056	73.4%	17.3%	12.7%	5.2%

*Because Hispanic is not a "race," and not all "races" are accounted for, the percentages in this table are not supposed to add up to 100. The percentages of each of these population groups should be considered individually in relation to the total population.

At this juncture, I'm going to ask you to consider what you've learned in this chapter and to apply this demographic information to your business acumen.

What do you take away from this demographic sketch of the regions and commentary on a few states? That you should avoid the Northeast and Midwest and focus on the South and West? That Texas, California, and Florida represent boomtowns, while Michigan, West Virginia, and Rhode Island are turning into wastelands? That Connecticut's healthcare sector is about to be overburdened to the point of catastrophe?

Well, not exactly what I was looking for from you, but if such thoughts are crossing your mind it means that you are considering the implications of the demographics. And that is the point of this whole book—to show you the demographics while encouraging you to always consider their implications. And thus far you have learned how to count the people and figure out who they are, and now you are learning about where they are and where they are likely to go and/or grow. Please keep considering the potential implications as we explore these three dynamics with a closer look at each of the regions and their states.

12

The Northeast Beholden to International Immigration

AS MENTIONED, I live in Connecticut, one of nine states designated as the U.S. Northeast region of our country, and one of the six New England states. Connecticut is a study in contrasts. On the one hand Connecticut has the highest per capita income of any state in the union, owing in large part to Fairfield County being a bedroom community for New York's financial district. On the other hand Connecticut's cities, New London, New Haven, Bridgeport, and yes, Hartford, struggle financially. Go figure.

The Northeast has been competing with the Midwest for the past twenty-five years as to which region is the most demographically challenged, and by most measures would take the trophy. It has the smallest population (about 56 million, or about 17.5 percent of the total U.S. population), is experiencing the lowest growth rate (1.7 percent—roughly 960,000—from 2010 to 2015), and losing the most domestic residents (more than 1.2 million from 2010 to 2015) through out-migration. States in the Northeast also have the oldest populations by median age, and the lowest birth and fertility rates. Perhaps the region's only saving grace is that it took in the second highest number—almost 1.4 million—of international migrants from 2010 to 2015 for a net migration gain of about 152,000.

The U.S. Census Bureau delineates the Northeast region as the states of Maine, Vermont, New Hampshire, New York, Massachusetts, Rhode Island, Connecticut, New Jersey, and Pennsylvania. It is geographically the smallest region by a significant margin, and historically has been the most densely populated. Currently it is estimated that more than 80 percent of the Northeast population lives in urban areas.

The Northeast population has grown only a cumulative 10.8 percent since 1990, when the population was pegged by the Census Bureau at just under 50.1 million. This is measly growth when compared to the country as a whole, which experienced about 29 percent population growth during the same time, and is considered downright anemic when compared to the South, which saw a 41.8 percent population rise. And, on a decade-wise basis, the population increase numbers are dwindling down.

Between 2010 and 2015, the Northeast's natural increase (the difference between births and deaths) was 871,276, with 3,350,436 births and 2,479,160 deaths, with all three counts being the lowest among all regions, and the 26 percent birth-to-death ratio also being the lowest of the regions.

With the exception of Maine, with 1,646 more deaths than births, all of the Northeast states experienced natural increases. The most populated state, New York, at more than 19.3 million people, experienced the biggest natural increase with more than 467,000, while the least populated state, Vermont, with just over 600,000 people, saw a natural increase of just over 3,000, but at least, unlike Maine, it marked an increase. All of the states experienced domestic migration population losses, with four experiencing net migration losses: Connecticut, -16,342; New York, -22,308; Rhode Island, -3,445; and, Vermont, -2,432.

TABLE 12.1

COMPONENTS OF POPULATION CHANGE 2010–2015

PLACE	NATURAL INCREASE	DOMESTIC MIGRATION	INTERNATIONAL MIGRATION	NET CHANGE IN POPULATION*	2015 POPULATION
Connecticut	38,144	-104,537	88,195	16,768	3,590,886
Maine	-1,646	-4,143	7,041	967	1,329,328
Massachusetts	97,841	-46,933	202,434	246,605	6,794,422
New Hampshire	9,535	-5,524	10,377	14,142	1,330,608
New Jersey	173,618	-269,194	270,306	166,077	8,958,013
New York	467,883	-653,071	630,763	417,704	19,795,791
Pennsylvania	75,417	-132,073	164,475	99,616	12,802,503
Rhode Island	7,306	-25,743	22,298	3,367	1,056,298
Vermont	3,178	-6,482	4,050	297	626,042
The Region	871,276	-1,247,700	1,399,939	965,543	56,283,891

*As noted on the Components of Population Change table in Chapter 11, If you take the time to calculate the numbers in the table you will notice that the sums of the natural increases, domestic migration, and international migrations do not necessarily add up to the net changes in population. This is because the U.S. Census Bureau includes a "residual" in this number to account for "changes in the population that cannot be attributed to any specific demographic component." I toyed with using the "true" net change in population numbers according to calculating the aforementioned sums but decided that for the sake of consistency I should utilize the "official" numbers despite the odd variance and potential confusion that might ensue should a reader count my sums.

The numbers in the table above are indicative of the big story with regard to the demographics of the Northeast and have pretty much been playing out in this fashion for at least the past twenty years.

So, in looking at the numbers in the table above, what can you tell me?

Right, Maine's numbers do a pretty good job of showing why the hypothetical restaurateur named Ted in Chapter 11 never opened any new McDonald's restaurants and is currently struggling to get his second kid through college.

What else?

With the exception perhaps of New York, the natural increase populations do not seem to be particularly robust, especially given the size of the states' respective overall populations. In fact, the

UPSIDE THE NORTHEAST BEHOLDEN TO INTERNATIONAL IMMIGRATION

natural increase numbers are downright anemic. Based on those natural increase figures alone, it would take Pennsylvania more than 800 years to double its population, New Hampshire would need almost 700 years, and my own state of Connecticut would need more than 450 years. Even New York would need more than 200 years to double its population if relying on the five-year natural increase numbers of 2010 to 2015.

Notice anything else of note?

Bingo! People seem to be moving out—big-time!

On a regional basis, hardly enough international migrants are filling the gap left behind by the departing domestic migrants, and some states are fully reliant on the natural increase to maintain their populations. Without international migration numbers, Connecticut, New Jersey, New York, Pennsylvania, Rhode Island, and Vermont would have joined Maine in suffering population declines, as seen in the table with the scary theoretical population numbers below.

TABLE 12.2

THEORETICAL POPULATION CHANGE ABSENT INTERNATIONAL MIGRATION 2010–2015

STATE	NATURAL INCREASE	DOMESTIC MIGRATION	THEORETICAL NET CHANGE IN POPULATION
Connecticut	38,144	-104,537	-66,393
Maine	-1,646	-4,143	-5,789
Massachusetts	97,841	-46,933	50,908
New Hampshire	9,535	-5,524	4,011
New Jersey	173,618	-269,194	-95,576
New York	467,883	-653,071	-185,188
Pennsylvania	75,417	-132,073	-56,656
Rhode Island	7,306	-25,743	-18,437
Vermont	3,178	-6,482	3,304
The Region	871,276	-1,247,700	-376,424

Now let's take a closer look at the region's population change with a couple of tables showing short- and longer-term rates of growth for each state. Unfortunately, as with the previous tables in this chapter, the numbers are going to be underwhelming.

TABLE 12.3

RATES OF POPULATION CHANGE 2010–2015

PLACE	2010 POPULATION	2015 POPULATION	NUMERIC CHANGE	PERCENTAGE CHANGE
Massachusetts	6,547,817	6,794,422	246,605	3.7%
New York	19,378,087	19,795,791	417,704	2.1%
New Jersey	8,791,936	8,958,013	166,077	1.9%
New Hampshire	1,316,466	1,330,608	14,142	1.1%
Pennsylvania	12,702,887	12,802,503	99,616	0.78%
Connecticut	3,574,118	3,590,886	16,768	0.47%
Rhode Island	1,052,931	1,056,298	3,367	0.32%
Maine	1,328,361	1,329,328	967	0.07%
Vermont	625,745	626,042	297	0.04%
The Region	55,318,348	56,283,891	965,543	1.7%

TABLE 12.4

RATES OF POPULATION CHANGE 1990–2015

PLACE	1990 POPULATION	2015 POPULATION	NUMERIC CHANGE	PERCENTAGE CHANGE
Massachusetts	6,016,425	6,794,422	777,997	12.9%
New York	17,990,455	19,795,791	1,805,336	10.0%
New Jersey	7,730,188	8,958,013	1,227,825	15.9%
New Hampshire	1,109,252	1,330,608	221,356	19.9%
Pennsylvania	11,881,643	12,802,503	920,860	7.7%
Connecticut	3,287,116	3,590,886	303,770	9.2%
Rhode Island	1,003,464	1,056,298	52,834	5.2%
Maine	1,227,928	1,329,328	101,400	8.2%
Vermont	562,758	626,042	63,284	11.2%
The Region	50,809,229	56,283,891	5,474,662	10.8%

Can you say "anemic"?

Well, excepting Massachusetts, I suppose.

But let's stretch the time period out twenty-five years and see what happens.

OK, so not nearly as bad as the shorter-term numbers, but when you consider that the nation as a whole during this time frame grew by about 29 percent, well then, states from the Northeast would appear to be laggards.

Also of interest are the changes in racial and ethnic populations in the region. Have a look at this table:

TABLE 12.5

RACIAL AND ETHNIC POPULATION CHANGE IN THE NORTHEAST 2000–2014

RACE OR ETHNICITY	2000 POPULATION	2014 POPULATION	NUMERICAL CHANGE	PERCENTAGE CHANGE
White	41,533,502	41,157,961	-375,541	-0.9%
Non-Hispanic White	39,327,262	37,384,854	-1,942,408	-4.9%
Black	6,099,881	6,682,109	582,228	9.5%
Hispanic	5,254,087	7,729,357	2,475,270	47.1%
Asian	2,119,426	3,498,544	1,379,118	65.1%
All	53,594,378	56,152,333	2,557,955	4.8%

This would seem to indicate that the White folks aren't having babies and/or they are the primary members of the domestic migration outflows from the region.

As with the rest of the country, the Northeast is seeing strong growth in its Hispanic and Asian populations, while Black population growth can be considered healthy. Little doubt that on a proportional basis all of these populations are going to make gains in the coming years.

TABLE 12.6

RACIAL AND ETHNIC COMPOSITION OF U.S. POPULATION 2014

PLACE	2014 POPULATION	PERCENTAGE WHITE	PERCENTAGE HISPANIC	PERCENTAGE BLACK	PERCENTAGE ASIAN
Northeast	56,152,333	73.3%	13.8%	11.9%	6.2%
South	119,771,934	71.3%	16.9%	19.4%	3.1%
Midwest	67,745,108	84.2%	7.5%	10.4%	3.0%
West	75,187,681	69.5%	29.5%	4.6%	9.9%
United States	318,857,056	73.4%	17.3%	12.7%	5.2%

Looking forward, the Census Bureau as of 2005 released projections based on the 2000 Census that indicated that the Northeast's growth rate will continue to stagnate. For whatever reason, the Census Bureau "does not have a current set of state [or regional] population projections and currently has no plans to produce them."[2]

In its 2005 projections the Bureau determined that the Northeast will see the slowest growth in the country, with its population projected to increase by about 4.1 million, a 7.6 percent increase between 2000 and 2030. Meanwhile, the South "will rise again"—It is projected to experience a 42.9 percent increase in its population, which will grow by about 43 million.

Of the Northeast's nine states, the largest, New York, is projected to have the least growth, with its population theoretically adding only about 500,000 for 2.6 percent growth over the thirty-year period. Pennsylvania comes in with the second-lowest projected growth, with about 490,000 new residents for 4.0 percent growth. Projections for all the Northeast states are indicated in Table 12.7 on the following page.

We're halfway through the thirty-year time frame for the projections, and thus far I would say their accuracy is mixed. Both New York and Pennsylvania have already exceeded their 2030 projections, with New York's current population more than 300,000 larger than the 2030 projection, and Pennsylvania's 34,000 larger. The current population of Massachusetts suggests that it will likely exceed the 2030 projection by 2025, while the current population of Connecticut suggests that it could meet its 2030 projection with some

UPSIDE THE NORTHEAST BEHOLDEN TO INTERNATIONAL IMMIGRATION

significant help from natural increase and migration. The current populations and last fifteen years of growth for the remaining states suggest that they will definitely not meet 2030 projections.

TABLE 12.7

PROJECTED POPULATION CHANGE 2000 TO 2030—NORTHEAST

PLACE	2000 POPULATION	PROJECTED 2030 POPULATION	NUMERIC CHANGE	PERCENTAGE CHANGE
New Hampshire	1,235,786	1,646,471	410,685	33.2%
Vermont	608,827	711,867	103,040	16.9%
New Jersey	8,414,350	9,802,440	1,388,090	16.5%
Maine	1,274,923	1,411,097	136,174	10.7%
Massachusetts	6,349,097	7,012,009	662,912	10.4%
Rhode Island	1,048,319	1,152,941	104,622	10.0%
Connecticut	3,405,565	3,688,630	283,065	8.3%
Pennsylvania	12,281,054	12,768,184	487,130	4.0%
New York	18,976,457	19,477,429	500,972	2.6%
The Region	53,594,378	57,671,068	4,076,690	7.6%

TABLE 12.8

PROJECTED VERSUS ACTUAL POPULATION CHANGE 2000 TO 2015

PLACE	2000 POPULATION	PROJECTED 2015 POPULATION	ACTUAL 2015 POPULATION	NUMERICAL DIFFERENCE
Connecticut	3,405,565	3,635,414	3,590,886	-44,528
Maine	1,274,923	1,388,878	1,329,328	-59,550
Massachusetts	6,349,097	6,758,580	6,794,422	35,842
New Hampshire	1,235,786	1,456,679	1,330,608	-126,071
New Jersey	8,414,350	9,255,769	8,958,013	-297,756
New York	18,976,457	19,546,699	19,795,791	249,092
Pennsylvania	12,281,054	12,710,938	12,802,503	91,565
Rhode Island	1,048,319	1,139,543	1,056,298	-83,245
Vermont	608,827	673,169	626,042	-47,127
The Region	53,594,378	56,565,669	56,283,891	-281,778

With regard to New Hampshire I can only believe that the Census Bureau forecast the strong growth of more than 33 percent by 2030 due to its relative strong economy and low tax policies. Apparently that has not been enough to stimulate the strong population growth forecast by Census Bureau analysts.

Crunching the numbers of population growth is relatively easy—determining the reasons behind the Northeast's stagnating population growth[3] presents far more difficulties. Opinions abound, and added all together most of them probably have relevance and contribute to the problem.

The economy, naturally, would be a primary determinant of the migratory metric of population growth, as people tend to move where the jobs are. On a historic basis the region as a whole has long enjoyed one of the strongest economies in the country, and some economic indicators—such as strong per capita income growth and high GDPs—suggest that this strength may have ebbed but is still powerful. However, a large portion of this historic economic strength is primarily carried by the states of New York, New Jersey, Massachusetts, Connecticut, and Pennsylvania. Moreover, the region's economic health fluctuates over time and varies widely on a sub-regional, county-by-county, and even city-by-city basis, with some areas being economic powerhouses, others being destitute, and many somewhere in between.

While space in this book does not allow an in-depth examination of all the economic factors that may be contributing to the region's stagnating population growth, the loss of manufacturing jobs in the region is definitely having a significant impact. According to analysts, the United States on the whole lost 5.7 million manufacturing jobs representing 33 percent of all manufacturing jobs in the 2000s, with the historical manufacturing centers in the Northeast and Midwest seeing the greatest declines. Not that the loss of manufacturing jobs in the Northeast started in the 2000s, as the region has been bleeding manufacturing jobs since the 1970s.

According to Kenneth M. Johnson, senior demographer at the Carsey School of Public Policy, the Northeast is growing slower than the rest of the country in large part because many of these states, especially the Northern ones, do not attract immigrants like states in the rest of the country (immigrants being the key in supporting the entire U.S. demographic, he notes), and domestic residents are migrating out because of the loss of manufacturing jobs. "There has been a significant population loss from what had been traditionally manufacturing counties," he said, adding that an unrecognized factor is that "a larger part of the rural workforce works in manufacturing than the urban." Many of these areas have experienced difficult economic times for the past ten to twenty years, he said, and, as a result, significant out-migration.

Mark Mather of the Population Reference Bureau says, "It's all about jobs," noting that parts of the Northeast "have been losing population for decades due to loss of employment opportunities, especially in manufacturing and farming." Mather adds that the out-migration "is most pronounced for young adults," and once that segment of the population declines, "the number of children and families starts to dwindle."

While employment opportunities are certainly having an impact on the region's population trends, the cost of living also plays a role. The *Boston Globe*, which chronicled Massachusetts's stagnating population throughout the 2000s, conducted a poll of former state residents that indicated better jobs and lower housing costs were the top reasons for leaving the state, with 73 percent saying their new home was more spacious than their former Massachusetts one, 54 percent indicating that they were enjoying a higher standard of living, and half reporting that housing costs were a major factor in their departure.

Rich States, Poor States, the 2015 State Economic Competitiveness Index from the American Legislative Exchange Council (ALEC), calls the Northeast "America's New Rust Belt," and blames high taxes (both personal and corporate), irresponsible government spending, and overregulation as the primary cause of job losses, and resultant population declines. Using fifteen parameters that primarily deal with taxation and regulation, the index gives the states of the Northeast region among the worst economic outlook rankings, and suggests that the extensive out-migration of people will continue absent state government policy changes.

ALEC's report describes how residents and companies in the region, with the exception of New Hampshire, pay state taxes "high above the national average." The report notes that "high taxes don't redistribute income, they redistribute people."

While most of the Northeastern states' personal income and property tax rates are "well above the national average," *all* of their corporate tax rates are far above the average, notes the report. Other than these high taxes, powerful unions "may be the single greatest factor impeding economic competitiveness in the region." Add these factors together and "it is no wonder migration out of these states was more than 2.6 million on net over the past 10 years."

Given that ALEC is recognized as a "conservative" organization, not everyone subscribes to this viewpoint. In fact, the states in the Northeast region rank exceptionally high in a periodic study by the Kauffman Foundation and Information Technology and Innovation Foundation that tries to determine which states are best positioned to capitalize on America's transformation to the "New Economy." The term *New Economy* was coined in the 1990s to describe a set of qualitative and quantitative changes that have been transforming the structure, function, and rules of the economy. The New Economy is described as global, entrepreneurial, and knowledge-based "in which the keys to success lie in the extent to which knowledge, technology, and innovation are embedded in products and services."

In the most recent rankings—"The 2014 State New Economy Index"—Massachusetts, Connecticut, and New Jersey were ranked in the top 10 for being furthest along in transitioning into the New Economy, while New Hampshire, New York, Vermont, and Rhode Island were ranked in the top 20.

The report suggests that many of these higher-ranked states may not be growing rapidly in employment, but it argues that they will be "best able to face the challenges brought on by the New Economy transformation."

. . .

While economic factors are obviously a key component driving migration-induced population stagnation in the Northeast, retirement to warmer climates should be considered as well. Of course, economic considerations ultimately play a role in people's retirement decisions, as evidenced by domestic migration patterns before, during, and after the Great Recession. Census data for the 2007 to 2010 period showed a significant decrease in domestic migration into the top states—Florida, Arizona, Nevada, Georgia, and North Carolina—known to be drawing retirees from the North. This corresponded with a noticeable decline in domestic migration out of the Northeastern states, with Massachusetts recording its first positive net inflow of domestic migrants for the decade, and New Jersey and New York also recording much higher population growth for the period.

Well, with the recession's end, Northern retirees again started moving South, and all indications suggest that the numbers of them moving to warmer climates is rapidly rising again and should soon, if not already, reach pre-recession levels. And with the number of Baby Boomers reaching retirement age slowly accelerating, I would guess that these numbers are going to far surpass pre-recession levels within the next ten years.

Remember what I told that audience of Florida municipal financial workers, as described in Chapter 1? Well, I've been down to Florida recently and can tell you that the state is going absolutely gangbusters with building infrastructure to support a rapidly growing population, but I'm not sure whether it is building it fast enough.

In concluding this chapter, let me restate that there are many explanations for the stagnating population of the Northeast, and it appears that levels of population growth will continue to be lackluster in the years ahead, especially in comparison with the South and West. But what do you make of this?

. . .

Sure, "Don't invest in or work for companies based in the Northeast" would be an easy answer, but nothing is that simple, is it?

No, it's complicated, and just because people seem to be fleeing the region in droves and its population is on the precipice of potential decline doesn't mean that the Northeast is going to become a wasteland in the next fifty years. It's not like New York City is going to disappear. . . .

Again, this is just an exercise designed to show you the demographics while teaching you how to always be cognizant of the potential implications of population dynamics. So, while the demographic and economic health of the Northeast may not currently seem to be especially healthy, both demographics and economics are almost always in a state of change, and within change one can find opportunity. And perhaps the Northeast's change will include that successful transition into the "New Economy" model. If so, the Northeast could become an economic powerhouse again, which would also likely spur a healthy transition of its current demographic dynamics.

13

The South Has Indeed Risen Again

CAN YOU ANSWER the following three questions?

1. How many college football teams from the South ended up on the Associated Press Top 25 list at the end of the 2015 season?
2. Teams from which National Collegiate Athletic Association (NCAA) conference have been dominating most college athletics for the past twenty-five years?
3. Which NCAA college football team has won the most national championships over the past ten years?

The answer to the first question is fifteen college football teams from Southern universities were on the AP Top 25 list at the end of the 2015 season.

The correct answer to the second question would be the Southeastern Conference (SEC), whose fourteen member universities have both competed in, and won, far more National Championships in all the college sports combined than any other conference.

Additionally, teams from the SEC tend to be highly ranked every season in most of the NCAA-sanctioned sports.

With wins in four of the last seven college football championship games, the SEC's University of Alabama has won the most college football national championships over the past ten years. Oh, and college football teams from the South have ended up as national champion or the equivalent[1] for twenty of the past twenty-five years.

What am I getting at here? Why, demographics, of course.

The South has long held football and other sports in high regard, but the South's universities, while winning various championships over the years, truly became dominant in the various sports only with the rise of their population starting in the 1970s. Prior to 1975, college football teams from the South won the equivalent of only seventeen national championships from among the 146 years in which a national champion has been named. Since 1975, Southern teams have taken twenty-nine of the past forty national titles.

I would posit that the South's dominance in sports is due in large part to the vast pool of talent that has arisen with its population over the past forty years. And I am not alone in this thinking. Several years ago a *Wall Street Journal* article bemoaned the declining fortunes of the once-vaunted NCAA Big Ten Conference, which is composed of nine teams from the Midwest and one from Northeast.

According to the article "The Big Ten: Down and Out?" "college's biggest, richest and oldest major conference" has lost its powerhouse status and its teams have been on a bowl game losing streak because of a lack of local talent. The conference consists of ten schools stretching across the demographically challenged Midwest into Pennsylvania and includes nationally recognized football teams from the University of Michigan, Ohio State, and Penn State.

The article states that:

The main problem seems to be rooted in the population growth of the South and West, and the greater zeal for high-school football in those regions. Historically, Pennsylvania and Ohio ranked third and fourth all-time in terms of the number of NFL players born within their borders. Florida was fifth. But today, Florida has nearly twice as many active players as Ohio and more than three times as many as Pennsylvania. The South and West continue to benefit because of the national population trend: 47 of the 50 fastest-growing metropolitan areas between 2007 and 2008 were in those regions, according to the Census Bureau. Playing football also is just not as important to Northerners. In the last school year, more high schoolers in Georgia played football than in Pennsylvania, according to data from the National Federation of State High School Associations, even though Pennsylvania has nearly three million more residents.

With demographic trends forecast to favor the South and West over the Midwest and Northeast for at least the next twenty years, the Big Ten faces a continued struggle to find local talent. And if demographics is the talent key, the SEC is best poised to dominate college football, and other collegiate sports, in the coming decades.

The South, with just over a Census Bureau–estimated 121 million people as of 2015, representing about 36 percent of the U.S. population, is by a wide margin the most populated of the country's four regions, and on a numeric basis has been experiencing the greatest growth for decades. And despite a few hiccups along the way—population declines in Louisiana following Hurricane Katrina, and a first-time Florida population decline after the housing market meltdown and subsequent recession—the region is expected to maintain its population boom for at least the next twenty years, if not beyond.

At the turn of the 20th century, the South, with a population of 24.5 million and an overall percentage share of the population of about 32.3 percent, was big, but the Midwest was more populated—26.3 million—and had a greater percentage share—34.7 percent—of the nation's overall population. The Northeast, with 21.1 million people and 27.7 percent of the total U.S. population, did not lag the South by all that much, and combined the three regions held about 95 percent of the nation's population, with the at-the-time sparsely populated West holding the last 5 percent or so.

By the year 2000, the South had more than quadrupled in population size, growing at a rate almost twice that of both the Midwest and Northeast, and led the nation in population both numerically and as a percentage of the U.S. total. It achieved this growth during a period that saw at least sixty years of relative economic stagnation as compared with its Northern and Midwestern neighbors, and despite a sixty-five-year, 6.6 million–strong, out-migration of its Black population primarily to those neighboring regions. In short, the South's population managed to more than double during a sixty-year period of economic stagnation and population out-migration, and then almost doubled again during the next forty years, a period of strong economic expansion and reversal in migration patterns.

And while the South's population growth is not projected to double again by 2040, its growth so far in the 21st century leads the nation on many metrics, and should continue to do so for many years to come, according to U.S. government projections.

The U.S. Census Bureau delineates the South Region as the states of Delaware, Maryland, Virginia, West Virginia, Kentucky, Tennessee, North Carolina, South Carolina, Georgia, Florida, Mississippi, Alabama, Arkansas, Louisiana, Oklahoma, Texas, and the District of Columbia.

Between 2010 and 2015 the South's natural increase (remember, difference between births and deaths) was 2,741,639, with 7,944,524 births and 5,202,885 deaths, with all three counts being the highest among all regions, and the 34 percent birth-to-death ratio being the second highest of the regions. If not for most states in the region having among the highest mortality rates in the country, the South would undoubtedly have the highest birth-to-death ratio.

On this note, I am going to pause to ask you to consider what might be a prime business to be engaged with in the South based on what you've read in the above paragraph.

If you've immediately come up with several ideas, I commend you for your demographic acuity. If among your ideas you've included the "end-of-life" industry, you get a gold star!

With the exception of West Virginia, with 5,558 more deaths than births, all of the Southern states experienced natural increases between 2010 and 2015. The most populated state, Texas, with about 27.5 million people, experienced by far the region's biggest (and country's second biggest after California) natural increase with more than 1.1 million, followed by Georgia, with just under 300,000, and Virginia, with almost 215,000. West Virginia was the sole anomaly with a natural decline rather than increase, though Delaware, Washington, D.C., and Alabama experienced low natural increases relative to their populations. While the region as a whole experienced the highest domestic migration increase in the country for the period, six—Kentucky, Louisiana, Maryland, Mississippi, Virginia, and West Virginia—of the region's sixteen states and District of Columbia experienced domestic out-migration. Texas and Florida were the most popular destination for domestic migrants, followed by the Carolinas. Texas and Florida also gained the most from international migration, followed by Virginia, Maryland, Georgia, and North Carolina. Other pertinent details can be derived from the table on the following page.

Much like a picture is worth a thousand words, so is a table, and as a budding demographer you should be able to discern a plethora of information from the table. All of those numbers tell a demographic story so, based on those numbers, can you tell me a story or two?

Like, say, what can you tell me about Texas?

Sure, it's big . . . Texas big! Everyone knows that.

How about something along the lines of "They must be having a lot of babies down in Texas"? Of course, because I haven't broken down the natural increase birth-to-death ratio in the table, it could be that not many folks are dying down in Texas. But death is pretty much a given, so, an initial reaction to attribute the high natural increase observation to births would be spot-on. In fact, Texas, with more than 2 million births during the 2010 to 2015 period, has the highest birth-to-death ratio in America at about 120 percent.

TABLE 13.1

COMPONENTS OF POPULATION CHANGE 2010–2015

PLACE	NATURAL INCREASE	DOMESTIC MIGRATION	INTERNATIONAL MIGRATION	NET CHANGE IN POPULATION*	2015 POPULATION
Alabama	47,896	2,005	27,276	78,852	4,858,979
Arkansas	44,508	249	17,755	62,246	2,978,204
Delaware	15,969	18,038	13,715	47,998	945,934
Wash., D.C.	23,683	25,596	20,837	70,461	672,228
Florida	179,728	650,660	610,495	1,466,649	20,271,272
Georgia	299,340	82,493	134,971	526,179	10,214,860
Kentucky	64,922	-12,292	34,455	85,743	4,425,092
Louisiana	107,922	-10,567	39,473	137,245	4,670,724
Maryland	143,658	-56,054	148,515	232,616	5,773,785
Mississippi	49,029	-38,499	12,952	24,230	2,992,333
North Carolina	198,111	180,189	116,875	507,110	10,042,802
Oklahoma	81,469	43,544	33,359	159,722	3,911,338
South Carolina	72,535	159,023	31,974	72,535	4,896,146
Tennessee	96,386	104,944	49,546	254,024	6,600,299
Texas	1,107,434	736,492	463,449	2,323,009	27,469,114
Virginia	214,607	-17,437	182,418	381,948	8,382,993
West Virginia	-5,588	-8,166	6,259	-8,883	1,844,128
The Region	2,741,639	1,860,218	1,944,324	6,619,894	121,182,847

*As noted in previous "Components of Population Change" tables, the sums of the natural increases, domestic migration, and international migrations do not necessarily add up to the net changes in population. This is because the U.S. Census Bureau includes a "residual" in this number to account for "changes in the population that cannot be attributed to any specific demographic component." I toyed with using the "true" net change in population numbers according to calculating the aforementioned sums but decided that for the sake of consistency I should utilize the "official" numbers despite the odd variance and potential confusion that might ensue should a reader count my sums.

With that story told, what can you tell me about Florida?

If you were able to quickly discern that Florida, with a large population but relatively small natural increase, likely has one of

TABLE 13.2

RATES OF POPULATION CHANGE 2010–2015

PLACE	2010 POPULATION	2015 POPULATION	NUMERIC CHANGE	PERCENTAGE CHANGE
Wash., D.C.	601,767	672,228	70,461	11.7%
Florida	18,804,623	20,271,272	1,466,649	7.7%
Georgia	9,688,681	10,214,860	526,179	5.4%
Delaware	897,936	945,934	47,998	5.3%
North Carolina	9,535,692	10,042,802	507,110	5.3%
Virginia	8,001,045	8,382,993	381,948	4.8%
Texas	25,146,105	27,469,114	2,323,009	4.4%
Oklahoma	3,751,616	3,911,338	159,722	4.2%
Maryland	5,773,785	6,006,401	232,616	4.0%
Tennessee	6,346,275	6,600,299	254,024	4.0%
Louisiana	4,533,749	4,670,724	137,245	3.0%
Arkansas	2,915,958	2,978,204	62,246	2.1%
Kentucky	4,339,349	4,425,092	85,743	2.0%
Alabama	4,780,127	4,858,979	78,852	1.6%
South Carolina	4,625,401	4,896,146	72,535	1.6%
Mississippi	2,968,103	2,992,333	24,230	0.8%
West Virginia	1,853,011	1,844,128	-8,883	-0.45%
The Region	114,562,953	121,182,847	6,619,894	5.8%

the lowest birth-to-death ratios in the South, then your demographic acumen is growing by leaps and bounds, because Florida, with a birth-to-death ratio of 19 percent, has among the lowest ratios in the country.

Of course, that brings us to West Virginia, and . . . ?

Yep, with that state you can hardly call it a "birth-to-death" ratio because it's more of a "death-to-birth" ratio, what with there being about a negative-5 percent ratio of births to deaths.

Well done!

Another factor you should have been able to deduce from that table was that the South's growth is not by any means uniform among the states. Anyone can tell from that table that Texas led the region in growth on a numerical basis for the 2010 to 2015 period, while West Virginia suffered with a population loss, but less clear might be how the other states fared. Well, as you can see from the table on the previous page, on a percentage basis Washington, D.C., saw the highest growth with 11.7 percent, followed by Florida at 7.7 percent. Despite the disparity among the states, and the few laggards, all in all the region experienced healthy growth, especially when measured against the Northeast and Midwest.

Now if we stretch the time period out twenty-five years, the rates of growth are downright phenomenal, as seen in the next table. Four states—Texas, Georgia, Florida, and North Carolina— saw population growth in excess of 50 percent during this period, while another four experienced growth exceeding 30 percent. Five states' populations grew by more than 20 percent, with another two and the District of Columbia seeing more than 10 percent growth. West Virginia, with 2.8 percent, proved to be the only laggard of the bunch.

TABLE 13.3

RATES OF POPULATION CHANGE 1990-2015

PLACE	1990 POPULATION	2015 POPULATION	NUMERIC CHANGE	PERCENTAGE CHANGE
Texas	16,986,510	27,469,114	10,482,604	61.7%
Georgia	6,478,216	10,214,860	3,736,644	57.7%
Florida	12,937,926	20,271,272	7,333,346	56.7%
North Carolina	6,628,637	10,042,802	3,414,165	51.5%
Delaware	666,168	945,934	279,766	41.9%
South Carolina	3,486,703	4,896,146	1,409,443	40.4%
Virginia	6,187,358	8,382,993	2,195,635	35.5%
Tennessee	4,877,185	6,600,299	1,723,114	35.3%
Arkansas	2,350,725	2,978,204	627,479	26.6%

PLACE	1990 POPULATION	2015 POPULATION	NUMERIC CHANGE	PERCENTAGE CHANGE
Maryland	4,781,468	6,006,401	1,224,933	25.6%
Oklahoma	3,145,585	3,911,338	765,753	24.3%
Alabama	4,040,587	4,858,979	818,392	20.2%
Kentucky	3,685,296	4,425,092	739,796	20.0%
Mississippi	2,573,216	2,992,333	419,117	16.3%
Wash., D.C.	606,900	672,228	65,328	10.7%
Louisiana	4,219,973	4,670,724	450,751	10.7%
West Virginia	1,793,477	1,844,128	50,651	2.8%
The Region	85,445,930	121,182,847	35,736,317	41.8%

The Southern birthrate is certainly a contributing factor supporting the South's population boom, as more than half of the Southern states tend to maintain birthrates above the U.S. mean. However, the state rates have varied significantly over the years, and while providing an overall boost to the region's growth, have been much more of a factor in some states than in others. While the rate in Texas, the South's biggest and fastest-growing state, has been among the nation's largest the past two decades, ranging from roughly 14.6 to 17 births per thousand, the rate in Florida, another of the region's top-growing states, has been fluctuating at a much lower 11-to-13-births-per-thousand rate.

As suggested earlier in the chapter, the bigger driver of the Southern population boom, both in the latter half of the 20th century and more recently, is migration, both domestic and from abroad. Florida, with its warm weather and lack of state income tax, has been attracting ever-increasing domestic and international immigrants since the 1940s, while Texas has long been a primary destination of immigrants from Mexico. However, in the early 1980s, most of the other Southern states began receiving noticeable numbers of domestic migrants from the Northeast and Midwest, a trend that, for the most part, has continued to accelerate.

While these domestic immigrants go to the South for a wide variety of reasons, there seems to be two primary groups: retirees looking for warmer weather and a more relaxed, low-cost lifestyle; and job seekers chasing employment in a rapidly expanding economy in a region with a relatively low cost of living. Among both groups are large numbers of African Americans who represent a reverse of the "Great Migration North" by Blacks between 1900 and 1970. Both those returning "home" to reconnect with their family communities and those new to the area are finding the region to be welcoming and progressive, and that a highly visible Black middle class has emerged.

The primary driver of international immigration to the South has been the huge influx of Hispanics, a trend that began accelerating in the early 1990s; the region's overall Hispanic population almost doubled to 11.5 million by 2000, with the states of North Carolina, Arkansas, and Georgia experiencing growth of more than 300 percent. The Census Bureau estimated that the Southern region's Hispanic population almost doubled again by 2014, when the population was pegged at 20.2 million. While immigration has been adding to the population, an emerging driver of the Southern Hispanic population boom has been natural, that is, due to births, which, according to the Census Bureau, were responsible for more than 60 percent of the increase in the overall U.S. Hispanic population from 2000 to 2010.

The breakdown of recent racial and ethnic population change is perhaps most noteworthy because the South has the highest rate of change for all the primary racial and ethnic groups excepting Whites and Asians (the latter of which, surprisingly, is held by the Midwest).

TABLE 13.4

RACIAL AND ETHNIC POPULATION CHANGE IN THE SOUTH 2000–2014

RACE OR ETHNICITY	2000 POPULATION	2014 POPULATION	NUMERICAL CHANGE	PERCENTAGE CHANGE
White	72,819,399	85,456,554	12,637,155	17.3%
Non-Hispanic White	65,927,794	69,695,515	3,767,721	5.7%

RACE OR ETHNICITY	2000 POPULATION	2014 POPULATION	NUMERICAL CHANGE	PERCENTAGE CHANGE
Black	18,981,692	23,200,966	4,219,274	22.2%
Hispanic	11,586,696	20,280,582	8,693,886	75.0%
Asian	2,267,094	3,758,909	1,491,815	65.8%
All	100,236,820	119,771,934	19,535,114	19.5%

The Hispanic population growth is especially robust, and suggests the region's Hispanic population will be the largest of all regions, and surpass that of the West, within a few years. The Asian population growth is also exceptionally strong; however, on a proportional basis the Asian population remains below 5 percent of the overall population.

TABLE 13.5

RACIAL AND ETHNIC COMPOSITION OF U.S. POPULATION 2014

PLACE	2014 POPULATION	PERCENTAGE WHITE	PERCENTAGE HISPANIC	PERCENTAGE BLACK	PERCENTAGE ASIAN
Northeast	56,152,333	73.3%	13.8%	11.9%	6.2%
South	119,771,934	71.3%	16.9%	19.4%	3.1%
Midwest	67,745,108	84.2%	7.5%	10.4%	3.0%
West	75,187,681	69.5%	29.5%	4.6%	9.9%
United States	318,857,056	73.4%	17.3%	12.7%	5.2%

The healthy Black population growth of more than 22 percent falls in line with the region having the largest proportional and numerical Black population of all the regions. And the Non-Hispanic White population, unlike the Northeast and Midwest, appears to be growing. However, the numbers beg the question of how much of this growth might be related to migration coming from those two regions.

Looking forward, the Census Bureau as of 2005 released projections based on the 2000 Census that indicated that the South's population growth rate will remain strong going toward 2030. As mentioned in the preceding chapter, the Census Bureau "does not have a current set of state [or regional] population projections and currently has no plans to produce them."

Those 2005 projections estimated that the South will account for more than 50 percent of the expected 82.2 million increase in the U.S. population between 2000 and 2030. The estimated 43 million gain in the South's 2030 population represents a 42.9 percent increase over its 2000 population of 100.2 million and would give the South 39.4 percent of the overall U.S. population. These projections estimated that the South's population would be 120.4 million as of 2015, which is off by only about 780,000 from the current estimates of 121.2 million.

As with historical rates, the growth patterns are far from uniform on a regional basis, as the states of Texas, Florida, and North Carolina are projected to account for 36 percent of total national population growth on their own, while the states of Virginia, Maryland, Tennessee, Delaware, South Carolina, and Arkansas are expected to see their populations increase by 20 to 40 percent. West Virginia is projected to lose over 88,000 people for a 4.9 percent population decline, and the District of Columbia is projected to lose more than 138,000 people for a 24.2 percent decline.

All of the projections are provided in the table below:

TABLE 13.6

PROJECTED POPULATION CHANGE 2000 TO 2030—SOUTH

PLACE	2000 POPULATION	PROJECTED 2030 POPULATION	NUMERIC CHANGE	PERCENTAGE CHANGE
Florida	15,982,378	28,685,769	12,703,391	79.5%
Texas	20,851,820	33,317,744	12,465,924	59.8%
North Carolina	8,049,313	12,227,739	4,178,426	51.9%
Georgia	8,186,453	12,017,838	3,831,385	46.8%
Virginia	7,078,515	9,825,019	2,746,504	38.8%
Maryland	5,296,486	7,022,251	1,725,765	32.6%
Tennessee	5,689,283	7,380,634	1,691,351	29.7%
Delaware	783,600	1,012,658	229,058	29.2%

PLACE	2000 POPULATION	PROJECTED 2030 POPULATION	NUMERIC CHANGE	PERCENTAGE CHANGE
South Carolina	4,012,012	5,148,569	1,136,557	28.3%
Arkansas	2,673,400	3,240,208	566,808	21.2%
Oklahoma	3,450,654	3,913,251	462,597	13.4%
Kentucky	4,041,769	4,554,998	513,229	12.7%
Alabama	4,447,100	4,874,243	427,143	9.6%
Mississippi	2,844,658	3,092,410	247,752	8.7%
Louisiana	4,468,976	4,802,633	333,657	7.5%
West Virginia	1,808,344	1,719,959	-88,385	-4.9%
Wash., D.C.	572,059	433,414	-138,645	-24.2%
The Region	100,236,820	143,269,337	43,032,517	42.9%

Given these projections, and everything else you've learned about the South's demographics, do you think that the hypothetical Ted from Chapter 11 needs to sell his franchise rights for Maine, pack his bags, and try again in one of these states? Other than West Virginia, I would guess that Ted would have an easier time trying to get that second kid through college were he to set up shop in one of these states.

The accuracy of these projections halfway through their thirty-year time frame can be considered quite good, especially when compared to the projections for the Northeast. The two largest states saw the biggest variances between projected and actual populations as of 2015, with Texas exceeding projections by almost 900,000 and Florida short by just over 900,000. South Carolina and Oklahoma beat their projections by about a quarter million, and Alabama and the District of Columbia handily beat their projections by more than 150,000. All in all, the midpoint check suggests that most of the states will likely meet or exceed the 2030 projections. While Maryland and Florida seem to be lagging, both can catch up during the next fifteen years, and, with Boomer retirement about to kick into high gear, I expect that Florida will handily beat the projections. The only real outlier of the bunch appeared to be Washington, D.C., which looks like it plans to completely ignore the Census Bureau's belief that it will lose significant population by 2030.

TABLE 13.7

PROJECTED VERSUS ACTUAL POPULATION CHANGE 2000 TO 2015

PLACE	2000 POPULATION	PROJECTED 2015 POPULATION	ACTUAL 2015 POPULATION	NUMERICAL DIFFERENCE
Alabama	4,447,100	4,663,111	4,858,979	195,868
Arkansas	2,673,400	2,968,913	2,978,204	9,291
Delaware	783,600	927,400	945,934	18,534
Florida	15,982,378	21,204,132	20,271,272	-932,860
Georgia	8,186,453	10,230,578	10,214,860	-15,718
Kentucky	4,041,769	4,351,188	4,425,092	73,904
Louisiana	4,468,976	4,673,721	4,670,724	-2,997
Maryland	5,296,486	6,208,392	6,006,401	-201,991
Mississippi	2,844,658	3,014,409	2,992,333	-22,076
North Carolina	8,049,313	10,010,770	10,042,802	32,032
Oklahoma	3,450,654	3,661,694	3,911,338	249,644
South Carolina	4,012,012	4,642,137	4,896,146	254,009
Tennessee	5,689,283	6,502,017	6,600,299	98,282
Texas	20,851,820	26,585,801	27,469,114	883,313
Virginia	7,078,515	8,466,864	8,382,993	-83,871
Wash., D.C.	572,059	506,323	672,228	165,905
West Virginia	1,808,344	1,822,758	1,844,128	21,370
The Region	100,236,820	120,440,208	121,182,847	742,639

Along with a booming population, the South has experienced massive economic growth since the mid-1970s. To ask which of these two factors was most responsible for begetting the other is essentially a "chicken or the egg" question, as each propagates the other.

And while the region's strong population growth offers business and industry an abundant workforce, the region also offers numerous other incentives, such as low development, construction, and operating costs; ready access to a fast-growing consumer market; low unionization levels; advantageous tax rates; and excellent transportation and communications infrastructure that is generally not impacted by the weather. All of these factors together suggest continued growth, in both the population and economy.

Rich States, Poor States, ALEC's 2015 State Economic Competitiveness Index, calls the South the "hotspot for economic growth" and attributes low tax rates and pro-growth economic policy as the primary driver of the South's strong economy, and resultant population increases. Using fifteen parameters that primarily deal with taxation and regulation, the Index ranks nine Southern states in its top twenty slots, with the remainder coming in between 22nd and 33rd, except West Virginia, which received the worst ranking at 36 (which is still better than most of the Northeastern states). The Southern states also tend to score relatively high on the ALEC-Laffer "2003–2013 Economic Performance Rankings," with both indexes suggesting that the region will continue to gain in population due to economically induced migration from other states.

Jonathan L. Sangster, a nationally recognized business and site location consultant, says the South's demographics combined with a favorable cost environment and fully developed and reliable infrastructure create a "perfect storm" in a positive sense for the South's continued economic development, particularly in the technology sector. Sangster adds that most of the Southern urban areas will experience 2 percent or greater growth in the coming years that, combined with numerous "leading-edge research universities" and a strong economic development–geared community college system, will provide a flowing pipeline for a knowledge-based workforce.

The promise of a young, healthy, educated workforce bodes well for the region and for the nation overall. I believe the South will drive the nation's economic engine going forward, especially as Asia's cheap manufacturing dominance declines with serious labor-force issues stemming from decades of low fertility. This should drive high-end manufacturing back to the States and to the South in particular. But we'll explore this dynamic more closely in Chapter 24.

14

Doldrums in the Midwest

THE MIDWEST, WITH about 66.5 million people as of 2008 representing about 22 percent of the U.S. population, has a demographic profile similar in many ways to that of the stagnating Northeast but has more pockets of favorable population growth. While the Midwest overall is experiencing significant net out-migration, numerous urban areas are bucking the trend and experiencing healthy population growth fueled in large part by incoming migrants, both domestic and international.

At the turn of the 20th century the Midwest, with a population of 26.3 million representing 34.7 percent of the nation's overall population, was the largest region by population. By the year 2000, the population of the Midwest had more than doubled; however, this growth was far surpassed by that of the West, which saw its population increase by more than fifteen times, from about 4 million to 63 million, and that of the South, which more than quadrupled, from 25 million to more than 100 million.

The Midwest's first population boom began after the American Revolutionary War, as settlers from the East flooded into the region to claim federal government land grants and to till the region's fertile soil. The region remained predominantly rural and became known as the nation's "breadbasket" thanks to an abundant harvest of cereal crops such as corn, oats, and wheat. Population growth accelerated in the late 1800s and the first half of the

1900s due to the industrialization of the Midwestern Great Lake states—Illinois, Indiana, Ohio, Michigan, and Wisconsin—which, joined with the Northeastern states of New York, Pennsylvania, and New Jersey, along with West Virginia, served as the nation's steel-driven manufacturing belt. This industrialization drew in millions of migrants, from Easterners looking for new opportunities, to Europeans bypassing the East, to Black Southerners fleeing the segregationist South in what was known as the "great migration." This industrialization was seen in the rise of Midwestern cities such as Chicago, St. Louis, Detroit, Minneapolis, Cincinnati, Cleveland, and Milwaukee, among others, but much of the Midwest remained rural and thinly populated on a relative basis.

The manufacturing belt began a slow decline in the 1960s, a decline that in the ensuing years has been exacerbated and accelerated by numerous factors—such as recessions, high state tax rates, worldwide free-trade agreements, and exceptionally high labor costs, to name a few—and perhaps reached its apogee during the Great Recession that started in 2008. As the manufacturing belt metamorphosed into the "Rust Belt," it lost its appeal as a destination for incoming migrants, and spurred significant out-migration of its residents, a key factor in the population stagnation in both the Midwest and Northeast that seems to be continuing to this day.

The U.S. Census Bureau delineates the Midwest Region as the states of Illinois, Indiana, Iowa, Kansas, Michigan, Minnesota, Missouri, Nebraska, North Dakota, Ohio, South Dakota, and Wisconsin.

And without further ado, and because you are getting so good at this demographics stuff, I think we'll turn immediately to the tables and let the numbers tell you the story, which you should then be able to relate back to me.

TABLE 14.1

RATES OF POPULATION CHANGE 2010–2015

PLACE	2010 POPULATION	2015 POPULATION	NUMERIC CHANGE	PERCENTAGE CHANGE
North Dakota	672,591	756,927	84,336	12.5%
South Dakota	814,191	858,469	44,278	5.4%
Nebraska	1,826,341	1,896,190	69,849	3.8%
Minnesota	5,303,925	5,489,594	185,669	3.5%
Iowa	3,046,869	3,123,899	77,030	2.5%
Indiana	6,484,229	6,619,680	135,451	2.1%
Kansas	2,853,132	2,911,641	58,509	2.1%
Missouri	5,988,927	6,083,672	94,745	1.6%
Wisconsin	5,687,289	5,771,337	84,048	1.5%
Ohio	11,536,725	11,613,423	76,698	0.7%
Michigan	9,884,129	9,922,576	38,447	0.4%
Illinois	12,831,549	12,859,995	28,446	0.2%
The Region	66,929,897	67,907,403	977,506	1.5%

With the exception of North Dakota, and perhaps to a smaller degree, South Dakota, I imagine that you're ready to tell me that the Midwest's population change numbers for 2010 to 2015 are fairly anemic. Probably reminds you a bit of the Northeast's numbers, though not quite as bad.

But did you notice anything about the different states' rates that might have struck you as a bit odd? Not necessarily in comparison with the Northeast states, but if you recall the Northeast table for this period you might have noticed that, excepting Pennsylvania, the states with the largest populations (and those considered the most economically powerful) experienced among the highest rates of population growth.

Not in the Midwest, as the three largest states by population (and size of their economies)—Illinois, Michigan, and Ohio—experienced the smallest percentage increases in population. I have not conducted any research yet, but based on this anomaly I can almost assure you that these three states are suffering economic challenges above and beyond those of the large Northeastern states. Now let's see how the region has fared over the past twenty-five years.

TABLE 14.2

RATES OF POPULATION CHANGE 1990–2015

PLACE	1990 POPULATION	2015 POPULATION	NUMERIC CHANGE	PERCENTAGE CHANGE
Minnesota	4,375,099	5,489,594	1,114,495	25.5%
South Dakota	696,004	858,469	162,465	23.3%
Nebraska	1,578,385	1,896,190	317,805	20.1%
Indiana	5,544,159	6,619,680	1,075,521	19.4%
Missouri	5,117,073	6,083,672	966,599	18.9%
North Dakota	638,800	756,927	118,127	18.5%
Wisconsin	4,891,769	5,771,337	879,568	17.9%
Kansas	2,477,574	2,911,641	434,067	17.5%
Illinois	11,430,602	12,859,995	1,429,393	12.5%
Iowa	2,776,755	3,123,899	347,144	12.5%
Ohio	10,847,115	11,613,423	766,308	7.1%
Michigan	9,295,297	9,922,576	627,279	6.7%
The Region	59,668,632	67,907,403	8,238,771	13.8%

OK, as with the Northeast, not as bad as the shorter-term numbers, but still below the national average of about 29 percent for this time period. As with the shorter 2010 to 2015 time period, the large population states considered the region's economic powerhouses are tending to see the least growth. One also needs to keep in mind that growth in the region has been decelerating, with 7.9 percent growth recorded in the 1990s, followed by 3.9 percent in the 2000s, and currently on track for 2.8 percent growth this decade.

And what about components of this decelerating growth?

TABLE 14.3

COMPONENTS OF POPULATION CHANGE 2010–2015

PLACE	NATURAL INCREASE	DOMESTIC MIGRATION	INTERNATIONAL MIGRATION	NET CHANGE IN POPULATION*	2015 POPULATION
Illinois	295,920	-425,954	170,366	28,446	12,859,995
Indiana	129,089	-47,311	57,474	135,451	6,619,680
Iowa	56,019	-7,170	29,280	77,030	3,123,899
Kansas	77,085	-52,597	33,848	58,509	2,911,641
Michigan	122,133	-191,130	111,091	38,447	9,922,576
Minnesota	152,035	-36,723	72,374	185,669	5,489,594
Missouri	101,770	-51,818	47,373	97,745	6,083,672
Nebraska	56,402	-7,731	21,893	69,849	1,896,190
North Dakota	22,285	53,048	8,057	84,336	756,927
Ohio	142,046	-152,296	95,444	76,698	11,613,423
South Dakota	25,761	10,267	7,924	44,278	858,469
Wisconsin	98,689	-52,211	38,001	84,048	5,771,337
The Region	1,279,234	-962,626	693,125	977,506	67,907,403

*As noted in previous "Components of Population Change" tables, the sums of the natural increases, domestic migration, and international migrations do not necessarily add up to the net changes in population. This is because the U.S. Census Bureau includes a "residual" in this number to account for "changes in the population that cannot be attributed to any specific demographic component." I toyed with using the "true" net change in population numbers according to calculating the aforementioned sums but decided that for the sake of consistency I should utilize the "official" numbers despite the odd variance and potential confusion that might ensue should a reader count the sums.

No doubt you determined that out-migration combined with low fertility is the cause of the deceleration. I mean, it's hard not to notice that with the exception of the Dakotas, people are fleeing from the Midwest. And while the number of people fleeing the Midwest is not as extreme as in the North, unlike the North the Midwest is not making up for the domestic migration loss with a significant international migration gain. While the North experienced a small net 152,239 migration gain, the Midwest experienced a net migration loss of 269,501.

TABLE 14.4

THEORETICAL POPULATION CHANGE ABSENT INTERNATIONAL MIGRATION 2010–2015

PLACE	NATURAL INCREASE	DOMESTIC MIGRATION	THEORETICAL NET CHANGE IN POPULATION
Minnesota	152,035	-36,723	115,312
Indiana	129,089	-47,311	81,778
North Dakota	22,285	53,048	75,333
Missouri	101,770	-51,818	49,952
Iowa	56,019	-7,170	48,849
Nebraska	56,402	-7,731	48,671
Wisconsin	98,689	-52,211	46,478
South Dakota	25,761	10,267	36,028
Kansas	77,085	-52,597	24,488
Ohio	142,046	-152,296	-10,250
Michigan	122,133	-191,130	-68,997
Illinois	295,920	-425,954	-130,034
The Region	1,279,234	-962,626	316,608

As with the previous tables, the numbers suggest something is rotten in Illinois, Michigan, and Ohio. And, as alluded to in previous chapters, I would guess that it has something to do with the decline in the region's manufacturing jobs.

With regard to the region's racial and ethnic composition and recent change, there are no real surprises. As you may recall from Chapter 11, the Midwest has the greatest proportion of Whites, smallest proportional representation of Hispanics and Asians, and second smallest proportion of Blacks.

Similar to the rest of the country, the Hispanic and Asian populations are experiencing robust growth, while White population growth is stagnant. As with the North, the Non-Hispanic White population is in decline, and I would guess that out-migration is playing a role in this decline. Black population growth is the smallest of all regions, and I assume that out-migration—the reverse migration to the South—is also playing a role in its anemic growth.

TABLE 14.5

RACIAL AND ETHNIC COMPOSITION OF U.S. POPULATION 2014

PLACE	2014 POPULATION	PERCENTAGE WHITE	PERCENTAGE HISPANIC	PERCENTAGE BLACK	PERCENTAGE ASIAN
Northeast	56,152,333	73.3%	13.8%	11.9%	6.2%
South	119,771,934	71.3%	16.9%	19.4%	3.1%
Midwest	67,745,108	84.2%	7.5%	10.4%	3.0%
West	75,187,681	69.5%	29.5%	4.6%	9.9%
United States	318,857,056	73.4%	17.3%	12.7%	5.2%

TABLE 14.6

RACIAL AND ETHNIC POPULATION CHANGE 2000–2014—MIDWEST

RACE OR ETHNICITY	2000 POPULATION	2014 POPULATION	NUMERICAL CHANGE	PERCENTAGE CHANGE
White	53,833,651	55,084,212	1,250,561	2.3%
Non-Hispanic White	52,386,131	51,895,649	-490,482	-0.9%
Black	6,838,669	7,021,172	182,503	2.7%
Hispanic	3,124,532	5,071,160	1,946,628	62.3%
Asian	1,197,554	2,012,054	814,500	68.0%
All	64,392,776	67,745,108	3,352,332	5.2%

Looking forward, the Census Bureau as of 2005 released projections based on the 2000 Census that indicated that the Midwest's population growth rate will remain relatively weak going toward 2030, with most Midwestern states expected to have lower growth rates than the Northeastern states.

The projections estimate that the Midwest's overall growth will be only slightly better than that of the Northeast, and excepting the Dakotas, no Midwestern states are likely to reach the national projected 2030 population increase of 29.2 percent. The projections call for the Midwest's population to grow by about 6.1 million people between 2000 and 2030, a 9.5 percent increase, just above the 7.6 percent increase expected for the Northeast, but far below the West's 45.8 percent or the South's 42.9 percent. With a projected 2030 population of about 70.5 million, the Midwest's share of total U.S. population is expected to drop to 19.4 percent, from a current 22 percent.

TABLE 14.7

PROJECTED POPULATION CHANGE 2000 TO 2030—MIDWEST

PLACE	2000 POPULATION	PROJECTED 2030 POPULATION	NUMERIC CHANGE	PERCENTAGE CHANGE
Minnesota	4,919,479	6,306,130	1,386,651	28.2%
Missouri	5,595,211	6,430,173	834,962	14.9%
Wisconsin	5,363,675	6,150,764	787,089	14.7%
Indiana	6,080,485	6,810,108	729,623	12.0%
Kansas	2,688,418	2,940,084	251,666	9.4%
Illinois	12,419,293	13,432,892	1,013,599	8.2%
Michigan	9,938,444	10,694,172	755,728	7.6%
Nebraska	1,711,263	1,820,247	108,984	6.4%
South Dakota	754,844	800,462	45,618	6.0%
Ohio	11,353,140	11,550,528	197,388	1.7%
Iowa	2,926,324	2,955,172	28,848	1.0%
North Dakota	642,200	606,566	-35,634	-5.5%
The Region	64,392,776	70,497,298	6,104,522	9.5%

Eight of the twelve Midwestern states are projected to have among the lowest growth rates in the country for the 2000–2030 time frame, joining seven other states (primarily from the Northeast) and the District of Columbia with projected growth rates below 10 percent.

And based upon a midpoint check of these projections, it appears that Census Bureau analysts overestimated growth for some

Midwestern states, and that few states will likely be able to reach the estimates for 2030. As of the midpoint year of 2015, Michigan was more than 650,000 short of its midpoint estimates and Illinois was almost a quarter million short. Other laggards include Minnesota, by about 180,000, and Wisconsin, by more than 100,000.

The Bureau underestimated both North and South Dakota, with North Dakota's 2015 population already exceeding the projections for 2030, and that of South Dakota almost meeting the 2030 projected number. Of course, the vibrant shale oil–based economy of these states is likely responsible for stimulating this population growth, and should the boom collapse I would expect a reversal in these states' migration trends.

TABLE 14.8

PROJECTED VERSUS ACTUAL POPULATION CHANGE 2000 TO 2015

PLACE	2000 POPULATION	PROJECTED 2015 POPULATION	ACTUAL 2015 POPULATION	NUMERICAL DIFFERENCE
Illinois	12,419,293	13,097,218	12,859,995	-237,223
Indiana	6,080,485	6,517,631	6,619,680	102,049
Iowa	2,926,324	3,026,380	3,123,899	97,519
Kansas	2,688,418	2,852,690	2,911,641	58,951
Michigan	9,938,444	10,599,122	9,922,576	-676,546
Minnesota	4,919,479	5,668,211	5,489,594	-178,617
Missouri	5,595,211	6,069,556	6,083,672	14,116
Nebraska	1,711,263	1,788,508	1,896,190	107,682
North Dakota	642,200	635,133	756,927	121,794
Ohio	11,353,140	11,635,446	11,613,423	-22,023
South Dakota	754,844	796,954	858,469	61,515
Wisconsin	5,363,675	5,882,760	5,771,337	-111,423
The Region	64,392,776	68,569,609	67,907,403	-662,206

While birthrates in the Midwest states are generally lower than those of the Southern and Western states, most are higher than those of the Northern states, with eight coming in higher than the 2014 national average of 12.5 births per thousand, and four coming in lower. And like the rest of the country, all Midwest state rates, excepting North Dakota, have been trending down in recent years. North Dakota, with a rate of 14.7, has the highest rate, followed by South Dakota, 14.6; Nebraska, 14.0; Kansas, 13.4; Minnesota, 12.8; Iowa, 12.6; Indiana, 12.6; and Missouri, 12.5. As seen with other parameters, Midwestern states with higher populations seemed to have lower birthrates, with the lowest rates held by Michigan, 11.5; Wisconsin, 11.6; Ohio, 12.1; and Illinois, 12.4. Thus, while the region's birthrate is not the primary cause of lagging growth, it is certainly not providing much of a boost to the population as it is in the South and, more particularly, the West.

The stagnating population is perhaps more obvious in the Midwest than the North because it seems to be more pronounced in specific areas of the region. While population stagnation in the North is generally more spread out across that region, and far fewer cities are experiencing outright decline, in the Midwest stagnation and outright decline are noticeable in dozens upon dozens of municipalities across the region. On the other hand, some Midwestern municipalities are experiencing healthy growth.

A primary example of decline is Detroit, once proudly known as Motor City, but now perhaps best known as capital of the Rust Belt. The city has lost more than 1.1 million residents since its heyday in the 1950s as the world's largest auto manufacturing center. As with other cities that have experienced population losses over the past fifty years, some of Detroit's exodus was short-range, local migration to the suburbs. However, suburban Detroit has also suffered intermittent population declines, especially from 1970 to 1990.

This ongoing exodus has long impacted the city's housing market, but the last fifteen years have been exacerbated by the collapse of the U.S. auto industry. The median cost of a Detroit house in 1994 was $42,000 while the median price has dropped to as low as $11,000 in some neighborhoods as recorded in 2015[1].

Other Midwestern steel and auto industry cities experiencing noticeable population losses include Cleveland, Ohio, down more than 115,000 since 1990; Dayton, Ohio, down more than 41,000; Flint, Michigan, down more than 41,000; and Gary, Indiana, down more than 38,000. And I could keep going with this list, but you get the general idea.

And actually, it's scarier than these numbers suggest because 1990 doesn't represent these cities' population peaks. The declines are much greater when recorded from each of their population peaks: Cleveland, Ohio, down about 525,000 from its 1950 peak; Dayton, Ohio, down about 121,000 from its 1960 peak; Flint, Michigan, down about 97,000 since 1960, and you get the picture....

But out-migration and population loss isn't restricted to steel and auto industry cities. Census Bureau data shows that hundreds of counties across the Midwest lost population between 2000 and 2014, with all but five states—Indiana, Wisconsin, Missouri, South Dakota, and North Dakota—recording more population declines by county than increases.

However, every state had pockets of growth, and in some cases—particularly those urban areas not heavily reliant on the steel or auto industries—significant growth. And while no Midwestern city or urban area can really be considered a boomtown, more than twenty metropolitan areas—including Minneapolis–St. Paul, Minnesota; Indianapolis, Indiana; Madison, Wisconsin; Columbus, Ohio; Kansas City, Missouri; Springfield, Missouri; and Des Moines, Iowa, to name some of the largest—experienced population growth between 2010 and 2015 above the U.S. average of 4.1 percent.

In short, the Midwest as a whole is experiencing population stagnation, with some areas, particularly in Michigan and Ohio, facing significant population declines; but other areas, primarily those urban areas not associated with the auto and steel industries, seeing fairly healthy growth.

The region's mixed economic performance and related population dynamics are noticed by economic analysts, such as the American Legislative Exchange Council (ALEC), which points to mixed economic performance among the region's states. Using fifteen parameters that primarily deal with taxation and regulation, five Midwestern states—Michigan, Ohio, Illinois, Wisconsin, and Missouri—join four Northeastern states and Mississippi as having among the worst economic performance rankings for the 2003 to 2013 period, with the report strongly suggesting that the extensive out-migration of people will continue from these states absent state government policy changes. Both Dakotas scored high in the rankings, while Iowa, Nebraska, Minnesota, and Kansas came in more or less in the middle, with Indiana nearing the bottom 10.

Noting that people "vote with their feet and move to states that offer better economic opportunities," ALEC's 2015 State Economic Competitiveness Index—*Rich States, Poor States*—calls out Illinois and Michigan as being the Midwestern states suffering the worst out-migration due to economic conditions. However, while the report applauds Michigan—as well as Indiana and Wisconsin—for recently enacting pro-growth reforms "after decades of poor policy choices," it chastises Illinois and Minnesota for continuing to pass "tax and spend policies." In short, the report suggests that recent state government fiscal policy moves could alleviate out-migration from Michigan, Indiana, and Wisconsin; while Illinois and Minnesota will likely see continued population out-migration until the fiscal policy changes to encourage a return of business growth.

However, this return of business growth doesn't necessarily mean a return of "manufacturing" jobs. In fact, some analysts believe that 2015 was a record year for U.S. manufacturing in both the Midwest and the country as a whole. But, as noted by economist Michael J. Hicks, director of the Center for Business and Economic Research at Ball State University, the high manufacturing output of the region and nation is being done by "far fewer workers." Hicks believes that "folks with master's degrees in robotics working in Palo Alto, California" have caused far more manufacturing job losses than have cheaper workers in Juarez and Beijing, and that there isn't going to be a mass return of manufacturing jobs to the United States.

Despite that dire prognostication, Hicks notes that for every manufacturing job lost, the country has created ten jobs elsewhere, while other economists increasingly point to the nation's manufacturing sector as being in transition. A transition based on innovation, automation, and technology, and one that should spur associated job growth to support the transition and its means.

And if the aforementioned Kauffman Foundation and Information Technology and Innovation Foundation's report on the "New Economy" is any indicator, some Midwestern states may be starting to make such a transition. As noted, the annual report tries to determine which states are best positioned to capitalize on America's transformation to the "New Economy," with the term describing a set of qualitative and quantitative changes that have been transforming the structure, function, and rules of the economy. The New Economy is global, entrepreneurial, and knowledge-based "in which the keys to success lie in the extent to which knowledge, technology, and innovation are embedded in products and services."

No Midwestern states made the top 10 in New Economy Index overall scores in the most recent rankings—"The 2014 State New Economy Index"—though Minnesota, Illinois, and Michigan did make the top 20. Minnesota was named eighth in the country with having a "knowledge-based" workforce with New Economy skills, and second in having a "digital economy" necessary for transitioning into the New Economy. Michigan was ranked fifth, and Wisconsin eighth, in the "digital economy" category. Michigan also earned ninth place for having "innovation capacity" as measured by patents issued, share of high-tech jobs, number of scientists and engineers, and other parameters that suggest ease in transitioning into the New Economy.

Of course, several Midwestern states received low overall rankings and low rankings in the various New Economy indicator parameters. But let's stick with the positives and focus on how some states are positioning themselves for future success, and close with the thought that any such success could spur these states' economies and change the anemic Census Bureau projections for future population growth.

15

Is the West the Best?

THE U.S. WEST has experienced the greatest regional population growth by percentage and second greatest by number since 1900, with its 1900 population of 4.1 million increasing almost twenty-fold to about 76 million in 2015. More than half of this current population resides in the state of California, with a population topping 39 million, with the bulk of the other half residing in the states of Washington, 7.1 million; Arizona, 6.8 million; Colorado, 5.4 million; Oregon, 4.0 million; Utah, 2.9 million; and Nevada, 2.9 million. The remaining 6 percent of the West's population can be found in New Mexico, 2.1 million; Idaho, 1.6 million; Hawaii, 1.4 million; Montana, 1 million; Alaska, 638,000; and in the nation's least populated state, Wyoming, 586,000.

The West is a study in contrasts, both demographically and with regard to other metrics. For example, it contains the largest state by population, as well as the smallest state by population.

It has by far the largest landmass of any region, encompassing more than half of the entire United States, but is the least densely populated, with an estimated 49.5 inhabitants per square mile. Only California, with 251.3 inhabitants per square mile; Hawaii, with 222.9; and Washington, with 107.9, exceed the national average of about 89.5 per square mile.

Many of the region's states have among the youngest populations in the country by median age, but the region also has one state—Montana—that has one of the oldest median ages.

The region contains the largest number of minorities in the United States, with a greater percentage of Hispanics, Asians, and Native Americans, but its percentage of Black Americans, at about 5.8 percent, is well below the national proportion of almost 13 percent. The region also contains three of the country's four states that have non-White and/or Hispanic populations that outnumber the White population.

The West includes the wettest state—Hawaii—in the country, as well as the driest—Nevada. For the most part the region is considered "semiarid" in climate; however, its temperate rain forests in the Northwest, along with the state of Hawaii, receive the highest annual precipitation in the country. And while the states of Washington, Oregon, Hawaii, and Alaska are rich with water resources, the lack of water resources in the region's other states could prove to be a limiting factor on future growth, especially in those areas already experiencing explosive growth.

The U.S. Census Bureau delineates the West Region as the states of Alaska, Arizona, California, Colorado, Hawaii, Idaho, Montana, Nevada, New Mexico, Oregon, Utah, Washington, and Wyoming, and in the table below you can see the most recent population estimates and the change since the 2000 Census.

TABLE 15.1

RATES OF POPULATION CHANGE 2010–2015

PLACE	2010 POPULATION	2015 POPULATION	NUMERIC CHANGE	PERCENTAGE CHANGE
Colorado	5,092,324	5,456,574	427,250	8.5%
Utah	2,763,888	2,995,919	232,031	8.4%
Nevada	2,700,691	2,890,845	190,154	7.0%
Arizona	6,392,307	6,828,065	435,758	6.8%

PLACE	2010 POPULATION	2015 POPULATION	NUMERIC CHANGE	PERCENTAGE CHANGE
Washington	6,724,543	7,170,351	445,808	6.6%
Idaho	1,567,652	1,654,930	87,278	5.6%
Hawaii	1,360,301	1,431,603	71,302	5.2%
Oregon	3,831,073	4,028,977	197,904	5.2%
California	37,254,503	39,144,818	1,890,315	5.1%
Montana	989,417	1,032,949	43,532	4.4%
Alaska	710,249	738,432	28,183	4.0%
Wyoming	563,767	586,107	22,340	4.0%
New Mexico	2,059,192	2,085,109	25,917	1.3%
The Region	71,946,907	76,044,679	4,097,772	5.7%

Now I'm not seeing anything especially remarkable about the table above, but do you see anything? Sure, New Mexico's population growth is rather lackluster, but other than that, the table appears to show healthy growth throughout the region, right? OK, so then let's look at the components of change table on the next page.

Other than domestic migration outflows from Alaska, California, Hawaii, and New Mexico, there don't seem to be any especially noteworthy components of population change. And for California and Hawaii, anyway, international migration more than compensated for the domestic migration losses. The large domestic migration outflow in New Mexico goes a long way in explaining the state's lackluster 1.3 percent population growth for the period. And this, in turn, can be explained by the state's economy, which still hasn't recovered from the Great Recession, from which it is still more than 17,000 payroll jobs short of the number it had in 2007, prior to the downturn.

The other states—especially Arizona, Colorado, Washington, and Nevada—seem to have enjoyed strong population increases from domestic migration. But with a closer look, do you notice anything about Utah?

TABLE 15.2

COMPONENTS OF POPULATION CHANGE 2010–2015

PLACE	NATURAL INCREASE	DOMESTIC MIGRATION	INTERNATIONAL MIGRATION	NET CHANGE IN POPULATION*	2015 POPULATION
Alaska	38,763	-22,265	12,072	28,183	738,432
Arizona	188,278	160,346	77,464	435,758	6,828,065
California	1,332,394	-266,115	834,999	1,890,315	39,144,818
Colorado	169,535	192,337	59,257	427,250	5,456,574
Hawaii	43,560	-18,423	46,728	71,302	1,431,603
Idaho	56,713	19,788	9,689	87,278	1,654,930
Montana	16,226	22,811	3,692	43,532	1,032,949
Nevada	74,734	69,231	41,949	190,154	2,890,845
New Mexico	53,203	-43,041	15,296	25,917	2,085,109
Oregon	81,469	43,544	33,359	197,904	4,028,977
Utah	188,559	14,576	29,344	232,009	2,995,919
Washington	191,006	124,326	127,116	445,808	7,170,351
Wyoming	16,110	3,129	2,932	22,340	586,107
The Region	2,433,677	350,108	1,297,501	4,097,772	76,044,679

*As noted on previous "Components of Population Change" tables, If you take the time to calculate the numbers in the table you will notice that the sums of the natural increases, domestic migration, and international migrations do not necessarily add up to the net changes in population. This is because the U.S. Census Bureau includes a "residual" in this number to account for "changes in the population that cannot be attributed to any specific demographic component." I toyed with using the "true" net change in population numbers according to calculating the aforementioned sums but decided that for the sake of consistency I should utilize the "official" numbers despite the odd variance and potential confusion that might ensue should a reader count my sums.

With your demographic acumen, you must have noticed that Utah's natural increase was relatively high in relation to its population. Care to take a stab as to why this might be?

If you said "Mormons," well, I can't dispute that as six in ten Utah residents identify as members of the Church of Jesus Christ of Latter-day Saints, which promotes large families. This probably helps explain why the average Utah woman has somewhere between (depending upon the source) 2.6 and 3.4 children and tends to marry far earlier than women in other states. Utah, with a median age of 30.5, has by far the youngest population in the country, and I generally find that the lower the median age the higher the natural population increase.

The longer-range view of population change is the most interesting as it shows part of the phenomenal growth the region has been experiencing for the past 100 years or so.

RATES OF POPULATION CHANGE 1990–2015

PLACE	1990 POPULATION	2015 POPULATION	NUMERIC CHANGE	PERCENTAGE CHANGE
Nevada	1,201,833	2,890,845	1,689,012	140.5%
Arizona	3,665,228	6,828,065	3,162,837	86.3%
Utah	1,722,850	2,995,919	1,273,069	73.9%
Colorado	3,294,394	5,456,574	2,162,180	65.6%
Idaho	1,006,749	1,654,930	648,181	64.4%
Washington	4,866,692	7,170,351	2,303,659	47.3%
Oregon	2,842,321	4,028,977	1,186,656	41.7%
New Mexico	1,515,069	2,085,109	570,040	37.6%
Alaska	550,043	738,432	188,389	34.2%
California	29,760,021	39,144,818	9,384,797	31.5%
Montana	799,065	1,032,949	233,884	29.3%
Hawaii	1,108,229	1,431,603	323,374	29.2%
Wyoming	453,588	586,107	132,519	29.2%
The Region	52,786,082	76,044,679	23,258,597	44.1%

Yep, phenomenal growth, but no real surprises given all that I know. It would be nice to see the components of change, but unfortunately the Census Bureau doesn't offer it for that time period. The especially robust population growth of Nevada and Arizona is no real surprise, as they've both been near the top of the fastest growing state rankings for at least the past two decades. And sure, they both saw population stagnation for a couple of years due to the Great Recession, but that was just a blip on the overall picture, as evidenced both by this table and the shorter-time-framed 2010 to 2015 one.

Like the South, most of the states in the West have birthrates higher than the 2014 national average of 12.5 births per thousand, and higher than most of the states in the Northeast and Midwest. This is likely due in large part to the relative youth of these states' populations, as in general the lower a state's median age the higher its birthrate. Utah, which, as mentioned, has by far the youngest median age in the country, also has the highest birthrate, with 17.6 per thousand. Alaska, with the nation's second youngest median age, at 33.3, has the second highest birthrate, 15.5. Conversely, the two Western states with the highest median ages, also have the lowest birthrates. Montana and Oregon, with median ages at 39.6 and 39.3, respectively, have birthrates of between 11.5 and 12.1, well below the national average. However, Hawaii, which also has a relatively high median age, at 38.1, bucks the trend, as its birthrate is a healthy 13.5. Birthrates for the other Western states are Arizona, 13.1; California, 13.1; Idaho, 13.9; Nevada, 12.6; New Mexico, 12.6; Colorado, 12.4; and Wyoming, 13.1.

On a proportional basis the West is seeing far more births than deaths than any other region. As suggested earlier, this is probably due to the relative youth of the population in many of the Western states, several of which—I mentioned Utah—have the youngest median ages in the country. While the West experienced 1.9 births for every death between 2010 and 2015, the more populated South experienced about 1.5, the Midwest just over 1.4, and the Northeast just over 1.3.

On a statewide basis, Utah, the youngest median age of all the states, has the country's highest birth-to-death ratio, at about 3.3. Alaska, the second youngest state by median age, has a ratio of 2.8, and California, with the seventh youngest median age—36.0—has a ratio of 2.3. Conversely, Montana, which is in a three-way tie for having the fifth oldest median age—39.6—in the country has a ratio of 1.3, comparable with most states in the Northeast, which also have older populations.

Perhaps the most surprising factor regarding the breakdown of recent racial and ethnic population change is the relative low rate of change for the Hispanic and Asian populations. While the growth is healthy, on a percentage basis it represents the lowest rate of growth for all the regions, which is surprising because the West holds the biggest populations of both groups. The surprise is somewhat muted, though, when considering that on a *numeric* basis the West had the largest increase of its Asian population, and second largest after the South of its Hispanic population.

TABLE 15.4

RACIAL AND ETHNIC POPULATION CHANGE IN THE WEST 2010–2014

RACE OR ETHNICITY	2000 POPULATION	2014 POPULATION	NUMERICAL CHANGE	PERCENTAGE CHANGE
White	43,274,074	52,264,401	8,990,327	20.8%
Non-Hispanic White	36,911,587	38,433,335	1,521,748	4.1%
Black	3,076,884	3,474,819	397,935	12.9%
Hispanic	15,340,503	22,198,353	6,857,850	44.7%
Asian	5,003,611	7,417,453	2,413,842	48.2%
All	63,197,932	75,187,681	11,989,749	19.0%

And while the South has the fastest-growing Hispanic population, the West's large and still growing Hispanic population is a key component of its overall demographics. With the exception perhaps of the South's Texas, no other region has such a strong Hispanic heritage, nor has a Hispanic base that is so influential on all levels.

According to the most recent data from the U.S. Census Bureau, more than 44 percent of the roughly 53 million U.S. residents of Hispanic origin, many of whom are second-, third-, and fourth-generation citizens, reside in the West. Hispanics have become the ethnic majority in New Mexico and are expected to become the majority in California by 2020, and in Arizona by 2050. Currently there are about 15 million Hispanics in California, 2 million in Arizona, and

almost 1 million in New Mexico. The other state Hispanic populations are Colorado: with about 1.1 million, comprising 21.2 percent
of the population; Washington, 860,000, or 12.2 percent; Nevada,
790,000, for 27.8 percent; Oregon, almost 500,000, or 12.5 percent;
Utah, almost 400,000, for 13.5 percent; Idaho, almost 200,000, for
12.0 percent; Hawaii, 143,000, or 10.1 percent; Wyoming, almost
60,000, for 9.4 percent; Alaska, with almost 50,000, representing 6.2
percent; and Montana, with 34,000, representing 3.2 percent.

It should be noted that Asians will also play a key role in Western growth, especially in California, where their numbers are projected by the state government to double by 2050 to almost 8
million, making them the third largest ethnic group comprising
almost 14 percent of the state's population. Asians also have a significant presence in the states of Hawaii, 37.6 percent of the population; Washington, 7.8 percent; and Nevada, 7.8 percent.

The West also had the second largest numerical increase of its
White population, though this represented the largest increase of
the regions on a percentage basis. The increase in its Non-Hispanic
White population was second largest after the South by number
and percentage, perhaps due more to birthrates than migration
from the Midwest and Northeast.

TABLE 15.5

RACIAL AND ETHNIC COMPOSITION OF U.S. POPULATION 2014

PLACE	2014 POPULATION	PERCENTAGE WHITE	PERCENTAGE HISPANIC	PERCENTAGE BLACK	PERCENTAGE ASIAN
Northeast	56,152,333	73.3%	13.8%	11.9%	6.2%
South	119,771,934	71.3%	16.9%	19.4%	3.1%
Midwest	67,745,108	84.2%	7.5%	10.4%	3.0%
West	75,187,681	69.5%	29.5%	4.6%	9.9%
United States	318,857,056	73.4%	17.3%	12.7%	5.2%

As previously mentioned, the West has the smallest Black population, both by number and proportion, but its 12.9 percent growth
with an almost 400,000 increase is respectable, especially when

TABLE 15.6

PROJECTED POPULATION CHANGE 2000 TO 2030—WEST

PLACE	2000 POPULATION	PROJECTED 2030 POPULATION	NUMERIC CHANGE	PERCENTAGE CHANGE
Nevada	1,998,257	4,282,102	2,283,845	114.3%
Arizona	5,130,632	10,712,397	5,581,765	108.8%
Utah	2,233,169	3,485,367	1,252,198	56.1%
Idaho	1,293,953	1,969,624	675,671	52.2%
Washington	5,894,121	8,624,801	2,730,680	46.3%
Oregon	3,421,399	4,833,918	1,412,519	41.3%
Alaska	626,932	867,674	240,742	38.4%
California	33,871,648	46,444,861	12,573,213	37.1%
Colorado	4,301,261	5,792,357	1,491,096	34.7%
Hawaii	1,211,537	1,466,046	254,509	21.0%
Montana	902,195	1,044,898	142,703	15.8%
New Mexico	1,819,046	2,099,708	280,662	15.4%
Wyoming	493,782	522,979	29,197	5.9%
The Region	63,197,932	92,146,732	28,948,800	45.8%

compared to that of the Midwest. The Asian population growth is also strong, and despite strong gains in both the Northeast and West, the West should continue to have the largest Asian population by both number and proportion for quite some time.

Looking forward, the Census Bureau projects that the West will experience the greatest growth on a percentage basis of all regions. In its 2005[1] interim projections based on the 2000 Census, the Bureau determined that the West's population would grow by almost 29 million people between 2000 and 2030, an increase of 45.8 percent, just above the near 43 percent increase expected for the South, but far below the South's numeric increase of an estimated 43 million. The West's projected growth is far above that of either the Midwest, about 6.1 million for a 9.5 percent rate of growth, or Northeast, with about 4 million for a 7.6 growth rate. With a projected 2030 population of about 92.1 million, the West's share of total U.S. population is expected to increase to 25 percent, from a current 23 percent.

Nine of the thirteen Western states are projected to have among the highest growth rates in the country for the 2000–2030 time frame, joining five Southern states with growth rates above 34 percent. While California is projected to experience by far the greatest numeric population increase, 12.5 million for a 37.1 percent increase, the states of Nevada and Arizona are expected to experience the greatest growth on a percentage basis. Wyoming is the laggard of the group, both on a numeric and percentage basis.

In considering the projections at the halfway mark, Census Bureau analysts have done a decent job on the regional basis and are within a one-percentage-point basis of being on the mark.

TABLE 15.7

PROJECTED VERSUS ACTUAL POPULATION CHANGE 2000 TO 2015

PLACE	2000 POPULATION	PROJECTED 2015 POPULATION	ACTUAL 2015 POPULATION	NUMERICAL DIFFERENCE
Alaska	626,932	732,544	738,432	5,888
Arizona	5,130,632	7,495,238	6,828,065	-667,173
California	33,871,648	40,123,232	39,144,818	-978,414
Colorado	4,301,261	5,049,493	5,456,574	407,081
Hawaii	1,211,537	1,385,952	1,431,603	45,651
Idaho	1,293,953	1,630,045	1,654,930	24,885
Montana	902,195	999,489	1,032,949	33,460
Nevada	1,998,257	3,058,190	2,890,845	-167,345
New Mexico	1,819,046	2,041,539	2,085,109	43,570
Oregon	3,421,399	4,012,924	4,028,977	16,053
Utah	2,233,169	2,783,040	2,995,919	212,879
Washington	5,894,121	6,950,610	7,170,351	219,741
Wyoming	493,782	528,005	586,107	58,102
The Region	63,197,932	76,790,301	76,044,679	-745,622

Analysts overestimated Arizona, California, and Nevada by a fairly wide margin; however, pretty much everyone overestimated the growth of those regions back when the projections were being made, which was at the height of the housing boom. As it stands now, Colorado, New Mexico, Hawaii, Montana, and Wyoming look like they will easily meet, if not exceed, the 2030 projections, while the other states, especially Arizona, will come up short if growth is similar to the past fifteen years.

Like the South, the West's population boom has in part been fed by migration. However, while migration to the South has been significantly increasing over the last few decades, migration to the West—which was largely responsible for its seventeen-fold population increase between 1900 and 2000—has been decreasing. In fact, since at least the mid-1990s more people have been migrating from Western states to Southern states than from Southern to Western states. Nevertheless, the West, unlike the Northeast and Midwest, is still drawing in net gains of migrants, primarily due to the large influx of international migrants.

The California Gold Rush of 1848 started the first large migration boom to the West, drawing in about 300,000 settlers to the area by 1855. Meanwhile, the numbers of settlers looking for other opportunities throughout the West increased every year, arriving first by rugged overland trails such as the "Oregon," "Mormon," and "Bozeman," or by ship via the long and perilous journey around Cape Horn in South America. These migration flows accelerated with the enactment of the Homestead Act, which offered free Western land to settlers, and with the building of transcontinental railroads, the first of which was completed in 1869.

Of course, this migration came with a price, as the region's original settlers, the 500,000 to 1 million (estimates vary greatly) Native Americans of 1850, were, if not outright killed, pushed aside and had their land essentially stolen from them, all within the space of about forty years. They are still recovering from that brief period of history, as their population in the region does not top 1.5 million.

Migration flows from other regions into the West continued in the 20th century, as the West, and particularly California, was still seen as America's land of opportunity. Migration flows were helped by the rise of the automobile, which was in turn enhanced by the building of the Interstate Highway System in the 1950s. While data containing actual numbers of migrants to the West in the 20th century is lacking, one Census Bureau report estimated that about 4.5 million residents of other regions migrated to the West between 1900 and 1940, with another 10.5 million migrating to the West between 1940 and 1990.

The inflow of migrants from other regions seems to be easing, with the South emerging as the current most popular destination of choice for domestic migration. A study by the Pew Research Center using U.S. Census Bureau data showed that while the West received a net gain of more than 1.1 million domestic migrants from 1975 to 1980, this inflow had slowed to a trickle by 2000, with a five-year net gain of only about 20,000 domestic migrants. While the West received a net gain of 166,000 from the Northeast and 115,000 from the Midwest from 1995 to 2000, it experienced a net loss of 261,000 from its overall migration flows to the South. More recent data suggests that though the West continues to receive net domestic migration gains from the Midwest, it also continues to experience net migration losses to the South.

The migratory attraction of the West was perhaps largely a result of the perception of it being the "Land of Opportunity." And yes, that is often how America as a whole is referred to. But for U.S. residents, especially those of us here on the East Coast, that expression has been used to refer to the West, and in particular, California . . . though the sheen on that state seems to have rubbed off in recent years.

That said, by many economic indicators, the West is still a land of opportunity. Five Western states are ranked in the top 10 for "economic outlook" in *Rich States, Poor States*, the 2015 State Economic Competitiveness Index from the American Legislative Exchange Council (ALEC), with another three ranked in the top 25. While the remaining six states ranked below 25, the historical economic performance was exceptional, with six ranked in the top 10 for 2003 to 2013 economic performance and another four making the top 15. Only New Mexico, ranked in the middle, and California, ranked 37th, were not top performers. Narrative in the report points to Utah, Wyoming, and Nevada as being the most likely hot spots for future growth.

California, with an ALEC economic outlook ranked 44th in the nation, has been a laggard in recent years because of its excessively high personal and corporate state tax rates, and corporate disincentives such as strong unions and high state debt levels.

Despite the somewhat negative view from ALEC, California's high-tech industry may give it a leg up for future growth. In fact, California ranks third in the nation in the Kauffman Foundation and Information Technology and Innovation Foundation's periodic study to determine which states are best positioned to capitalize on America's transformation to the "New Economy." As noted in Chapter 12, the term "New Economy" was coined in the 1990s to describe a set of qualitative and quantitative changes that have been transforming the structure, function, and rules of the economy.

Along with California's third place in the most recent rankings—"The 2014 State New Economy Index"—Washington, Colorado, and Utah were ranked in the top 10 for being furthest along in transitioning into the New Economy, while Oregon and Arizona were ranked in the top 20. The laggards of the group happen to be the four states with the smallest populations, and, though there is not necessarily a correlation, being a demographer, I can certainly say there might be.

As a final note on the West, it needs to be pointed out that successful future growth—both population and economic—is highly dependent on how the states utilize the region's scarce water resources. And water, or lack thereof, will undoubtedly influence domestic migration patterns in the future, and may already, in fact, be doing so.

PART TWO

THE SUPPLY SIDE OF THE EQUATION:
The Impact of Demographics

16

Put All These People Together and Stir the Pot

NOW THAT YOU know who and where all these people are, what do you do with this information? How do you utilize demographics on a day-to-day basis in business or everyday life?

Easy! Think back to that quote I gave you in Chapter 2: "Everything in business—everything—is affected by supply and demand."

And what are people? They are the demand part of the equation. And as a budding demographer you count them, figure out where they are and where they are going, and try to determine what they need and want.

Do all that and you can effectively and economically provide the "supply" part of the equation. Kind of like Phil Visintainer and his barbecue chicken.

Simple, right?

So at this point, let's be like Phil and apply our vast demographic knowledge to the real world. Let's further examine how it has been used in the past to determine "supply," figure out what demographics tell us about various supply needs of the present, and see if we can use it to predict future supply.

During the course of this exercise, I will be providing you with my subjective opinions about what the demographics mean for the various scenarios, but I want you to try to beat me to the punch—posit your own opinions before I offer mine. And always feel free to second-guess me. Demographic forecasting is, to some degree, more of an art than a science, and demographers do occasionally get it wrong. Though—*"ahem"*—my demographic-based forecasts have proved prescient far more often than not. . . .

In drafting this section of the book I must admit that I was challenged by how to organize it. I am so used to looking at things via the eyes of the specific generations that I wanted to proceed on a generational basis—that is, providing another chapter on each generation and then showing how each has impacted the various businesses and sectors in the past, and then weigh in on how I think they will impact them in the future.

But I worried that this could get quite muddled, and that as I moved through the generations I might often need to backpedal to remind the reader how an earlier generation's impact affected the business. In short, I came to believe that this approach might lead to the reader needing to pause too often in order to consider previous generational impacts. For example, motorcycles play a significant role with Baby Boomers, Generation X, and Gen Y, and though the impacts on the business were, and are, different depending upon each generation, would those differences get lost between my discussion of the Boomers and then, two generations later, of Gen Y?

So I determined that it perhaps makes more sense to examine specific business sectors—along with the occasional case-study company—and show how they've been impacted in the past and how I believe they might be impacted in the future by whichever generations are responsible for the impacts.

Space in this book does not allow for the inclusion of all business sectors, nor have I, by any means, conducted demographic research that covers all the sectors. And the targeted research I've done to determine demographic impacts on individual companies is extremely limited, especially given that more than 5,000 U.S. companies are publicly traded on the U.S. stock exchanges, and that there is just me and my colleagues conducting research for this book and other projects.

Speaking of publicly traded companies, at this juncture I need to make the following proclamation:

> The information and data provided in this book reflect the views and opinions of Ken Gronbach and his KGC Direct colleagues. The views expressed may change at any time. The opinions expressed in this communication are those of the author(s). No representation is made concerning the accuracy of cited data. Nor is there any guarantee that any projection, forecast, or opinion will be realized.
>
> Readers using this information are solely responsible for their own actions and invest at their own risk. Before making specific investments, further investigation is recommended. Although information contained in this book is derived from sources that are believed to be reliable, they are not always necessarily complete and cannot be guaranteed.
>
> The value of investments, and the income from them, can fall as well as rise, and you may not get back the original amount invested. Past performance is not a guide to future performance. Publicly traded securities of companies referenced in this book may be held by the author and/or his colleagues. References to these securities should in no way be deemed as an understanding of any future position, buying or selling, that may be taken by them.

In other words, conduct your own due diligence if and when considering the purchase of securities. Just because I might think Harley-Davidson, Inc., is a prime candidate for short selling does not mean you should just run out and put everything you own on a short position in HOG. And really, anyone willing to buy and sell stocks based solely on what someone else says about a specific position has no business being in the game.

Right! Now where was I?

Ah yes, businesses and sectors, and that's how this section of the book is going to be organized.

But where should I start? Which business or sector should we examine first? Which business or sector is about to feel the full upside strength and tsunami-like power of any of the particular generations?

I've got it!

And you'll have to pardon the pun, but we're going to begin this section with the end. . . .

17

Death Comes Knocking for Us All

ABOUT FIVE YEARS ago I received a call from Joe Budzinski, the COO of the ICCFA, The International Cemetery, Cremation and Funeral Association. The ICCFA is the second largest organization in the world involved with the death care industry. Joe had read my first book and thought that maybe I could explain why the number of funerals and cremations in the United States had fallen off dramatically in the last ten or so years while his industry had been preparing for the exact opposite. Apparently a famous futurist, demographer, and author had keynoted an ICCFA conference in the early 1990s, during which he had advised the industry to prepare for an avalanche of dead Baby Boomers starting in the year 2000.

It never happened. In fact, the number of annual funerals and cremations plummeted. Joe wanted to know what was going on and whether the Boomers were secretly being buried at home. I told him it had everything to do with the fact that on a relative basis few people were born seventy to eighty years ago and that most people die between the ages of 70 and 80.

That well-known futurist was obviously part of the cadre of

demographic experts who in the late 1980s and early 1990s started predicting a "graying of America" that would overwhelm the country starting in about the year 2000.

But wait a minute . . . what's going on here? The "graying" *hasn't* happened? Were the experts wrong?

Well, kind of, because they were fifteen to twenty years too early, which suggests to me that they can't count. And, if you can recall what I wrote about the Silent Generation in Chapter 6, then you know what I'm about to say.

Remember?

How about: The Silent Generation (born 1925 to 1944) is tiny in comparison to the generations that preceded and followed it. The Silent Generation boasted only about 52.5 million live births and, due to anti-immigrant sentiment (sound familiar?), the Great Depression, and then World War II, their ranks were never really boosted by any significant immigration numbers. The G.I. Generation that preceded them was 70 million-plus (thanks in part to immigration), while the Boomers were close to 80 million strong.

For whatever reason, so many of the "experts" ignored this crucial difference between the generations, and the diminutive Silent Generation has proved to be a real problem for businesses that geared up for the graying of America—funeral homes, among other businesses, have gone begging for the past twenty years. But that's all about to change because . . .

Anyone?

That's right, hello Baby Boomers!

As of 2015 the first of the Baby Boomers turned 70 years old, and the grand marshals of this generational parade cohort are heralding in a population of potential death care customers that absolutely dwarfs the customer base of the last twenty years.

And yes, we Boomers think we're going to live forever. And yes, a fair number of us will enjoy longevity above and beyond that experienced by our own parents. Nevertheless, there are so many more of us than the preceding generation, and so many more of us with lifestyle-related health issues—think smoking and obesity as two prime examples—that the annual number of deaths in the United States going forward is going to skyrocket, despite those super-healthy Boomer outliers.

I haven't talked to Joe in a couple of years, but my guess is that funeral homes across the country are already noticing a significant uptake in the number of funerals.

The death care industry is at a demographic crossroads and needs to prepare and collectively lose its fear of capital spending, now. Right now. Yes, the industry probably spent far too much back in the 1990s gearing up for that "graying of America" that never arrived.

But it is finally arriving, and from what I can tell the "cry wolf" phenomenon created by the false prophets of graying and dying has caused the industry to gear down. According to the National Directory of Morticians Redbook, the number of funeral homes in the United States has declined by more than 2,000 in the past ten years.

Not to pat myself on the back or anything, but I have yet to see anyone attribute the decline in the number of funeral homes—or related declines in elderly care—to the especially small size of the Silent Generation. I honestly wonder whether anyone else bothered to count them.

OK, pat me on the back, because I've been talking about the small size of the Silent Generation for years, and warning people that there was going to be a ten- to fifteen-year dearth of business related to elderly issues as they aged. But perhaps people didn't hear that part because I was much more focused on the massive "boom" (pardon the pun) that was following close on the heels of that bust.

Meanwhile, the number of Americans nearing the prime years for dying is about to soar.

Just consider the vast difference between the population numbers in the table on the next page as recorded by the Census Bureau in 2000, when the graying was theoretically set to begin, and the numbers for the same populations just ten years later and for two[1] components of the population fourteen years later:

TABLE 17.1

SELECT POPULATIONS BY AGE—2000 VERSUS 2010 AND 2014

CENSUS YEAR	AGE 65 AND OLDER	AGE 65 TO 74	AGE 75 TO 84	AGE 85 AND OLDER
2000	34,991,753	18,390,986	12,361,180	4,239,587
2010	40,267,984	21,713,429	13,061,122	5,493,433
Difference	5,276,231	3,322,443	699,942	1,253,846
2014	46,243,211	N/A	N/A	6,162,231
Difference	11,251,458	N/A	N/A	1,922,644

Talk about an increase in one's customer base!

And did you notice how the 2000–2010 increase in the numbers of the Age 65 and Older population almost doubled again in just four short years? That, my friends, is the power of the Baby Boomers, and I really don't think the funeral industry is quite ready for it.

Consider also that the number of people dying every year remained relatively static at roughly 2.4 million per year during the first ten years of this century. In fact, in 2011, the U.S. death rate hit an all-time low of 740.6 deaths per 100,000 population, according to the U.S. Centers for Disease Control. However, that same year marked a milestone of sorts, as the Center reported that total annual U.S. deaths topped 2.5 million for the first time ever, a number that has continued to rise in the subsequent reporting years, jumping by almost 100,000 in two years, and another 30,000 by 2014, the last year of reported CDC data. Despite a U.S. life-expectancy-at-birth rate of 78.8 years and rising, I have little doubt that the annual number of deaths will continue to climb and will soon near 3 million.

As of 2013, the number of Americans turning the key life expectancy age of 78.8 started to slowly increase, and it is set to rapidly accelerate beginning in 2018, to reflect the steady increase in Silent Generation births that began in 1940, and then turned into a flood with the Baby Boomers starting in 1945.

Unfortunately, it's not just the Boomers who are adding to the death care customer base. I say unfortunately because children just shouldn't predecease their parents. But some of them do, and given the immense size of Generation Y, and the fact that the second growth spurt years of this generation are entering the primary accidental death age bracket of 15–24, the years in which accidents are the leading cause of death, well then the number of accidental youth deaths will likely rise.

Let's again compare Census numbers, looking at the population of this vulnerable group in 2000 and compare it with the same population as of 2010 and 2014:

TABLE 17.2

SELECT POPULATIONS BY AGE—2000 VERSUS 2010 AND 2014

CENSUS YEAR	AGE 15 TO 24
2000	39,183,891
2010	43,628,964
Difference	4,445,073
2014	43,979,821
Difference	4,795,930

And thus another increase in the potential customer base. Now there might not be a huge difference between 2014 and 2010, but it is showing a continued increase . . . unfortunately.

Perhaps a small saving grace might be that all indications point to Generation Y having less of an affinity for the automobile culture, when compared to previous generations, especially that of the Boomers. Given that motor vehicle accidents are by far the leading cause of accidental death, if fewer Millennials are getting their driver's licenses and driving, well then hopefully fewer of them will be dying on the highways.

To recap, starting about now the number of funerals and cremations in the United States will increase dramatically and not look back for thirty years. A market shift of this magnitude is not always good news, especially for folks whose strategic plan is "Wait and See." There is a real threat of a big-box death care concept attempting to overwhelm the industry, much like Home Depot did to hardware stores. This does not have to happen if the existing business model is prepared and reinforces the barriers to entry. Marketing, merchandising, and salesmanship are disciplines that will need to be embraced by the death care industry if it plans to make its way in the new millennium.

And speaking of big-box death care, don't think I'm joking, as Walmart and Amazon.com offer a large line of discount caskets and urns with a wide range of price points, along with forty-eight-hour shipping. While the impact on the overall business by these two upstart retailers is considered relatively small, some analysts believe that they are growing market share.

While driving home from the airport in Hartford a couple of years ago, I noticed a billboard on the interstate advertising complete cremations for $995. I thought to myself, now there is a company that has figured it out. It is riding the crest of two trends. One, Baby Boomers are aging into the dominant years for dying. Two, Boomers will favor cremations. Bingo. In marketing you always want to position yourself in front of trends. Positioning your product or service in front of two trends is more than twice as good. My long-standing axiom for selling to Boomers is: *Make my life easy. Save me some time. Don't rip me off.* This $995 cremation service company nailed all three. Now if it can add in some kind of religious service on premises, it will hit it out of the park.

Cremations are already the death care handling of choice for almost 50 percent of funerals in the United States. This number is expected to grow dramatically over the next twenty years, with the National Funeral Directors Association forecasting it to reach more than 55 percent of services by 2020, and more than 70 percent by 2030. Boomer spouses and their Generation Y kids will embrace the memorialization of cremation. There is no reason cremations cannot be as profitable as traditional funerals. None.

Keep in mind that though African Americans do not favor cremation for cultural reasons, and Catholic Hispanics tend to choose traditional burials favored by the church, Asians choose cremation almost exclusively. Asians are moving into this country every year by the hundreds of thousands . . . to live, and to die. A significant opportunity.

What have I forgotten here?

Death is not an equal-opportunity distributor. Mortality rates tend to be highest in the South, and the South has the largest population of all the regions. So, if you want to open a funeral home, I'd suggest that you perhaps look South first.

Keep an eye on pre-need insurance and planning going forward, as this form of death care sales had been increasing even in the face of the small Silent Generation market. Now that the Boomers are coming of age, I expect to see astronomical growth.

If you are thinking about investing in the death care industry, a $15 billion to $20 billion per year industry depending upon which potential components are included in the tally, there are about seven primary publicly owned companies that dominate the industry, absent the 15,000 or so smaller—usually family-owned—companies that conduct most of the nation's funerals. At this juncture, I could pat myself on the back again for recommending three of these companies as "buys" back in 2009. However, given that most stock prices have climbed dramatically since then, perhaps I don't deserve that much of a pat.

Companies to look at include:

- Service Corp. International (SCI)
- Carriage Services Inc. (CSV)
- StoneMor Partners L.P. (STON)
- Hillenbrand, Inc. (HI)
- Matthews International (MATW)

Back in 2009, most of these companies had been beaten down to the single-digit range, but they have since climbed back up, with a couple reaching all-time highs. At current (as of early 2016) prices, my colleagues and I do not believe they offer an especially attractive entry price, though they have for the most part sold off from those highs. Additionally, a couple of them offer decent dividends, with StoneMor's yield topping 5 percent now for many successive years. As mentioned in Chapter 16, conduct your own due diligence.

18

Kicking Back During the Golden Years

O K, SO YOU can now forget everything I wrote in the previous chapter because we Boomers aren't going to die. Nope, we're going to kick off our shoes, relax, and change the face of retirement and assisted living like Medusa getting a facelift and new hairweave.

Actually, you can take everything I wrote in the previous chapter and just replace "death care" with "retirement/assisted living," because the same dynamics that will impact the death care industry are at work with retirement and assisted living. Though with a huge difference in scale and scope, as retirement and assisted living encompass so many more parameters than dying. In fact, the "retirement" component can't really be called a "sector," as it is multidimensional and potentially impacts so many other sectors both on the macro and micro level (for example, retirement housing would be macro, while retirement leisure activities such as golf would be micro). The assisted living component does serve as a distinct sector, but one that also incorporates to some degree healthcare (which will be covered in the next chapter).

Those folks currently working in businesses that cater to retirement and assisted living can't perceive the size of the wave that's about to roll over them like . . . well, like a tsunami! And with this tsunami the seismologists have detected the earthquake under the seabed, and have activated the warning bells and sirens to let everyone know it's coming, but no one really sees a tsunami until it hits land. Everyone knows it's big, but because of the vastness of the ocean and the undulation of the waves, people cannot discern how truly massive a tsunami can be. And let me tell you, this Baby Boomer tsunami is a giant.

The Baby Boomers will make the population of those 65 years and older in America the largest such cohort ever both because of their existing size and because they are expected to live longer than any previous generation. In fact, the Harvard School of Public Health, among others, projects that those Boomers who make it to age 65 can expect on average to live to the age of 83. So, the population of those 65 years and older is about to expand like a bicep on steroids.

In fact, the expansion has already begun, as in just six short years since 2010 the population of this age group has grown by more than 5 million. This is the leading edge of the tsunami and, despite its size, it hasn't really been noticed yet. Boomers don't like the idea of growing old, are not turning "elderly" as their parents did, and, due in large part to the Recession of 2008, postponed their retirement plans. Well, the recession is over and the retirement party has begun!

And what a party! The population of those over age 65 is projected to more than double from 2010 to 2050, from the 40.2 million in 2010 to an estimated 88.5 million in 2050.

If you think finding a tee time at your local golf course is tough now, wait a few years.

If you're one of those people who work in the assisted living sector and have been seeing a lot of empty beds over the past fifteen years, well that bed space will soon enough start getting filled. And yes, I know that you've heard that before, but that's because you listened to those "graying of America" geniuses who couldn't count and were fifteen years too early with their projections.

Well, *I can count,* and I know that the number of people age 85 and older—those most likely to need assisted living services—has grown by about 700,000 in just the past six years and is only going to keep growing. In fact, the Census Bureau estimates that the population of this age group will almost triple by 2050, from some 6.3 million now to a projected 17.9 million by 2050. Now that's a lot of potential assisted living bed space.

I was born in 1947. Do the math. If I were my parents, I would be old. I am not old. Apart from a couple of minor maladies, everything still works, and I plan on keeping it that way with good nutrition and quality healthcare. I don't really feel any different than I did when I was younger. And put me behind the wheel of a high-powered car and the age disappears completely. I still love to go through the gears and hear the motor wind tight. I hope I never grow out of this. I know I am not alone, so I don't see the Boomer love affair with the automobile disappearing anytime soon. I hope Detroit doesn't forget us.

If ever there was an economic opportunity to position yourself in front of a demographic wave it would be in the South or one of the prime Western retirement states selling anything to Baby Boomers. Can you imagine Baby Boomers' consumption of everything pharmaceutical and geriatric?

Remember that Boomers have redefined just about everything in America as they passed through the different stages of life, and there is little doubt that they are going to redefine retirement and everything retirees consume. So it's a new ball game. I don't think they will be buying rocking chairs. Boomers have already redefined the golf cart in communities that use them for the principal transportation. Golf carts that look like cars that are hot-rodded. This should partially satisfy the Boomers' love affair with the automobile. Boomers will never grow up. Remember, Baby Boomers are not going to suddenly want to listen to big band music. Can you picture an 80-year-old Boomer doing air guitar to Led Zeppelin? Not a pretty picture, but we're undoubtedly going to be seeing it in the not-so-distant future.

I am certain that Boomers will consume the latest electronics until they die. So everything computer and television, whatever form it morphs into, will be big with the Baby Boomers until further notice.

Boomers will never lose their affection for sweatshirts, jeans, T-shirts, sneakers, and sandals. The new elder uniform.

Say good-bye to the Harley-Davidsons. They won't be able to hold them up at traffic lights (more on this in Chapter 21). Sure, Harley is managing to entice some Boomers with its three-wheeler, but I doubt it will ever enjoy the popularity that the bikes did. Maybe Harley needs to design a golf cart.

That axiom for selling anything to Boomers? If you've already forgotten it, you're probably a late-stage Boomer, as I just mentioned a few pages back: *Make my life easy, save me some time, don't rip me off, and I will buy from you.* And try not to forget it again because it still works.

Baby Boomers love to have their houses cleaned, cars washed, and stuff delivered—bodes well for cleaning services, car washes, UPS, and Federal Express.

Boomers have always loved to travel, and with more free time and money to spend, they are going to go see those parts of the world that they didn't see in their youth.

Cruises will continue to flourish, but their personalities will adapt to Boomer culture. A Motown Cruise? A heavy metal cruise? A marijuana cruise? I don't believe it's as far-fetched as you might think.

Remember, Boomers like to change things. They are not their parents and never will be.

What about Baby Boomer food? What's next? What will they eat? Based on the number of Boomers who are obese, they will apparently eat anything and all the wrong things. Baby Boomers can thank Generation Y kids for the big changes that are coming in the supermarkets. Think prepared foods and total transparency about nutrition. I think the meat counter will go away because Generation Y can't deal with the concept of raw meat. I believe they will still eat meat, but not in any form that they can identify. Spaghetti with meat sauce is fine. A sirloin steak? No way. Indirectly, the changes in the supermarket will benefit Boomers. Prepared foods are easy to serve. Boomers like easy and will better be able to control their portions.

Transparency about nutrition is a no-brainer that will benefit everyone. I believe that eventually food will be sold and valued based on nutrition and not on weight. Think about it, as it makes sense on so many levels.

So what about restaurants? Trust me, they are Baby Boomer-driven. Think big portions and doggy bags (remember them?). The way we buy food is changing. We now routinely buy several days of food when we eat out. My office is in my home. What I have for lunch is very often a repeat of what I didn't finish at an earlier dinner or lunch at a restaurant. Essentially we are doing a lot of our prepared food shopping at restaurants. The only difference between a restaurant and a supermarket is the fact that we eat some of the prepared food in the restaurant before we bring it home. In a supermarket we will bring our entire prepared food purchase home.

Do you ever think about doggy bags? Why were they called doggy bags? They were called doggy bags because thirty- or forty-plus years ago the only time you would ever bring leftovers home from a restaurant was to feed it to a dog. Worked back then, but not the case so much today.

A friend of mine related a recent restaurant story about his wife asking that her unfinished T-bone steak be put in a doggy bag. When the bag arrived at the table, it was big and heavy. The waitperson, aiming to please, included other bones from other tables for the dog to enjoy. My friend and his wife did not have a dog, or a cat for that matter. His wife simply wanted to enjoy the remaining steak at home, but she did not tell the waitperson of her intentions because that was not done. Everything is changing.

The issue of Baby Boomers and sleep should definitely be looked into by somebody, as it probably represents several untapped markets—something I realized back when our advertising agency, KGA, was doing about $40 million in billing a year in the late 1990s.

We were not a big national agency by any means, but on the regional level we were a force to be reckoned with. We were very successful with mass media, especially broadcast and specifically television. We could buy television surgically because we analyzed where the viewers were and knew exactly who was watching what. Young male blue jean buyers clustered around sports and entertainment shows. Cosmetics and household products found their efficiencies in television spots bought on the soaps where women viewers abounded. When we wanted to sell high-end Rolex watches to middle-aged men, we bought the *CBS Evening News*. I can remember being somewhat vexed when one of our clients wanted to sell a product called a Stair-Glide, a chair on rails that would transport an elderly or physically challenged person up and down stairs in a two-level home. The chair system enabled folks to be able to stay in their homes longer at a fraction of the cost of an elevator. Elderly people loved it and loved the idea of staying in their homes. So how do we reach the seniors? At first I believed the answer was a four-color Sunday newspaper insert. Problem was you could not see the chair in action and feel comfortable that it could really solve your problems, maintain your freedom, and keep you in your own home. Television was the obvious answer, but where was the efficient buy? In what time slot could you entice senior viewers without wasting money on viewers who were way too young to care about Stair-Glides?

Our senior media buyer knew exactly what time slots to buy. "Overnights," he said. The television shows that air between 1:00 A.M. and 5:00 A.M.

"Why is that?" I asked.

He replied, "Old people can't sleep; they wake up and watch television."

He was right. We bought overnight programs and successfully sold Stair-Glides to seniors using a ninety-second infomercial-type spot that told the whole story. And it didn't cost a lot of our client's money.

Baby Boomers can't sleep now and they are not elderly yet. Are we going to have a whole generation of vampires? Baby Boomers never slept like babies; I don't know why. Maybe we have too much brain activity. Want to print money? Help Baby Boomers get a good night's sleep. This is the largest generation in the history of the United States ever to face the sleepless years. I don't know what the answer is, but there must be one. My lovely wife of forty years used to accuse me of having a second family somewhere that I would visit at night because I stayed up so late. Then we bought a very high-end Tempur-Pedic–type mattress with memory foam. Now I don't sleep—I go into nightly comas. I dream vivid dreams like never before. I look forward to and look for excuses to go to bed early. My wife says I still snore. I am addressing that issue now.

A new industry, Baby Boomer sleep? It is worth billions with a capital *B*.

Wherever Baby Boomers age, they establish new dimensions, set new boundaries. Don't expect anything less from Baby Boomer retirement. As I've said, it will be retirement on steroids.

I do not specifically follow businesses that serve retirement and assisted living needs but assume that hundreds (if not thousands) of them will undoubtedly benefit from the Boomers' vast numbers as they age into this last (and likely long) stage of their life span. No doubt that you were thinking about which companies might be involved with any of the aging-Boomer subjects I touched upon in the preceding pages, but let's not forget about healthcare and its cousin assisted living.

Think about it: Money spent on healthcare needs for the age 65 and older set is going to double in the years ahead, while money spent on related assisted living needs for the over 85 set will likely triple. With this in mind, hundreds of healthcare companies will undoubtedly benefit from the aging Boomer population.

Which publicly traded companies make hip and knee replacements, or perhaps stents and pacemakers? You think their sales are going to increase in the years ahead? Ka-ching! I certainly do.

And how about drugs? Sure, a lot of Boomers were into drugs back in the 1960s and 1970s, but they're going to be way more into drugs going forward than they were back then . . . just not the kind designed to get you high. Drug makers who offer pharmaceuticals that treat arthritis, diabetes, heart disease, and hypertension will undoubtedly see a massive increase in sales in the coming years.

Assisted living? What did I say a few pages back about the population of those 85 and older? Something about a potential customer base that is poised to triple over the next twenty-four years? Ka-ching!

Now, just because the potential customer base is going to triple doesn't mean that the estimated $330 billion assisted living industry is going to triple. Perhaps up to one-third of spending by this growing customer base will be limited by how much Medicare will be willing to pay. And the industry has been in transition over the past decade, with traditional nursing homes closing down while options for "independent living," "senior living communities," and "adult day care" have increased, which in some cases means higher costs that not all Boomers will be able to afford. Nevertheless, the industry's growth, even if it only doubles, represents a significant increase.

With that in mind, of the ten biggest players within the assisted living industry, only two are publicly traded:

o Brookdale Senior Living, Inc. (BKD)
o 5 Star Quality Care (FVE)

Both of these stocks were trading at the bottom end of their ranges as of mid-2016, probably due in part to the dearth of potential Silent Generation customers. Several other large players were taken private in the past few years, likely at bargain-basement prices, but there may be a few smaller publicly traded companies still listed. While neither Brookdale nor 5 Star offer a dividend, based strictly on demographics I would have to say that their long-range growth prospects look good.

As an outlier, and one with a 7 percent dividend yield, you could look at HCP, Inc. (HCP), a real estate investment trust that makes almost half of its earnings through senior housing. In fact, the above-mentioned Brookdale Senior Living is one of its biggest customers.

Do I have to mention "do your own due diligence"?

19

Boomers Driving the Future of Healthcare

WE KIND OF looked at healthcare from the Boomers' perspective in the previous chapter, in that aging Boomers are going to need a lot more healthcare than previous generations because of their size and expected longevity. And with the vast numbers of people needing near-end-of-life healthcare, the sector as a business is going to be bringing in the dollars hand over fist despite any real or perceived limitations caused by the Affordable Care Act. The same upside tsunami that is poised to sweep over the assisted living and death care sectors is going to be rolling over the healthcare sector first. The numbers of people needing or wanting everything from face-lifts to cataract removal to heart surgery is about to soar. And along with medical procedures, medicines, and general healthcare, Boomers will need and want all of the ancillary healthcare products that ease recuperation and assist with disability.

Remember, Boomers are a mobile generation, and they are not going to accept loss of mobility. So anyone who can design better crutches, wheelchairs, stair lifts, and other mobility aids is mining a potential vein of gold. The Boomer axiom of *Make my life easy—*

Save me some time—Don't rip me off will hold true with healthcare as well.

The Boomers have been a transformative force in every sector of the economy since their birth, and now they are going to transform healthcare. It's a transformation that opens up a plethora of potential opportunities but also presents a host of challenges. Consider:

○ While the Boomers' massive numbers will lead to increased sales of myriad medical products and services, to what extent will their expected overall high costs serve to hinder such sales increases?

○ As the customer base grows by leaps and bounds, the ranks of Boomers who work as healthcare providers will be plummeting, creating potential voids in clinical care and healthcare management. Who is going to replace them?

○ And then there's Medicare. . . . Fears abound in the medical profession and in Washington, D.C., that the Boomers are going to overwhelm the system. Given that the Congressional Budget Office is projecting that Boomers are going to increase Medicare enrollment by more than 30 percent within the next ten years, such fears may not be unjustified.

But even if not "unjustified," perhaps overblown? I say this for a number of reasons, key among which are the rising ranks of adult members of Generation Y. While I hate to put it on their backs, they will be crucial in saving the nation's healthcare system and Medicare. Think about it: The U.S. healthcare industry has always been both beholden to and vulnerable to the shifting sands of demography.

When the massive block of 80 million Baby Boomers dominated the 20- to 40-year-old segment of the U.S. population from about 1965 to 1985, the private shared-risk, insurance-based healthcare model was very successful. Boomers were paying insurance premiums into the system and not using many of the services in return because they were young and healthy. The much smaller Silent Generation, born 1925 to 1944, occupied the 40- to 60-year-old segment of the labor force, and because of their age at that time, used more services than they paid for in premiums. However, the critical mass of Boomers more than made up for this deficit. This demographic fact kept insurance premiums low and healthcare service providers profitable. Starting in 1984, the Boomers began to populate the 40- to 60-year-old segment of the labor force, and the value of the medical services they used began to exceed what they were paying in premiums. The private shared-risk insurance model began to fail. The young healthy generation right behind the Baby Boomers, Generation X, which was about 9 million people smaller by births than the Boomer Generation, was too small and economically impotent to compensate for the Boomers' escalating utilization of medical services.

But now Generation Y, the largest generation in American history, is beginning to enter the workforce in large numbers. Add in the millions of young Hispanic immigrants and socioeconomically advancing African American cohorts and you have a complex private healthcare insurance marketplace with the potential to significantly expand. In short, millions of new very desirable young healthy potential customers poised to flood the private shared-risk insurance-based model. And all of this was set to take place without a single piece of legislation or government involvement. Imagine that. Our current private healthcare system here in the United States was not broken, it was just suffering from a demographically induced setback that would have self-corrected as our demography shifts. In short, Generation Y would have saved the existing private shared-risk insurance-based model, and will undoubtedly solve the looming healthcare provider shortage, as well.

I am not sure how the Affordable Care Act is going to affect these demographic dynamics in healthcare going forward, but I have a feeling that it is going to end up as a dead horse. About two and one-half years ago I was hired to keynote an annual meeting for a healthcare-related company in the Midwest. This private company handled the complex administration of Medicaid and Medicare for an entire state. I was warned up front not to refer to the Affordable Care Act as ObamaCare as this would be offensive to the company's president. I am a mercenary, so I never mentioned ObamaCare. The president spoke before I did and extolled the merits of the Affordable Care Act, pointing out that this new 2014 federal legislation would increase the company's workload and compensation by 25 percent. Twenty-five percent is a mammoth increase in the number of takers to be introduced to an already struggling shared-risk healthcare system. I silently forecast that ObamaCare would die a slow but sure death, probably after President Obama left office. As of the last months of Obama's term, I believe I started hearing death rattles.

Another reason I believe the fears of a looming healthcare crisis may be overblown is the American people's incredible capacity for innovation. When confronted with problems or crisis situations, Americans rally and work hard to quickly bring the situation to heel. The massive population of aging Boomers definitely represents a challenge for the continued successful and affordable delivery of quality healthcare services. But in America, where there is challenge, there is opportunity. And we've got more than 80 million members of Gen Y reaching the primary age range in which people are generally at their best meeting challenges, and at seeking opportunity.

Finally, innovation—whether in treatment methods or delivery of care—should help reduce costs. In fact, "innovation" has been U.S. healthcare's catchall of late, with innovators across the country seeking out and testing new treatment methods and new means of delivering effective healthcare. "Mobile health" technologies such as smartphone apps, wireless sensors, remote monitoring, and even an iPhone-sized ultrasound are transforming patient-doctor interactions, offering savings in times, and giving patients more opportunities to self-manage their care. "Accountable-care organization," as encouraged through the Affordable Care Act, is working to pool healthcare provider resources and more effectively manage their operations in order to cut costs and reduce redundancies in care. Electronic-medical-record systems are being developed and revamped to ensure better delivery and ongoing monitoring of medical care. The list of ongoing and potential innovations certainly doesn't end here, and consider also that the ranks of the innovators are poised to rise with the aging of Generation Y. And remember, where there is challenge, there is opportunity.

The healthcare sector is so massive that space in this book doesn't allow for a complete overview of all its parameters, but perhaps we should look at a couple of health concerns that seem to be impacting all of the generations. Obesity has emerged in the past twenty years as the leading lifestyle-related cause of disease and death after smoking, with it being considered a major risk factor for a number of diseases, including type 2 diabetes, cardiovascular disease, stroke, and certain cancers. Some healthcare researchers believe that obesity-related healthcare costs have now exceeded those of smoking and problem drinking. The number of clinically obese adults in the United States is believed to have increased by more than 50 percent since 1980, while the number of overweight children and adolescents has tripled. The Centers for Disease Control and Prevention in its latest findings on obesity has determined that almost 35 percent of U.S. adults and 17 percent of children and adolescents aged 2 to 19 are obese.

While the obesity epidemic is affecting all of the generations, certain age, racial, and ethnic groups seem to be facing higher levels. Asians have the lowest rates of age-adjusted obesity, at just over 10 percent, while Blacks have the highest, at almost 50 percent. The Hispanic rate was pegged at just over 42 percent, while Non-Hispanic Whites came in at 32.6 percent. For children and adolescents, Hispanics had the highest rates, followed by Blacks, Non-Hispanic Whites, and Asians.

All of this means that healthcare impacts related to obesity will continue to rise; however, the demographics of the nation's obesity epidemic vary by region and by state. On a regional basis as of 2014, the Midwest experienced the highest prevalence of obesity at 30.7 percent; followed by the South, 30.6 percent; Northeast, 27.3 percent; and West, 25.7 percent. All states recorded prevalence above 20 percent, with California, Colorado, Vermont, and Massachusetts recording the lowest prevalence, and West Virginia, Arkansas, and Mississippi recording a prevalence greater than 35 percent.

And at this juncture, I'm going to ask you two questions: 1. What occupation is likely seeing a significant boom due to this healthcare-related demographic? And, 2. Where would be the best locations in America for a person to set up shop with this occupation?

You answered the first one correctly, right?

Bariatric surgeon? Well, that wasn't quite what I was looking for, but their numbers are definitely growing, too.

No, I was looking for dietitian/nutritionist.

As for the best places for a dietitian/nutritionist to set up shop, I assume you answered the three states with an obesity prevalence above 35 percent, and/or the "Midwest" and "South."

And yes, you have determined a good demographic starting point for where the need might be, but you will still want to figure out if that need is being met. Sure, the epidemic is out of control in Mississippi, but what if the state is already overrun with dietitians/ nutritionists? Well, you'll need to figure that out, and then look at the population of that group of workers in the other favorable states.

How? The U.S. Bureau of Labor Statistics has a fantastic website (www.bls.gov) with databases for examining the demographics of occupations.

And, by the way, of the three most obese-prevalent states, Arkansas definitely seems to have the greatest demand for dietitians/ nutritionists; however, West Virginia appears to offer significantly higher earnings potential.

Now that you know a bit more about the healthcare demographics of obesity, what other healthcare-related demographic might have a big impact on the nation's healthcare system?

Naturally, you've been reading carefully, saw the answer referenced a couple of pages back, and know that I am obviously referring to smokers and their habit, which is the leading cause of preventable diseases and death in the United States.

In some ways the demographics of smoking is more interesting than that of obesity. Perhaps the most noteworthy fact is that U.S. smoking rates have been falling for the past fifty years, and hit an all-time low in 2014, when the CDC estimated that only about 16.8 percent of the adult population was smoking. In 1965 it was estimated that 42 percent of the adult population smoked, a figure that decreased by half by 2005, and then dropped another 20 percent in just the past ten years.

While smoking affects all the generations, smoking rates vary widely among age, ethnic, and racial groups, as well as by sex, education, income levels, regions, states, and even sexual orientation.

Men are more likely to be current smokers than women, with almost 19 percent of men tagged as current smokers in 2014, compared to just under 15 percent of women. We older folks have the lowest rates, with only 8.5 percent of the population over 65 currently smoking. It's highly probable that some of us got smart and quit, but on the flip side, part of that lower rate is due to early death caused by smoking. Adults aged 25–44 had the highest rates, at 20 percent of the population, while 18 percent of the aged 45–64 population currently smoke. The younger adult members of Gen Y tend to smoke less than other generations, with only 16.7 percent of those aged 18–24 smoking.

As for smoking on a race or ethnicity basis, Native Americans have the highest rates at just over 29 percent; followed by multiracial individuals, 27.9 percent; Non-Hispanic Whites, 18.2 percent; Blacks, 17.5 percent; Hispanics, 11.2 percent; and Asians, 9.5 percent.

Those with lower levels of education tend to smoke the most, which kind of figures. However, those of less means also tend to smoke more, which almost doesn't make sense, as they are the least likely to be able to afford what has become an expensive addiction.

Almost 30 percent of those without a high school diploma smoke, but of more interest, 43 percent of adults with a General Equivalency Degree (GED) smoke. I have no idea what might be causing that spike, but find it so odd that I believe it deserves a study.

Other than the GED anomaly, smoking rates go down with the level of education, with 21.7 percent of high school diploma holders smoking, 17.1 percent of those with an associate's degree, 7.9 percent of those with an undergraduate college degree, and only 5.4 percent with a graduate-level degree. So, maybe all those student loans are worth it. . . .

While 15.2 percent of adults who live at or above the poverty level smoke, 26.3 percent of those who live below the poverty level smoke. As I noted, I'm not quite sure how this population can afford to smoke, and would posit that smoking most likely helps keep them below the poverty level.

On a regional basis smoking rates tend to follow in step with the rates of obesity, with the Midwest having the highest rate, at 20.7 percent; followed by the South, 17.2 percent; Northeast, 15.3 percent; and West, 13.1 percent. A quick glance at the states shows Utah with the lowest rates, at 9.7 percent, and West Virginia with the highest, at 26.7 percent.

And for yet another rate perhaps deserving of more scientific study, the gay/lesbian/bisexual adult smoking rate comes in at 23.9 percent, significantly above the straight adult rate of 16.6 percent.

So, what do these smoking-related demographics mean for healthcare? This is pretty much a rhetorical question as I did not provide you any hints in the previous pages, nor do I know the answer myself. What I do know is that the CDC believes that smoking still causes more than 480,000 deaths per year (along with the associated healthcare costs while they die), and that more than 16 million Americans are currently living with a smoking-related disease.

Depending on the data source, smoking-related mortality and disease numbers haven't changed all that much over the years, despite the significant 50 percent drop in smoking rates over the past fifty years.

How can that be, you ask?

Well, we're talking demographics here, and if you pause to think about it, I would surmise that you can answer this question.

Give up?

Easy. While the rate of smoking in the United States has pretty much dropped 50 percent since 1965, the overall population has increased by more than 60 percent, and thus the absolute number of smokers hasn't really changed.

I know that I've repeatedly inferred that this demographics stuff is easy, but I never said that it couldn't be tricky at times.

The majority of my focus in this chapter has centered on how the Baby Boomers will impact U.S. healthcare, so you're perhaps wondering if the other generations are going to affect the sector. As indicated, I see the Boomers as a tsunami hitting the healthcare sector, and no, I don't really foresee that the other generations are going to make much of an impact over the next twenty years, other than how Gen Y will:

- help fill the ranks of retiring Boomer healthcare workers
- bring in new innovations, and
- help pay for it all

I don't see any other healthcare tsunamis, nor do I believe that the other generations will create any significant sinkholes. I do not foresee Gen Y creating a new "baby boom" but believe we will see a healthy number of births going forward.

Now that you've been given some bare-bones basics regarding demographics and the U.S. healthcare sector, do you think that the demographics support investment in healthcare equities?

I would certainly say yes, but the question remains as to which ones. And there are hundreds to choose from. This is a sector in which my colleagues would advise you to go with "big" and "long-established" companies, because they are better able to weather the overall ups and downs of the economy and stock market and are more likely to pay a dividend.

You are probably familiar with "biotech" and have heard tales of biotech stock prices doubling, tripling, quintupling, and even growing by what seems to be a gazillion percent over short periods of time. A biotech, for the record, is similar to a pharmaceutical or medical device company; they all generally conduct clinical research and focus on novel drug and treatment development. However, a pharmaceutical/medical device company is already established with products on the market and therefore capable of managing and diversifying risk, whereas all but a few biotechs are usually working on a do or fail proposition. Thus, while a successful biotech can reap significant returns should its experimental product(s) receive regulatory approval, somewhere in the neighborhood of 85–95 percent of all biotech endeavors fail, with subsequent losses in equity pricing. Thus, a biotech is basically a wannabe pharmaceutical[1] or medical device company, so invest warily, if at all.

The bigger, long-established healthcare companies can be broken down into sub-sectors, such as pharmaceuticals, diagnostics, generic drugs, long-term care, medical insurance, hospitals, and medical instruments and supplies, among others. Some of the biggest players in these fields that offer stable dividends are:

- o GlaxoSmithKline PLC (GSK)
- o Pfizer (PFE)
- o Merck (MRK)
- o Bristol-Myers Squibb (BMY)
- o Amgen (AMGN)
- o Meridian Biosciences, Inc. (VIVO)
- o Becton Dickinson (BDX)
- o Stryker Corp. (SYK)
- o Select Medical Holdings Corp. (SEM)
- o St. Jude Medical (STJ)
- o UnitedHealth Group (UNH)

These are just a few examples of the many healthcare companies that might be worth investing in, and you could spend days, if not weeks, researching them all.

Another angle to explore would be an exchange-traded fund (ETF), which is basically a marketable security that owns a basket of assets (stocks, bonds, futures, etc.) and divides them into distinct shares traded on the exchanges. A typical healthcare ETF would own a variety of healthcare-related stocks and bonds, and its price would vary during each day based on market conditions and the cumulative strength of its portfolio. Some people consider ETFs a good investment because they spread the risk and let others take care of the detailed research. Many ETFs also offer dividends. Among the more popular healthcare ETFs are:

o Vanguard Health Care (VHT)
o Health Care Select Sector SPDR (XLV)
o iShares US Healthcare (IYH)

And . . . need I say it?

Conduct your own due diligence.

20

Where House Now?

GRADUATED HIGH SCHOOL in 1966—yes, before fire was discovered, as my Generation Y daughters would say. I used to feel "leading edge." In at least one way I am leading edge—a leading-edge Baby Boomer, born in 1947. Now I feel like an "antique" and am not going into this old age thing gracefully. I will go kicking and screaming.

I remember high school graduation very well. I recall that my graduation gift from my parents was a plaid set of cloth luggage.

"When would I use this?" I asked.

"Now," my parents replied. "You are out of here."

And I was, in fact, out of there. The last out of eleven children from two large merged families to leave, which I suppose in that case made me "ending edge."

My stepfather had seven kids and my mom had four. That's eleven. I was the baby. So I packed my plaid cloth luggage, bought a plane ticket, and flew from Connecticut to Los Angeles, California, at the end of June 1966. By September I had blown through my meager savings and came face-to-face with the facts of life. If I wanted to eat, I was going to have to figure this survival thing out.

I did, and then some. I worked forty hours a week and went to school full-time. I graduated California State University, Long Beach, in January 1971 and then got recruited into marketing at Volkswagen of America in Culver City, California.

What's my point?

I had to leave home and I had to make my own way. It was sink or swim. I chose to swim—out of necessity, not because I wanted to.

So what of it?

Well, right now the two largest generations in U.S. history are pretty much living under one roof: Baby Boomers and their Generation Y kids.[1]

Yes, these Gen Y kids are slow to move out (and some are even now in their 30s), but it is not entirely their fault. The Millennials have been having difficulty finding work in part because Boomers are proving to be very slow at leaving the workforce. Boomers have been slow to leave the workforce because they don't have enough money to retire because they can't sell their houses because of the housing market meltdown and resulting Great Recession of 2008.

But that is all changing as of this writing. The housing market, once riddled by foreclosures, is improving. The dominos are starting to fall. According to the latest[2] U.S. Census biannual American Housing Survey, there were almost 133 million housing units (houses, condos, and apartments) in the United States as of 2013, of which only about 75.5 million were "owner occupied," with the rest consisting of rental units (roughly 40.2 million), seasonal (vacation) units (4 million), and vacant units (12.9 million). Considering that there are about 78,000,000 Boomers and about 84,000,000 members of Generation Y living together, and that Generation Y is starting to move out, do you think we will need more housing?

How much more housing? Twenty million more units? Forty million more units? How much?

Remember, if 2008 taught us nothing, it taught us that housing is the U.S. economy and the economy is housing. The inevitable emergence of 9 million bad mortgages in 2008 and 2009 brought down the housing industry and the United States economy, precipitating a worldwide financial crisis.

The lesson that I hope we learned? Don't write stupid loans for folks who can ill afford the payments no matter how easy it is or how much money we are making. Wasn't anyone watching? We paid a dear price. Now we are seeing fewer and fewer foreclosures, and a strong housing market is reemerging. And guess what? We are discovering that we may be more than just a little bit short of supply in housing.

How can this be? Do the math. Count the two largest generations ever created in America and realize, as mentioned above, that they have uncharacteristically been living together under the same roof far longer than did previous generations. These two generations are starting to part company in big numbers, and more and more of the ones moving out are going to need housing.

The average age for first marriages in the United States is right around 26 to 29 years old. Generation Y is currently aged 13 to 32, and they are starting to get married in big numbers.

Don't believe me? Try to rent a hall on a weekend or find a caterer who isn't booked. It has started. Remember that the footprint of the services to meet the needs of newlyweds had adjusted to meet the needs of Generation X, with its much smaller birth population and economically challenged (for the most part) immigrant population. Well, now that footprint is about to get a lot bigger.

I bet you are all thinking about business opportunities. There will be so many, it will make your head spin. Weddings are just the beginning. What about household items? Appliances? Furniture? Strollers? Lawn mowers?

What about houses?

The idea of single people in their 20s living with their parents might have become almost commonplace over the past ten years or so, but I do not think the same will hold true with couples in their 20s and 30s living with one set of parents. For many couples, seeing the in-laws on holidays is tough enough. Living with them? Forget it!

Generation Y is already driving an upswing in housing. Consider these headlines from news articles written over the past two years:

"Millennial-Driven Housing Boom on the Horizon"
"How Millennials Could Be Housing Market Heroes"
"3 Reasons Millennials Are Driving the Housing Market"
"Millennial Generation Key to Housing Market Future"

Now here's a 2009 headline from *The Age Curve Report*, a demographic-based newsletter my colleagues and I used to produce:

"Gens X and Y to Spur Housing Recovery"

How about that? My colleagues and I called the Gen Y–induced housing market upswing some five years before just about everyone else. How did we do it?

And you *did* immediately respond "demographics," *right*?

OK, so that article was written in May 2009, one month after the release of the lowest monthly housing starts recorded since 1959. Housing starts that pointed to an annual rate of about 458,000, far below the nation's average annual for that time of about 1.6 million starts. We were pretty sure the bottom was near and that our take on the influence of demographics was going to make us look like geniuses.

And we were.

But a quick question for your consideration. Why would we have attributed the recovery in part to Gen X?

Anyone?

This was perhaps a tougher question than usual, but if you were reading carefully, you might recall from Chapter 8 that the second half of Gen X was marked by a significant increase in their numbers by birth. And with these younger—and more bountiful—members of Gen X starting to pass through their key first-time home-buying years, we felt that they would be first to help spur the recovery, followed immediately by the oldest (and more numerous) members of Gen Y as they hit their key first-time home-buying years.

And they did and have been, though admittedly not quite as quickly or robustly as we had forecast back in 2009. While we were thinking full recovery in two to four years, annual starts still haven't gotten back to the historical annual average, which is currently pegged at just below 1.44 million. But they are in a rising trend, as are other indicators of the economic health of the nation's housing sector. Combine this with the increasing numbers of Gen Y members who are in the midst of their key first-time home-buying years, and you've got a recipe for a healthy and growing housing market. And yes, I believe one that can surpass the previous 2.4 million peak for annual housing starts that happened in 1972. That peak, by the way, seems to have been caused in part by the first crop of Boomers—such as myself—reaching their key years for first-time home-buying.

As indicated by those recent headlines, I'm not alone in my prognostication for an oncoming healthy Gen Y–inspired housing market.

In fact, the National Association of Realtors (NAR) conducted a large survey—*Home Buyer and Seller Generational Trends*—that determined that Gen Y (which it delineates as having been born between 1980 and 2000) constituted the largest share of both overall home buyers (35 percent) and first-time home buyers (67 percent) in 2015.

The Demand Institute believes that Millennials are on the cusp of having significant influence on the economy and housing market. According to the institute's report—*Millennials and Their Homes: Still Seeking the American Dream*—Gen Y households will be spending more on a per-household basis than any other generation by 2018, and that between 2014 and 2018, Gen Y will spend $1.6 trillion on home purchases and $600 billion on rent. As of 2014, the think tank estimated that 13.3 million families are headed by Generation Y, a figure it expects to grow to 21.6 million by 2018.

While the older members of Generation Y have been tagged with the image of urban-dwelling hipsters with little interest in possessing things like cars, boats, and houses, a number of recent surveys point to Gen Yers being more like earlier generations in their desire for home ownership, if not even more eager to attain home ownership than the preceding generations. And while some Millennials aspire to the hip urban lifestyle, the surveys suggest that the bulk of this generation is much more interested in the typical suburban style of home ownership, with lots of space, safe streets, and expectations of a short drive to access most suburban amenities—

Wait a minute!

Short "drive"?

You didn't think Gen Y liked cars, did you? (More on this in Chapter 21.)

Not only do the recent surveys and research point to an elevated interest in home ownership by Gen Y, but these studies suggest that Gen Y home ownership already surpasses that of previous generations when they were at this age in their generational lives. Research by Zillow, an online real estate and rental marketplace, suggests that married Millennials already own homes at a rate close to or above historical norms for their demographic. If the generation's marriage habits were similar to previous generations, with more marriages sooner in life, Zillow estimates that Gen Y home ownership would be six percentage points higher than it currently is, and roughly the same as the rate for the same age cohort in the 1990s. Zillow also believes single employed members of Gen Y have a home ownership rate slightly above their counterparts from the 1970s, 1980s, and 1990s.

The previously mentioned Demand Institute survey[3] came up with similar conclusions. The survey, which examined how members of Gen Y were able to purchase homes and cars despite such high levels of student loans debt, determined that almost 40 percent of the oldest members (aged 26–31) of Gen Y who graduated college and have no student debt are current homeowners. Only 19 percent of college grads with student debt from the same age cohort are current homeowners, while 24 percent of non-college grads of this cohort are homeowners.

This survey concluded that the Gen Y desire for home ownership is especially strong but that turning the dream into reality is difficult for those under large student debt loads. The institute believes that the creation of "alternative mechanisms," such as lease-to-own finance models, presents "a significant innovation opportunity in both the business and public sectors."

Overall, research and surveys seem to indicate that Gen Y home ownership at this point in the generational time frame would likely have far surpassed all other generations if not for three key factors: economic impacts from the Great Recession of 2008, delay in the traditional years for first marriages, and high student loan debts. I am not sure that this means there's the equivalent of a tidal back surge, and that as these three factors play themselves out the surge will be released like from the opening of a dam and allow Generation Y to overwhelm the housing market like a tsunami.

Nope, I am not going to specifically say that, but Gen Y is definitely going to have an impact. Perhaps like a tidal storm surge, or maybe like a mini tsunami, and Gen Y could even surprise us by blowing the housing market wide open like their Boomer parents did in the 1970s and 1980s. Whichever outcome, it's already starting and will be upon us soon. So prepare, and figure out how to best profit from it.

So what of the other generations? What is their likely impact on the housing market?

Come on, you're a demographer now, aren't you? You can tell me how the other generations will influence the housing market going forward. Let's start with:

The G.I. Generation:

And you would be correct if your first response is that the G.I. Generation has effectively aged out of the housing market. Those who remain are most likely residing in assisted living facilities (if they can afford it) or are being cared for by other family members or "friends." Their needs are pretty much constrained to nursing and medical care and leave no room for consideration of housing or housing-related services.

Silent Generation:

In terms of housing, this generation is still a "mixed bag" (there's a phrase from the 1960s!). At the older age range, their current status is probably similar to the G.I. Generation survivors. At the younger end of the age range, their housing status is more mixed, with some aging in place in their own homes and others downsizing to "active adult" communities. Some of them are still moving to warmer climates and seeking states where retirement living is cheaper. And, yes, some of these older people are moving in with other family members.

In terms of their impact, this generation continues to contribute in a small capacity in new home purchases, renovations, furnishings, home services, and the like, but perhaps not to an extent at which its housing activity could make or break the market. But then again, the National Association of Realtors survey determined that members of the Silent Generation constituted 9 percent of all home buyers in 2015.

Baby Boomers:

You now know enough about demographics and the Boomers to tell me how the aging Boomers might impact the housing market. I mean, the Silent Generation isn't going to "make or break" the housing market, but how about the Boomers? Can they still make or break it?

Of course they can! They've been making and breaking markets since they were born, so why should that change now? In fact, they've pretty much influenced the direction of the housing market ever since their G.I. and Silent Generation parents started building and buying homes designed on the Levittown model, in large part to accommodate their growing brood of Boomer kids. Think about it: Back when the first Baby Boomers were turning 10 years old, the average size of a single-family house was less than 1,000 square feet. This average grew to 1,500 square feet by the mid-1970s, and to just over 2,200 square feet as of 2010. Think the

Boomers were largely responsible for this rise in housing size? Heck, those suburban starter castles that began sprouting up like mushrooms in the 1980s practically scream "Baby Boomer."

So what do the Boomers want and need out of housing now as they reach retirement?

Well, given that Boomers likely experienced the most financial pain during the housing bust with the loss of significant home equity, those Boomers planning a retirement-based change in housing just want to see the recouping of some of their losses and a widening of their economic options. And with so many options, there is no single answer as to how Boomers will affect the housing market going forward. Meanwhile, they are still very much in the market according to the National Association of Realtors survey, what with their share of 2015 home buying pegged at 31 percent.

It is estimated that Boomers are hitting age 65 and retiring at a rate of about one every ten seconds. A good number are still trying to recoup the losses from the Great Recession and will keep working and remain in their current castle. But in the coming years, a large number of these Boomers will end up making a move. Some will want to move closer to their children. Some will want to move to the less congested and more bucolic country, while others may opt for the cultural and gourmand offerings of the city. And a few will opt for the conveniences offered by adult retirement communities; however, surveys consistently show that only about 10 percent of Baby Boomers are making plans to move into such retirement communities. Nevertheless, as Boomers keep aging, more and more of them will need the services provided by such "assisted living"-style retirement communities.

As with previous generations, many will undoubtedly want to relocate to warmer climates and places where their retirement dollars go further. And the South and warmer areas of the West will be the beneficiaries of these moves. Remember what I told those Florida municipal workers in Chapter 1? Well, housing in Florida is back—perhaps not with a vengeance, but there has been steady and healthy increasing growth in housing starts since 2013. Economic forecasts suggest that this growth will continue to pick up steam in the coming years. While retiring Boomers are not the only driver of this growth, they are undoubtedly having an impact, especially on the Florida condo market, as surveys suggest that many Boomers will seek the ease of condo living when they downsize.

And while other Southern states are drawing in retiring Boomers, Florida holds an ace in its hand because of its lack of a state income tax. In fact, a study by Watchdog NY determined that roughly 40 percent of taxpayers who move out of New York relocate to Florida. This same report determined that in one year—2012—New York lost more of its Boomer population to out-migration than any other state in the nation.

Retirement-friendly Western states may also see a Boomer-enhanced housing boom. A 2014 survey by the California Administration on Aging determined that 44 percent of its Baby Boomer population plans to "move out of state after retirement," with Florida, Texas and Arizona considered top destinations, according to California Realtors.

All of this indicates that Boomer impact on housing might be more regionally specific than it has been in the past, with warm-weather states likely to receive the biggest Boomer-induced boost to their housing markets.

Generation X:

Based on what you've learned so far in this book, what can you tell me about Generation X and the housing market? Care to make any speculations? How about their share of recent home-buying? How much of a difference do you think there is between Gen X's share and that of the generations that bracket it?

If you guessed that its share is lower, you would be correct, so well done. In fact, according to the NAR survey, Gen X's share of home-buying in 2015 was only 26 percent. But why the difference given that Generation X's population numbers are roughly in line with that of Generation Y and the Boomers?

And that was a trick question to see if you've been paying attention. If you have, then you might have answered that Gen X's population numbers may have been boosted by immigration; however, first-generation immigrants' economic power is generally much lower than that of native-born Americans. That's a good answer from a demographer, and one I believe to be true, but there are other factors at play, as you'll see in the paragraphs to follow.

By chance did you wonder if Gen X's diminutive birth numbers might have caused a sinkhole of sorts that may have contributed to the housing market collapse?

Given that the collapse happened just when Generation X reached the peak home-buying years, I have certainly wondered as to the possible extent of their impact. Think about it: In 2008 the leading edge of Baby Boomers who were just bumping up against retirement age decided to sell their large "starter castle" homes at the height of the real estate bubble to maximize the recovery of their equity. However, Boomers soon discovered that there was not a sufficient market to buy them. The younger generation following, and most likely able to afford the castles, were 9 million fewer by birth, resulting in a deficit of people needed to purchase these homes at the level necessary to sustain the market. Add in some skullduggery, bad decisions, and greed by the banks, rating agencies, and regulators and you've got a recipe for disaster, which was then duly baked.

So of course Gen X did not outright cause the housing crisis and ensuing crash, and I have not seen any research or reports that point to Gen X as culprits; however, like me, others do speculate about the generation's role in the crash.

Interestingly, the largest percentage of households that ended up in foreclosure belonged to those in Generation X,[4] and Gen Xers currently make up the largest proportion of people now renting-but-used-to-own. According to Harvard University's Joint Center for Housing Studies,[5] home-ownership rates for the 35–54 age range Gen X currently sits within have dropped the most of any age group since 1993. Prior to the crash, the Census Bureau determined that people within the Gen X age range 25 to 34 had the highest rates of home ownership for that age group since it began collecting that data in the early 1980s.

The Harvard center does not foresee Gen X being especially active in the near future with regard to home-buying, due to stagnant wages, bad housing crisis memories, and high rents, which make it harder to save for a down payment. While the center expects some Gen Xers to move back into home ownership, it expects that members of Gen Y will have a bigger impact on the housing market as they continue to enter the job market in large numbers and build their careers.

Generation Y:

As we have already discussed Gen Y's potential influence on the housing market, we will move right on to:

Generation Z:

Who knows what this generation will want in a home—as of right now the best guess would be houses made out of Legos.

Given the not-so-far-in-the-past collapse of the housing market, should I even bother to suggest investing in the sector? Is what you have been learning about demographics, strong enough to override whatever fear you might have with regard to investing in what some would still consider a risky sector? Or, recent history aside, do demographics support investments in the housing sector?

Before considering demographics, understand that the housing market in total roughly represents more than one-fifth of the country's GDP, and thus is one of the major sectors of the economy. As such, inclusion of housing-related investments should make up at least part of any well-balanced portfolio.

As for the demographics, Generation Y is looking like a tsunami. However, with regard to the housing market, a portion of this tsunami's power is needed to fill a sinkhole. Thus, the demographics point to mixed performance in this sector. Additionally, I should point out that many housing-related companies have recovered from the collapse, and of this writing it seems that some housing market stock prices may be getting ahead of themselves as they climb back toward the highs seen prior to the crash, and a few even far exceeding those highs. So, be wary.

A few of the bigger Wall Street names in the housing market sector include:

- Lennar (LEN)
- KB Home (KBH)
- USG Corp. (USG)
- D.R. Horton Inc. (DHI)
- Masco Corp. (MAS)
- Continental Building Products, Inc. (CBPX)
- Home Depot (HD)
- Lowe's (LOW)
- Sherwin-Williams (SHW)
- Whirlpool (WHR)

The dividend yields of these particular housing market–related stocks are not especially generous, and several appear to be over-valued, though this is based on only a cursory examination. There are dozens of other companies out there that may be worth a look.

You might also want to consider real estate investment trusts (REITs), which tend to offer higher-than-average dividend yields. However, be advised that when REITs go south, they tend to fall harder, faster, and further than other stocks.

A couple of names to look at for your initial research could include:

- Duke Realty (DRE)
- Highwoods Properties (HIW)
- Franklin Street Properties (FSP)
- First Potomac Realty Trust (FPO)
- Redwood Trust (RWT)

With the exception of HIW, prices for the REITs above seem

relatively cheap when compared to their valuations prior to the market meltdown. There are a couple of dozen other REITs that could be examined as well.

Finally, please repeat after me: "Conduct your own due diligence."

21

Planes, Trains, and Automobiles . . . Not to Mention Boats

AFEW YEARS AGO we had some friends and their children over for a casual dinner. Their 7-year-old boy seemed bored, so I asked his dad if it was OK if I let him play with one of my metal model cars that we keep for visiting kids. His dad's response of, "He has no interest in cars and won't play with it," absolutely floored me.

Was this kid from outer space? When I was a kid, I loved cars, and I'm fairly positive that my first toy was a car. I even had stuffed cars. I could replicate the sound of going through the gears on a three-speed-on-the-column Ford with convincing authenticity. I can still tell you the difference between a 1949, 1950, and 1951 Ford with unfailing accuracy. I dreamed of the day I would turn 16 and get my driver's license. It was clearly one of the most defining times in my life, with childhood/teenage memories dictated by being either before or after I got my license. How could this 7-year-old not want to play with a die-cast model of a Mercedes Gull Wing? It seemed totally un-American, even accounting for the model's German origin.

Soon after meeting that odd child, I read somewhere that about 25 percent of Generation Y youth eligible for a driver's license were not bothering to get one. *What? This does not compute*, flooded my mind as I sat there mouth agape and reread the paragraph about Gen Y's apparent lack of interest in America's icon, the automobile. I was truly gobsmacked and remain a bit disconcerted that America's youth does not have the same affinity with car culture that my generation did.

But they don't. Various research has determined that the number of youth drivers has been in decline since at least 1995, which suggests that youthful apathy toward car culture started with the younger members of Generation X.

The Transportation Research Institute at the University of Michigan conducted a study in 2014 that found only 60 percent of American 18-year-olds had a driver's license compared to 80 percent of 18-year-olds in 1983. In comparing the same years, the Institute determined that licensing rates of those ages 16 to 44 decreased from 91.8 percent in 1983 to 76.7 percent as of 2014.

Transport scholars at the University of North Carolina conducted a cross-generational[1] study of driving habits for the years 1995, 2001, and 2009 that determined that the number of annual trips and miles traveled by age groups in the 19–42 range has been declining significantly since 1995, with younger age groups showing the most significant decrease in driving. Interestingly, and at odds with other research, the study determined that the youngest Gen Xers and oldest members of Gen Y were not supplementing their reduced driving habits with other modes of transportation, which perhaps suggests the influence of the Internet and related devices. In short, the study determined that these age cohorts were driving less due to a combination of changing attitudes about driving and lifestyle changes such as increased schooling, reduced employment, and a delay in marriage and childbearing. "Taken together, these trends lend credence to the idea that Millennials are increasingly 'going nowhere.'"

The Frontier Group determined that after steadily increasing since the end of World War II, annual per capita mileage driven by all Americans peaked in 2004, and has dropped 6 percent since that peak. The think tank attributes much of this decline to Generation Y and the youngest members of Gen X, and points to research suggesting that their annual per capita vehicle miles driven has dropped 23 percent since 2001. It attributes the decline to a variety of factors, including a preference by the younger cohorts to actively seek out alternative modes of transport. Between 2001 and 2009, younger people ages 16 to 34 years old increased their per capita public transit mileage by 40 percent, bicycle mileage by 24 percent, and walk-to-destination mode of travel by 16 percent, according to the group, which also noted that a 2012 survey determined that 45 percent of young people ages 18–34 consciously seek out alternatives to driving.

And along with the usual suspect alternative transportation modes such as buses, subways, taxis, bicycles, and feet, there are new driving options, such as "ride sharing" services like Uber and Lyft, which essentially serve as cheaper taxis that are summoned by smartphone apps. And there are "car sharing services" such as Zipcar and Getaround that provide relatively cheap hourly and daily rentals. The younger generations adopted these emerging services early, but the older generations are now jumping on the bandwagon. The consulting firm AlixPartners has determined that each vehicle dedicated to a car sharing service replaces sales of thirty-two new and used cars, and as the services grow in popularity could displace up to 1.2 million auto purchases through 2020.

If I were the president of General Motors, Ford, or any other automaker with a big presence in America, I would be watching this apparent disinterest in automobiles very closely. If, in fact, 25 percent of Gen Y has no interest in getting a license or driving, does this translate into 25 percent fewer new car sales down the road? Such a large drop in sales could crush the industry.

And what of impacts to the automobile industry by other generations? With the aging Baby Boomers retiring and leaving the daily commute behind, will they have less need for vehicles? If they are like me, they will never lose their love for the automobile, but on the whole I'm fairly certain their auto purchasing practices will moderate in the coming years. Those Boomers who used to buy a new car on a set two-, three-, or five-year schedule, or those who automatically upgraded once the lease or loan terms were met, might decide to stretch it out going forward. That represents a mighty large customer base that will likely change its car purchasing habits.

What of Gen X? Care to speculate?

I'm pretty sure you quickly said something along the lines of how automakers better not be waiting around for them to come in and save the day. If not, then you haven't been reading very carefully.

And, no, Gen X probably isn't going to jump in and supplant any loss of Boomer sales. In fact, I kind of doubt Gen X will make much of a difference up or down with future car sales. It may have killed the Japanese motorcycle market in the United States back in the late 1980s, but I doubt it's going to do the same thing to the country's auto market going forward.

Why not, you ask?

Well, immigration has helped boost its numbers, and if Gen X hasn't been able to significantly hinder auto sales so far in its life cycle I don't see how it could become a hindrance now.

In fact, recent U.S. auto sales haven't shown any demographic-based slippage of sales as far as I can see, and sales hit an all-time record in 2015 with almost 18 million sold. Part of the reason for the recent strong health of the auto sector could be related to Great Recession–influenced pent-up demand. And while Gen Y may not be displaying an affinity for automobiles, as more and more of them finally get jobs and start moving out of their parents' homes, many of them discover that they might *need* a car.

Because the auto market is very much a cyclical business, most experts believe that sales are nearing a peak and that lean years lie ahead. The recent cycle, which started moving up after 2009, with that year's 10.4 million sales being the worst since 1982, was spurred by an improving economy, low interest rates, falling gas prices, and the need for drivers to replace aging cars. While analysts firmly believe that interest rates will soon rise and auto sales soon decline, the question is how far will sales fall and how long will it take for them to recover? And the answer to this question could very well be dependent in part on the generational factors I highlighted in this chapter's previous pages.

With the U.S. auto market being so cyclical, I have found it difficult to find evidence of demographic influences. Auto sales have generally been on an upward trend since 1935's sales numbers of about 3.5 million, with several good years generally followed by a year or two of recession-inspired declining sales until the cycle renews, all with the numbers gradually rising. With the Silent Generation proving to be so relatively small, one might think that there must be evidence of demographically reduced sales as they came into their prime auto-buying years. But I don't really see any evidence of such. Care to make a stab at why?

Now, I haven't conducted any research to determine the reason, but I would surmise that it is because the Silent Generation came into that age during the rise of the "two- (and more) automobile" family. If you have a better idea as to the reason, I am certainly willing to entertain it.

Oh, and speaking of the two-car family, analysts believe that that four-decade trend is poised to go into decline. A recent study by KPMG determined that 57 percent of U.S. households owned two or more cars, a percentage the group felt had been holding steady for at least the past two decades. However, given the high price of today's cars, "changing travel preferences among younger generations," increasing urbanization, telecommuting, and the rise of car sharing services, KPMG expects the share of two-car households to fall to 43 percent by 2040.

I find this demise of the U.S. auto culture sad, but I guess one thing I can take away from this is that young children can prove to be good barometers of emerging trends. Interestingly, two of my colleagues have young Gen Y children and both report that their children also show a surprising lack of any interest in cars. Apparently, they are like the 35 percent of Gen Y who would sooner give up their rights to drive than give up their iPhones or related products.

All in all, the outlook for the auto industry seems quite bearish, and based on what I've written above I wouldn't be seeking out any auto-related investments . . . that is, other than perhaps a low-mileage, mint-condition 1967 Shelby Mustang GT500.

But there may be a ray of hope for the industry, as Autotrader and Kelley Blue Book issued a report earlier this year that determined that Generation Z[2] has far more interest in car ownership than Gen Y, with 92 percent planning to own their own car and 72 percent reporting that they would rather have a car than social media.

I should also remind you that people change as they age. For example, the same Baby Boomers who were driving VWs, lightweight muscle cars, and gas-friendly Japanese imports in the late 1960s and into the 1970s became the primary buyers of minivans and SUVs in the 1980s and 1990s. Likewise, the same members of Gen Y who eschew the automobile today might be singing a different tune when they settle down, have children, and move to the suburbs. And those members of Gen Y who participated in the various housing surveys certainly indicated as much.

OK, given that motorcycles helped me begin my career in demographics, I certainly cannot omit discussion about them in this chapter, now can I?

To my knowledge, sales of Japanese motorbikes never recovered to levels seen in the late 1970s and early 1980s. Generation X didn't save them, and Gen Y didn't seem to have the same affinity for them that the Boomers had. However, an American motorcycle company did benefit from the aging Boomer market, a benefit that has lasted well into the generation's older years.

While Harley-Davidson (HOG) has been around since 1903, it really didn't become a motorcycle powerhouse until the early 1990s, by which time its marketing strategy had fully adopted the retro outlaw biker appeal of the machine, and started to boost interest from aging Baby Boomers and younger members of Generation X. Well, Harley bikes are generally quite big, and there comes a time when such bikes are almost too difficult for older folks to handle. And the "cool" factor has to fade at some point in our lives. I mean, really, an old goat such as myself looks fairly silly all kitted out in leather sitting at a stoplight trying to keep my Hog from falling over. In short, I have been calling for the demise of Harley-Davidson since 2009, at which point my newsletter stated: "Harley-Davidson's success was built on a brand, the branding of the outlaw biker. In the 1960s and 70s the Harley Davidson logo was signature wear for the 'Hells Angels,' other biker gangs, and bad-boy wannabes—relatively rare and thus 'cool.' Today the logo seems almost ubiquitous on middle-aged and elderly bikers, who wear far more black leather and sport shinier chrome on their Harleys than any member of the Hells Angel ever did. The once cool, outlaw-style logo has been homogenized, and is now about as outlaw and cool as the Walt Disney mouse ears."

While HOG's market share hasn't been slipping as fast I thought, I still stand by that statement and believe that the company is facing stiff generational headwinds. All evidence points to Gen Y youth having far more interest in smaller Japanese bikes, and Boomers will continue to age out of the Harley market. Of course, Boomers being Boomers, we're just not aging out of the market with any haste.

So other than the apparent demographic sinkholes for cars and Harley-Davidson motorcycles, what might demographic change mean for other elements of the transportation sector? We've covered automobiles, so how about planes, trains, and boats? Think there are any potential demographic-induced tsunamis or sinkholes? Are you seeing potential upside or downside?

Quick, what about trains?

I'm guessing that some of you quickly guessed "downside." And while not correct, such thinking makes sense as passenger train service (metropolitan and airport subway/tram/streetcar lines excepted) as a standard transportation mode is much more familiar to members of the G.I., Silent, and older Boomer generations than it is to the generations that followed. In fact, U.S. intercity passenger train travel had pretty much been in decline since the rise of the automobile, with the number of passenger trains declining 85 percent between 1929 and 1965. Passenger train travel was almost declared dead in the early 1980s, after the last remaining private intercity passenger rail line was merged into the government-subsidized Amtrak system. But Amtrak, formed by the government in 1971 as a "last hurrah" of U.S. passenger rail service, managed to chug on with its stagnant 20-million-passengers-per-year traffic up until 2000, at which time ridership started to rise.

The inauguration of Amtrak's high-speed Acela Express is believed to have stirred increased ridership, but rising gas prices and highway congestion likely played a role, too. No matter the cause, ridership continued to increase and as of 2015 had reached almost 31 million passengers per year, with five consecutive years of ridership in excess of 30 million.

Acela's relative success has stirred proposals for other high-speed[3] passenger rail lines, with at least a half-dozen state, regional, and federally subsidized proposals currently being considered. Of these only one—California High-Speed Rail—is currently under construction, and the 520-mile San Francisco to Los Angeles line is not expected to be completed until about 2029.

Perhaps of more interest with regard to the apparent revival of passenger rail is that 2017 is expected to mark the return of *privately* owned and operated passenger rail. All Aboard Florida marks the first time in over 100 years that a significant investment has been made in private intercity rail. The line will offer thirty-two departures per day servicing a high-speed route between Miami and Orlando, with other stops along the way. The project is considered a blueprint for the future of passenger rail in America, and private freight railways will be watching closely to determine if it is time for them to bring back their own passenger lines.

While the future of passenger train service likely relies more on how it will compete with automobile travel than it does on demographics, highway congestion caused by large urban populations seems to be the prime motivator for its use. It also appears that, going forward, Gen Y will be a key supporter and rider of existing and new routes. Given what seems to be the ever-worsening congestion on the nation's highways, other generations will undoubtedly continue to jump on board in increasing numbers, too.

The bottom line in my opinion is that passenger rail has been sitting in a sinkhole for decades, but it might be slowly chugging a steep grade out of it. And while perhaps not strictly demographically induced, the ever-growing population is spurring the need for reliable transportation alternatives to the automobile.

Air travel? What do you think, sinkhole or tsunami?

Upside?

I certainly hope so, because downside and flying generally aren't compatible.

I fly a lot, and probably fly in and out of about thirty U.S. cities per year. Airports are always crowded, security lines always long, and the planes often running late. All indications point to a robust business that needs to expand. The business certainly isn't in a sinkhole, but I'm not so sure that it's about to be hit by a demographically induced tsunami of overwhelming demand.

While Gen Y is poised to become the airlines' largest passenger base, its current primary passenger base is starting to retire in large numbers. Thus, the changing demographics might represent churn more than anything else. In fact, various forecasts point to both short-term and long-term slow, steady, and healthy growth in passenger traffic numbers, but do not suggest that the already crowded airports and aircraft are going to be overwhelmed.

The Federal Aviation Administration (FAA) forecasts average annual growth of 2.1 percent in revenue passenger miles (RPM) for domestic airline traffic over the next twenty years. While not gangbusters, this can certainly be called healthy. Interestingly, the FAA forecasts that international travel into and out of the United States will experience the largest growth, with a projected annual increase of 4.2 percent in RPMs.

According to the Boston Consulting Group (BCG),[4] Generation Y will be the primary driver of airline travel going forward, with their spending on business travel expected to increase to a proportional 50 percent of all business travel by 2020. Meanwhile, during this same period, the Baby Boomers' proportional spending on business travel is expected to decline to 16 percent of the total by 2020 and down to 11 percent by 2025.

BCG also believes that Generation Y will exceed all other generations in flying for vacation purposes, and determined that the generation is more interested in traveling abroad than the older generations by a 23 percentage-point margin. Other sources provide support for this line of thinking, what with the United Nations estimating that 20 percent of all international travelers are young people under the age of 25, and surveys that have determined that Millennials would rather travel now than save for more extensive travel during their golden years.

While I respect these opinions, I beg to differ, as I believe Boomers will be the primary fliers for leisure/vacation purposes going forward. First off, they have far more money than the young Gen Y upstarts, and as they retire they will have far more time. Opportunities might look vast when you step out into the world of adulthood, but "life" gets in the way of such pursuits as flying off to an exotic country.

As of 2012, four out of every five leisure travelers were between the ages of 50 and 70, according to the American Association of Retired Persons (AARP), and I don't see that changing as more Boomers age into retirement. Nor do I see how the younger Millennials will have the time and money to travel as much as the Boomers in the coming years.

And moves from the airline industry suggest that it sees the Boomers remaining as a primary customer. Consider that an Aircraft Interiors Expo earlier this year focused on the needs and desires of airline passengers over the age of 65, and that Boeing started preparing for older Boomer travelers back in 2005 when it studied how older passengers interacted with aircraft interiors. Boeing's "Experience Aging Project" led to dozens of elderly-friendly design changes in the next generation "Dreamliner" aircraft that are coming online now as the Boomers edge into retirement.

So, are there any components of the transportation sector in which the Baby Boomers are going to cause a tsunami-like impact?

Well, what haven't we covered yet?

That's right, boats! And the tsunami has already started to hit the shore.

And I'm not talking about recreational motorboats and sailboats, because most Boomers interested in watercraft most likely already own a boat, if not two. No, I'm talking about vacation cruises, the segment of leisure/vacation travel that's experienced the most growth in recent years, in fact, more than 2,100 percent growth since 1970.

Overall, the cruise line industry expects 24 million passengers to set sail in 2016, an increase of 9 million over the 15 million who cruised in 2006, and a more than twenty-fold increase in the 1.4 million passengers recorded in 1980. U.S. residents account for more than half of all cruise ship passenger traffic. Annual U.S.-based cruise ship revenues are expected to double over ten years, from $15.7 billion recorded in 2010 to a projected $31.5 billion by 2020.

A 2015 survey conducted by the American Association of Retired Persons determined that while 16 percent of Boomers surveyed took a cruise in 2014, 27 percent expected to take a cruise in 2015, which, if it held true, would represent a growth rate of more than 75 percent.

For the record, not everyone is bullish on the idea of a Boomer-induced boom for the cruise ship industry. A 2015 MarketWatch analysis suggests that three-quarters of Boomers will not be able to afford to take cruises and warns that younger generations—in particular, Gen X—will not have the customer numbers to replace the aging cruisers who travel less. "Generation 'X' is small," notes the report, with "only about 51 million[5] versus the 76 million boomers, [and] is largely saddled with dependent children and parents, flat wages and significant debts." In short, the report suggests that Boomer cruise ship travel is already on the wane and that their past positive impact on the industry cannot be replicated by the younger generations.

The analyst makes some interesting points, but I don't think that the industry's Boomer customer base is ready to quit cruising as quickly as the analyst thinks. Members of the Silent Generation are still cruising in droves, especially on the fast-growing European river trip cruise routes. And the cruise ship industry certainly thinks boom times are ahead, given that as of 2015 the industry had 22 new vessels in production to add to the worldwide fleet of more than 420.

Oh, and while we aren't talking about the rest of the world yet, the analyst totally failed to acknowledge the burgeoning growth of passengers from Asia.

While I think I've covered the primary segments of the transportation sector, I've undoubtedly left portions out. But as a budding demographer you can apply your own counting skills to determine any potential demographic influences on transportation.

Interested in hover boards? My guess is that any developing market will be driven by Generations Y and Z, so get counting.

As for demographic-based investing in this sector, other than a U.S.–based automaker, I've never invested in transportation-related stocks. But I'll throw out some company names you can check out. And I am not even going to comment on these companies, which will force you to "do your own due diligence."

- o Southwest Airlines (LUV)
- o Delta Air Lines (DAL)
- o United Continental Holdings (UAL)
- o Ford Motor Company (F)
- o General Motors (GM)
- o Exxon (XO)

- Norfolk Southern (NSC)
- Union Pacific (UNP)
- Providence & Worcester RR (PWX)
- Carnival Corporation (CCL)
- Royal Caribbean Cruises (RCL)
- Norwegian Cruise Lines (NCLH)

22

Technology— A Language Best Spoken by the Young?

ONE HUNDRED YEARS ago, when the first members of the G.I. Generation were turning 10 years old, the one invention against which all others are often compared hadn't even been invented yet.

Any guesses as to what I may be referring to?

Perhaps the expression has become a tad archaic, but I am referring to "sliced bread," as in "that's the greatest thing since . . . " Hard to believe, but while the pop-up toaster first came to market in 1919, sliced bread didn't make the scene until 1928.

But those first ten years of the G.I. Generation's entry into the world were marked by numerous other technological advances. The previous decades' advancements in electrical engineering were finally being applied as suburban homes across the country became wired, and new electric-powered gadgets, such as vacuum cleaners and washing machines, entered the market. Transcontinental long-distance telephone calling became a reality, the Model T automobile started being mass-produced, and, instead of looking to the skies, man could actually look down from the sky onto the earth from man-made flying machines. Other inventions during those first G.I. Generation years included Bakelite, cellophane, stainless steel, tea bags, instant coffee, disposable razor blades, escalators, and the zipper.

Perhaps those young members of the G.I. Generation were amazed by all the newfangled gadgets and subsequent advancements in technology as the generation matured, or maybe they just took it all for granted, as seems to be the case with Gens Y and Z with all the amazing "new" technology that has become mainstream during their thirty-plus years of birth and aging.

As of the first year of Gen Y births in 1985, most of the cyber-related technologies we take for granted today did not exist.

In 1985 most folks thought "Morse" if you said the word *code*. I'm pretty sure that "computers" and/or "programming" would come to mind first when *code* is referenced today to a member of Gen Y or Z.

While the "Internet" had been invented by Al Gore[1] prior to 1985, only a relative handful of people knew of its existence until development of the World Wide Web in 1990 ushered in the age of the modern Internet. Back in 1985 "Amazon" was just a South American River, "Google" was something a 2-year-old might say, "Twitter" was a succession of sounds or trembling motion, and "Yahoo" was an epithet for a hick or redneck.

Back in 1985 "Apple" was found in pies or eaten as a snack. Today Apple is the world's largest information technology company, which offers a plethora of tools and gadgets that much of the world finds indispensable in their day-to-day lives.

While rare, there was a commercially available, handheld cellular mobile phone back in 1985. However, it was bigger than a brick, had limited service areas, and provided only about thirty minutes of use per ten-hour charge. Oh, and unlike today's cell phones that can do just about everything but toast the previously referenced slice of bread, that first cell phone could only send and receive calls.

In 1985 most televisions were still boxlike and offered little more than color or black and white. VHS was still the primary standard for recorded movies, and the compact cassette tape the most popular medium for listening to music.

I could go on . . . and on . . . and on . . . because the technological advances of the past thirty years are truly astounding, especially to us older folks who came of age when color TV was still considered somewhat of a novelty. For today's Gen Y and Z youth, all of this amazing technology is second nature. They can navigate through its complications with ease, and adapt to it quickly as it evolves.

All of this bodes well going forward as technological advancement is often a bastion of the young. Think about it: Many of the technologies of the past thirty years that I referenced above were developed by men and women when they were in their youth. Baby Boomer Steve Jobs initially invented the Apple desktop computer and operating system while in his teens and early 20s. Sure, he kept inventing new products and systems as he aged, but most of it as an evolution of his original inventions and with the help of a cadre of mainly youthful researchers.

Cyber-powerhouse Microsoft was created by two 20-year-old Boomers, Google by two 20-something-year-old Gen Xers, Twitter by young Gen Xers, and Facebook by young college students on either edge of the Gen X to Gen Y transition years.

With so much technological advancement tending to be fostered by the young, America's continued technological success and prowess will undoubtedly be assured by a large Gen Y that has grown up "speaking tech as a second language."

But don't count the Boomers out! While Silicon Valley's venture capitalists openly display bias by directing most of their start-up capital to youthful tech entrepreneurs, researchers have determined that this trend may be shortsighted. Prominent venture capitalist Vinod Khosla said, "People under 35 are the people who make change happen; people over 45 basically die in terms of new ideas." Or, perhaps more dismissive, Facebook founder Mark Zuckerberg's pronouncement that "young people are just smarter."

However, researchers have determined that this trend may be shortsighted. For example, researchers from the Kauffman Foundation and various universities beg to differ with such views, pointing to Apple's Steve Jobs, who continued to create amazing technology well into his 50s. A Northwestern University economist determined that the average age at which Nobel laureates of the 20th century performed their prizewinning work and the average age at which inventors had their greatest achievement was 39. Furthermore, he found that twice as many Nobel winners were older than 50 than younger than 26, and that the previously cited average age had climbed up to 45 by the second decade of the 21st century.

A Duke researcher acknowledges that young tech inventors will have an edge in developing new technology because they have grown up using existing technologies and understand them better than their Boomer and Gen X parents. However, the young tech whizzes generally lack cross-disciplinary skills and may not understand how to best utilize new and evolving technology in fields beyond computer gaming app building and social media development. Thus, older tech developers may be crucial for developing technologies that merge into and add to the modernization of other fields, such as healthcare and transportation.

Sounds like a win-win!

So what of the market for "tech"? you are undoubtedly wondering.

And yes, I have approached this sector in a different manner from the preceding "sector" chapters. I have done so because while technology in some regards (especially cyber) is a separate entity, it is also a significant component of all other sectors. And, because youth is *considered* the primary driver of technological advancement, I believed I should start there.

That said, from a demographic perspective I foresee "tech" remaining a bull market going forward. Gen Y and the oncoming Gen Z have grown up with technology infused in their day-to-day lives like no other generations before them, and I believe their members will continue to inhale all things "tech" in the years to come—from virtual-reality gaming systems, to electric cars, to the nascent hover boards, to some new technological wonder incubating in the mind of a 16-year-old—build it and they are going to buy it in droves.

And, as with tech development, don't count us Baby Boomers and Gen Xers out. While we may not be nearly as technologically savvy as the younger generations, we love our tech gadgets, too, and will continue to buy them. However, we are much more likely to retain our existing technological gadgets and services for as long as possible and may be more resistant to change.

And I'm not the only one who thinks Boomers will remain a potent force in the technology market. Just Google "Baby Boomers and technology" and you can find dozens of articles that describe how Boomers will continue to embrace technology as much as younger generations. Here are a few selected quotes:

"Contrary to many public and media perceptions, Baby Boomers have a real interest in continuing adoption of technology."

"Baby Boomers are no longer the inferior demographic when it comes to using modern technology and the web."

"Health related technology is much more important to [the Boomers] than social media or apps."

And take special note of that last one, as technology's intersection with healthcare seems to be a predominate theme with regard to Boomers' future relationship with technology.

With regard to Boomer tech preferences, a word of caution that Boomers will likely prefer tech products that aren't complicated and cluttered with excessive features. And, according to the American Association of Retired Persons, "Boomers expect technology to adapt to them." We will also need more hand-holding and assistance with making tech purchases than do younger customers.

Consider this: I used to enjoy walking into Best Buy. Now it just gives me a stomachache. It is not a big deal; I am just not comfortable there. When my favorite laptop developed a power problem, off I went to the Best Buy from where I had bought it. The power cord connection at the computer connected and disconnected independently. If I held it with my hand, it would stay on. But once I released it, the computer would switch from AC to battery. I tried various remedies like tape and glue but eventually my MacGyver fixes fell short.

So there I was, face-to-face with a Generation Y member of the Geek Squad. I explained the problem, an electrical connection gone south. I anticipated a quick reply about a simple fix, replace the connectors. Instead I got a bewildered silent stare and then a sympathetic smile.

"How old is this machine?" he asked.

I thought for a moment. "Three years old, I think."

"Why would you want to fix it?" he asked.

"Because it works perfectly and does everything I need and the only problem should be a simple fix." I realized that to him three years was an eternity and it was long since past time to upgrade. But I stood my ground. I was in the right. Common sense was on my side. I looked around to see if there were any supporters. There were none.

I used to love to shop. I still like to buy new clothes, and I don't think my look or color choices date me. I can hold my own in a car dealership, whether buying a new or used car. I am comfortable buying lawn mowers, generators, chain saws, tractors, and snow blowers. I am addicted to Harbor Freight. When I go there, I buy things I don't need, things that I will never use.

But now when I walk into Best Buy or similar stores, I am lost. I cannot buy a laptop, tablet, printer, television, or phone because I am not qualified and can't speak the lingo. Technology has passed me by. Thus tech retail stores like Best Buy need to provide more customer service oriented to helping older customers navigate this ever-changing world of technology. Whichever retail technology company can successfully cater to the older, tech-challenged population will undoubtedly earn a large cadre of devoted customers.

Bottom line with regard to any demographic impact on technology is that there appears to be no downside but instead just a steady upside surge.

As mentioned above, technology is way bigger than just itself, so let's look at another intersection between technology and demographics.

My Generation Y daughter Hayley and I both enjoy automobiles and we both have Mustangs. Hayley's Mustang is a 2006 300hp V6 automatic fastback that is modified and lowered. My Mustang is a 1965 271hp V8 4-speed K code coupe. And yes, my car can beat Hayley's car.

The cars serve as a metaphor for the technological comprehension differences between my daughter and me and are a clear indication of how technology really changes. It is easier to tell you what my car doesn't have than explain the differences. My 1965 Mustang does not have power ABS disc brakes, power steering, power windows, climate control, power seats, traction control, fuel injection, airbags, computers, heated seats, seat belts in the rear seat, rear defrosters, backup lights, automatic door locks, remote controls, FM radio or CD player, electronic ignition or seventeen-inch mag wheels. Cars are great examples of how technology is changing everything, for the better. Hayley's car could easily have a serviceable life of 300,000 miles if properly maintained. The 1960s-era cars were ready for the wrecking yard at 100,000 miles. Most important, of course, is the fact that Hayley's car is much safer than mine in the event of an accident. So if you invest in technology blindly, you could discover that your product or service is the equivalent of a 1965 Mustang.

If you had invested $1,000 in Apple stock after it went public in 1980, its value as of today would be worth well north of $300,000, not even accounting for annual dividend payments. Of course, you could have plowed that $1,000 into any one of dozens and dozens of other tech companies back in 1980 and lost every dime. I don't believe that tech is as bad as biotech with regard to the number of failed companies, or number of investors who've lost their shirts, but tech failures are legion and tech companies can get ahead of themselves. With this latter thought, consider the dot-com bubble of 1997–2000, which saw massively inflated tech stock prices collapse and dozens of companies subsequently fall into bankruptcy and/or dissolution.

There are hundreds of established tech companies from which an investor can choose and probably an equal number of nascent tech companies that are still working on bringing a new product to market. I am just going to list a few established companies, and, if interested in investing in the sector, I know that you will conduct due diligence by looking at these companies' histories, financials, fundamentals, etc., and gain an understanding as to what technology exactly the company is involved with. You will also carefully consider the world's current economic status and projections for America's continued economic growth. *Right?*

As for any possible Apple-like fliers, I'll leave that for you to find on your own. But don't run off and by a boatload of "Acme Start-Up Tech" because your coworker knows someone who works there who said the company was about to release a new killer app that's going to change the world.

Or go ahead! It's your money. . . .

o Apple (AAPL)
o Jabil Circuit (JBL)
o Microsoft (MSFT)
o Facebook (FB)
o Tesla Motors Inc. (TSLA)
o Micron Technology (MU)
o Google (GOOG)
o International Business Machines (IBM)
o Intel Corp. (INTC)
o Cisco Systems (CSCO)
o Linked In (LNKD)

23

Retail and Marketing—
When and How to Sell
What to Whom

WHAT DO YOU think, should I start this chapter off with a question?

    Oops, guess I already did, so here's a second question: How many different retail sectors are there within the retail industry?

Give up? Well, off the top of my head I couldn't come up with a concrete number either, and I believe that the number is somewhat fluid depending upon how you characterize different retail establishments and on how you characterize online shopping, or "e-tail." That said, there are five (or six, for those who would include "e-tail") retail industry areas that cover a total of about twenty industry sectors, give or take (with "e-tail" serving as a possible "give" for those who include it as a retail sector). Below are the retail areas and their related sectors (with "e-tail" included under "General Retailing").

WHOLESALE & LOGISTICS
o Wholesale and Logistics

GENERAL RETAILING

o Department Stores

o Discount and Variety

o E-Tail

SPECIALTY RETAILING

o Floristry

o Newsagents, Stationery, and Bookshops

o Local Pharmacies

o Jewelry

o Fashion, Clothing, and Footwear

o Other Specialty—Hobby Shops, Photography, Green
Stores, Novelty Shops, Tourist Shops

FOOD & BEVERAGE

o Supermarkets

o Liquor and Beer

o Fruit and Vegetable

o Fast Food and Takeout

o Casual and Fine Dining

o Specialty Food

WORK, HOME & LIFESTYLE

o Entertainment, Communication, and Technology

o Sport, Recreation, and Leisure

o Furniture and Housewares

o Hardware, Trade, and Gardening

Now, you've gotten so good at this demographics stuff that you can tell me how the country's current and projected demographics will affect each of these retail sectors? Right?

Right, but first let me give you a couple of examples and tell you a story: Back in January 2009, I launched a newsletter called *The Age Curve Report* that was developed to examine specific demographic trends to determine how they might affect the economy and, in particular, specific business sectors and publicly traded companies. It seemed like the absolute worst timing for starting up a new business venture, what with the world teetering on the edge of financial catastrophe during the height of the Great Recession. However, my colleagues in the venture, Logie Cassells and Jamie Moye (aka M.J. Moye, this book's editorial consultant and researcher), helped allay my trepidation by suggesting that market bottoms were the perfect time to start such ventures and reminding me that Gen Y presented a huge potential economic growth story on many levels. My fears were allayed even more when that first issue came out, and I saw how well we were able to meld demographic trends with real-world business and economic forecasting.

Over the next eighteen months we examined hundreds of publicly traded companies to determine potential demographic influences, picked out ones we felt would benefit the most from demographic change, wrote about them, and included some of their stocks in a model portfolio designed to profit off of demographics, sentiment, and valuation. Both the newsletter and model portfolio were developed in partnership with a boutique investment firm and were supposed to coincide with the establishment of a demographics-based fund, but that's another story.[1]

Anyhow, retail served as a core component of companies profiled and included in our model portfolio. By the end of the newsletter's run in 2010, the portfolio had risen almost 100 percent, compared to a 30 percent gain in the S&P 500.

And no, I am not going to claim that its success was the result of calling it correctly on the demographics. First off, the overall market was in recovery, and secondly the time frame was too short for demographics to really work their magic. Not that demographics didn't perhaps play a bit of a role, but having former U.K. "Hedge Fund Manager of the Year" Logie Cassells in charge of sentiment and valuation research was probably more key.

Looking back now over a much longer time frame, I can say that in many cases we called it correctly on the demographic influence on certain retail sectors and businesses. Sure, it turns out we made a couple of bad calls, too, but I don't think we were mistaken about the demographics.

Among the articles in our first newsletter issue was one titled "Beer Sales Set to Rise with Emergent Generation Y."

Now, having read this far into the book, you are probably thinking something along the lines of: *Wow, you guys probably nailed it!* And we did . . . kind of.

Among the observations made in that article were:

- Domestic beer consumption went flat in the late 1980s, coinciding with Boomers exiting their prime 21–27-year-old beer drinking years and a smaller Gen X moving in;
- The flat beer consumption started turning into a decline in the 1990s;
- That Gen X had shown a distinct interest in microbrewed beer, a trend that was likely to continue with Gen Y;
- That foreign brewers likely made a smart move in buying up the large U.S. beer companies;
- That Generation Y, by sheer force of numbers, was going to provide a significant boon to both major brewers and microbreweries;
- And, that the growing Hispanic population would also likely boost sales, especially for those brewers offering imported beer from Mexico.

Several issues later, when we debuted our "Model Portfolio," Boston Beer Co. (SAM) was a key stock pick in our retail sectors. We had picked up 1,080 "virtual" shares at a cost basis of $25.90, and saw a 15 percent gain in less than six weeks, and 100 percent gain within a year.

And no, Gen Y didn't just start quickly drinking a lot of beer. As noted, we started the portfolio during the stock market lows, and pretty much everything we bought went up nicely as the market started to recover. Too bad, though, that the "buys" were only virtual.

Especially given that SAM's stock price climbed more than 700 percent, reaching an all-time high of almost $315 per share in the last days of 2015, before surrendering about 50 percent of that high price, in part, according to analysts, because of strong competition from other microbreweries. All major breweries serving the U.S. market saw significant stock gains as Gen Y entered the beer drinking years, with Constellation Brands (STZ), a key importer of Mexican beer, experiencing a more than 1,000 percent increase in stock price since 2009.

So, I'd say we hit a home run with SAM, nailed the positive impact of Hispanics, and called it correctly on microbreweries, which have seen their overall share of the U.S. beer market double from the 6 percent estimated in 2008 to 12 percent today.

Unfortunately, I can't prove that we nailed it with regard to Gen Y, as the generation wasn't necessarily the primary driver of beer company stock price appreciation. In fact, despite the increasing numbers of potential Gen Y beer drinkers, per capita beer consumption in the United States kept declining until 2012, at which point it appears to have made a reversal. So, I can suggest that Gen Y "might be" responsible for the reversal, and point out that much of the significant price appreciation of beer stocks seemed to have started at about the time of the reversal, but I can't conclusively prove that it is connected to an increase in Gen Y beer drinkers. To put it another way, even though "correlation does not imply causation," it sure does suggest it at times.

Another "home run" was provided by Chipotle Mexican Grill, which we profiled in the newsletter and added to our Model Portfolio at a cost of $81 in 2009. Our research began by trying to determine which restaurants seemed to be most appealing to Generation Y. McDonald's proved favorable due to younger members of the generation, who, with their mothers, were a core component of the chain's customer base. But the relatively new Chipotle Mexican Grill sparked our interest as it seemed to be a big draw with Gen X and older members of Gen Y. We were also aware that Gen Y seemed to show a propensity for "green" businesses and for local produce, both of which are provided by Chipotle. Additionally, the "fast casual" chain relied on "traditional

Mexican cooking methods," which we felt would be a big draw for potential Hispanic customers.

In short, we thought the demographics would totally support the chain going forward, and they did. Since we first reported on it in 2009, the chain has added more than 1,100 new restaurants and its stock price reached an all-time high of almost $750 in July 2015, representing a gain of more than 800 percent.

Remember how I brought up Mattel and "Barbie" back in Chapter 1? The youngest members of Gen Y were 4 years old back when we started that venture. Do you think we considered toy companies as a possible solid demographics-based investment back then?

If you answered yes, you would be correct. On a relative basis compared to most companies, the stock prices of both Hasbro (HAS) and Mattel (MAT) held up fairly well during the Great Recession—i.e., beaten down like all, but not to any extremes. Given that both companies would continue to benefit from at least eight more years of Gen Y–populated childhood and a strong population of the first members of Gen Z, we saw them as good buys. And yes, our virtual buys (HAS at about $30, and MAT at about $20) enjoyed strong short-term gains, not to mention strong long-term performance for Hasbro, which recently hit an all-time high, breaching $87. Mattel enjoyed strength until the end of 2013, when declining sales marked the effects of declining Gen Z births that ensued in 2008.

Naturally you are wondering why this did not impact Hasbro as well. My quick and easy answer is that Mattel's line of toys seems to be much more generated toward younger children than Hasbro's line. Perhaps needless to say, but neither one of these companies currently looks favorable on a demographic basis.

With all this retail focus on Gen Y, what of other generational impacts on the retail sector?

A good question, and one we did not ignore back in 2009. We saw the Boomers as being potential significant drivers of organic food, wine, and nuts (go figure). Based on this, we wrote about and added to the model portfolio, Whole Foods Markets (WFM), Tree-House Foods (THS), Willamette Valley Vineyards (WVVI), and John Sanfilippo & Son (JBSS). And yes, all have performed admirably, but no, I cannot conclusively prove that the Boomers were the cause of this success.

Interestingly, for the longer term, the nuts sector has proved to be the biggest gainer, as the stock price of JBSS has climbed almost 400 percent since we named it a buy in 2010. I am not positive that the Boomers actually are the primary driver of the company's increasing profits and stock price, but we felt it likely back then. As we wrote: "We believe nut producers are well placed to reap the rewards of the changing U.S. demographic landscape. The Nut Spending Curve in the sector overview shows that older households spend the most on nuts. While many consumers limit their nut consumption because of concerns over fat and calories, more and more research is showing the true health benefits of nuts. We believe that as Boomers age into their prime nut-consuming age bracket, spending on nuts is likely to rise."

Perhaps our only specific call regarding Gen X was that the younger—and noticeably larger—half of this generation was aging into the peak spending years for cosmetics, perfume, and bath products. To add to the potential generational uptick in numbers, we also pointed out that this cohort would be immediately followed by an even larger cadre of Gen Y customers. Additionally, we noted the market would be enhanced by the increasing population of Hispanic women, as they spend on average 28 percent more on cosmetics than other customers. We profiled both Ulta Salon, Cosmetics & Fragrance, Inc. (ULTA), and Nu Skin Enterprises (NUS), and I've got to say that we hit one of them out of the park for a grand slam homer. Ulta recently hit an all-time high north of $230, representing a gain of almost 1,400 percent from the $16 cost at which we recommended it in 2009. NUS, which we recommended in 2009 at about $15, saw a 700 percent gain as of the end of 2013 but has since suffered significant declines.

And allow me to just toot our own horn again, as we were quite bullish on Apple Inc. (APPL), which we felt would benefit from all the generations. While APPL is a "tech" company, it is also a highly successful retail operation with products that appeal to all generations, even us tech-challenged Boomers. We wrote about its appeal extensively, and added it to the portfolio at a split-adjusted cost basis of $13.40. It since reached an all-time high of almost $133, representing a gain of about 950 percent. I remain bullish on the company, both because of demographics and its unique product line. Though I doubt I'll ever get around to figuring out the iWatch.

Now let's take a look at a big retailer. OK, the biggest. Walmart (WMT). I have been bearish on Walmart for what seems like forever. I wrote about Walmart's impending generational troubles in my first book, and sang about its impending demise in my blog and in the newsletter.

My basic premise was that Walmart is a Boomer-oriented business, and that its core Boomer customer was reaching the age at which people don't buy much anymore. Meanwhile, America's largest potential customer cohort, the 86.6 million members of Gen Y, were a fickle bunch, less interested in "low price" than in "selection," who would not be enticed by Walmart's limited selection of cheap merchandise.

I may have been overly pessimistic regarding my feelings for the future of Walmart, as "low prices" will always help drive retail sales. However, the giant retailer has been struggling of late, what with last year's announced closing of hundreds of stores, thousands of layoffs, flatlining sales growth, and early 2016's first reported year-over-year annual revenue decline since the company went public. So maybe I was correct when I wrote in 2007 that "there is no new market for Wal-Mart. No market unless it dramatically changes what it is, and it is too big and entrenched to make this change in a timely manner. It will begin to be eroded by the very concept it put out of business twenty years ago: small, fast-changing, entrepreneurial retailers offering selection and service."

What I failed to take into account when writing that blog was the impending power of Amazon (AMZN), now the world's largest e-tailer, and by valuation, the world's largest retailer. But we did have Amazon on our radar at the newsletter. We were bullish on its prospects due to our belief that the younger generations would be eager customers, and added it to our model portfolio at a cost of $120. With a recent all-time high north of $700, that would equate to a 500 percent gain, so yeah, another home run.

So, what of Walmart? Well, it reportedly has a reorganization plan in place, but many business pundits seem to be warning that Walmart has a limited amount of time to turn things around. As noted by Bloomberg, "declining sales might be okay for a year or two, but at some point a turnaround plan could become a failed strategy."

OK, your turn. Pick a retail sector and tell me what you think—do the demographics support the business? Absent all but demographic considerations, is this business likely to be boomtown or bust?

How about floristry?

I know what I'd say: *While not facing a tsunami, the floristry business is likely to see a healthy uptick in business in the coming years, as the two largest generations in America both age into life span time periods that are conducive to spending on flowers. The maturing members of Gen Y are increasingly entering the years in which they are most likely going to get married, while the Boomers are slowly aging into their funeral years. While holidays,[2] anniversaries, and special occasions constitute a larger overall share of a florist's business, weddings and funerals combined represent a healthy chunk.*

Unfortunately, not everyone agrees with my spur-of-the-moment demographic assessment. While demographics seem to support the business, the florist industry has "been withering away over the past five years," according to market analysts at IBIS-World. Due to a Great Recession-induced reduction in discretionary spending and increased competition from supermarkets and e-tailers, florist industry annual revenue growth suffered a 1.2 percent decline from 2010 to 2015. The analyst forecasts further declines in the florist business going forward. Additionally, the Bureau of Labor Statistics (BLS) foresees a 3 percent decline by 2024 in the number of U.S. florists job positions.

I wasn't able to read the full IBISWorld report, nor able to assess how the group determined the revenue decline, but according to Aboutflowers.com, total "floriculture" sales grew by more than $5 billion between 2010 and 2015. I also don't know whether or not the market analysts or BLS bothered to count people, though I would assume BLS did. Whatever the case, the contrarian views serve as a reminder that demographics is just one tool out of many, and that all parameters of a business should be examined during the decision-making process.

Given that my prior career was in marketing, I cannot leave this chapter without giving you my perspectives on marketing in today's generational landscape and, in particular, marketing to Generation Y. Consider the design of this enormous Y Generation. They are a kinder, gentler generation that has been taught not to name-call, bully, or be mean. They generally do not see color or race as a defining characteristic, so bigotry and racial prejudice are much rarer than what was once exhibited by earlier generations. They have been taught to be competitive but not combative, to disagree but not disrespect, to achieve but not condescend, and that the end does not justify the means. They tend to be "green," and seem to favor patronizing a businesses with a real "eco" or humanitarian story over one with a better product or lower price.

It is important to note that any company that is perceived by Generation Y to be disingenuous about "giving back" and tries to fake a green stand will be labeled a "green washer" and could face a crippling boycott. You should not and cannot lie to Generation Y.

They speak cyber as a first language and live in a world of instant information as evidenced by their mastery of social networking sites like YouTube, Facebook, Snapchat, Instagram, Myspace, and newly introduced ones that can hardly be pronounced. They have reinvented communication with their ability to text on their phones without looking at the keyboard.

Marketers are vexed by Gen Y's rejection of traditional media like radio, television, and newspapers. This makes them difficult to reach and brand with advertising messages. The messages themselves are also in jeopardy and have not found favor with Generation Y because much of the advertising copy has the attendant hyperbole and exaggeration often associated with promoting products and services. Marketers are quickly finding out that the best strategy is veracity and pragmatism. The "sales pitch" is history and has been replaced by relevant communication or "The Truth Well Told."

The truth, what a concept!

The caliber of products and services should definitely improve under Gen Y's watch. A good product or service with a fair price and an honest green story will find an endorsement of their offering coursing through Generation Y at light speed. It's called viral marketing, and it is a whole new ball game.

As we drill down to street-level selling to Gen Y, we need to be aware of some basic considerations, some dos and don'ts. Don't expect to hold their attention with a boilerplate PowerPoint presentation. These young people are capable of multitasking four and five things at a time. It is not uncommon for them to be listening to music while they are on Instagram, talking to a friend on Skype, texting on their phone, and watching television. In their world a minute is a long time, and they will probably find your technology primitive and a turnoff. Remember, you need to be relevant and even tailored to this generation or they will look at you like you have two heads. Generation Y will understand the concept of responsibility and long-term planning. It goes along with being green.

Just a quick word about prospecting to Generation Y: It is going to be tough. Telemarketers are going to have a difficult time finding them because they don't use conventional telephones. As we mentioned earlier, they don't respond to radio, television, or newspapers.

Has anyone found the silver bullet for reaching them online? No. So what is the answer? Relationships and referrals. So work hard, put in long hours, and do the right thing and this generation will beat a path to your door.

Demographic-based investing? Sure, but be careful. Among other demographically based selections in our model portfolio were several clothing retailers, including Ross Stores (ROST), Children's Place (PLCE), Aéropostale (ARO), Pacific Sunwear of California (PSUN), and Skechers (SKX). On a demographic basis we felt they were well positioned to capture Generation Y consumers as they aged through the key teen and young adult clothing-buying years.

Even with a large customer base, retail is a tough business. Competition is bitter, labor difficult, consumers fickle, and margins often slim. While Children's Place, Ross Stores, and Skechers proved successful, Aéropostale and Pacific Sunwear have recently filed for bankruptcy.

As with companies presented at the end of previous chapters, these are for informational purposes only for use while you contemplate demographics. And of course, say it please: *Do your own due diligence prior to making any investment decisions.*

- o Amazon (AMZN)
- o L Brands (LB)
- o TJX Companies, Inc. (TJX)
- o Ross Stores (ROST)
- o Costco Wholesale Corp. (COST)
- o Home Depot (HD)
- o Lululemon Athletica Inc. (LULU)
- o Blue Nile Inc. (NILE)
- o Overstock.com, Inc. (OSTK)
- o Shutterfly Inc. (SFLY)

24

Manufacturing—Coming Home to Roost?

AH, MANUFACTURING . . .

Those who have read my first book, heard me speak, or read my blog know how I feel about the U.S. manufacturing sector. My premise has long been that America's downtrodden manufacturing sector will recover and grow again due to the maturing of the country's largest and smartest generation ever, combined with a decline in China's labor force resulting from the country's decades-long "one-child" policy.

Eight years ago I wrote: "Yes, manufacturing will return to the U.S.—starting now, and its growth will accelerate over the next 10 years!" I posited that the offshoring of manufacturing that accelerated in the 1980s was partly a result of the small size of the native-born Generation X, and that their diminutive numbers led to a significant rise in labor costs. This in turn led to further offshoring of manufacturing to countries (especially China) with larger, and therefore cheaper, labor pools. While not labeling it as such then, I pointed out that China's one-child policy was going to create a labor shortage "sinkhole" that would lead to rising labor costs and help direct manufacturing back to the United States, which "has an abundance of natural resources, energy, technology, built-in consumer demand, money/capital, and now the biggest and best labor force in the nation's history."

I tend to be overly optimistic at times, and perhaps my ten-year time frame was a tad unrealistic, but as reported a couple of years ago in a CNBC news article about China's rising labor costs, "change is in the air," and "China is no longer a slam dunk for manufacturers looking for the lowest cost for operations." In fact, the article pointed to research that determined that outsourcing manufacturing to China would be equal to the cost of manufacturing in the United States by 2015.

How about that?

Now, I'm not sure if that parity was actually reached in 2015, but there certainly have been reports of companies pulling plants out of China to find cheaper labor, with some re-shored back to the United States, where any cost differences are "offset by higher productivity of American workers." That said, there probably isn't going to be a massive exodus of manufacturing out of China, in part because domestic consumer demand remains strong in the country and is still rising. But it seems that those companies with little or no China customer base who brought their manufacturing to China for the cheap labor are starting to skedaddle. Given that 27 percent of the 220 U.S.–China Business Council member companies reported in 2011 that they utilized China as an export platform to serve the United States, a significant number of companies may be eyeing re-shoring.

Is there evidence for this re-shoring, and is re-shoring leading to a comeback in U.S. manufacturing? Well, yes to the first question, but the evidence is mixed, at best, for the second question. According to the Reshoring Initiative, the number of manufacturing jobs returning to the United States—or coming in-country for the first time—from overseas hit a record level in 2014. The initiative reported that 60,000 re-shored and new foreign direct investment–created jobs were added to the United States in 2014, in contrast to the 50,000 jobs lost to offshoring that year. This net increase of 10,000 manufacturing jobs represented the first net increase in at least twenty years. Among the prime drivers of re-shoring, according to the initiative, were escalating wages, shipping costs, and a relatively skilled U.S. workforce. Additionally, the United States is now ranked second, behind only China, in cost competitiveness from among the world's top 10 export economies. The biggest companies bringing jobs back from China that year included Walmart, General Electric, Farouk Systems, and NCR.

Meanwhile, as to whether manufacturing is truly making a comeback, the latest Census Bureau data—*2014 Annual Survey of Manufacturers*—provides a mixed overview. While the U.S. manufacturing sector's annual payroll climbed 2.5 percent from 2013 to 2014, the total number of employees declined by about 70,000. However, some manufacturing sectors reported significant employment growth during this time. For example, household appliance manufacturing reported a 7.8 percent growth in employment, and all elements of automobile and auto parts manufacturing reported employment gains.

And data from the Bureau of Labor Statistics isn't providing much support in relation to my feelings about manufacturing. According to its latest (2015) *Employment by Major Industry Sector* projections, the number of manufacturing jobs will decline by just over 800,000 between 2014 and 2024. Mind you this is a lot better than the 2.1 million manufacturing jobs the BLS believes were lost between 2004 and 2014, so I could suggest that this represents a recovery of sorts. Additionally, I can point out that the Bureau's most recent manufacturing employment number of about 12.3 million (as of March 2016) is roughly 120,000 higher than the 2014 number used for its projections. Nevertheless, and perhaps needless to say, no manufacturing positions are listed by BLS as among the "fastest growing occupations, 2014–24."[1]

Despite the government's assessment of future manufacturing employment, I remain convinced that manufacturing is coming back to the United States, and that the country will once again become a manufacturing powerhouse. Unfortunately, it's not looking like the return of manufacturing will boost job numbers as robustly as I once thought, but perhaps it can at least stabilize them.

I suppose I need to confess to being a bit myopic at times, in that I focus on the demographics at the expense of other factors. Thus, while I focus on the potential increase in jobs with manufacturing's return to America, I might neglect the potential impact of automation and computerization on such potential employment. But this makes sense as I don't count machines and computers, I count people.

Bottom line, manufacturing is returning to America, but it is coming back in with extensive automation. For example, Foxconn, which has been manufacturing Apple devices in China, is investing more than $100 million for manufacturing facilities in the United States; however, $30 million of this investment includes construction of a robotic manufacturing facility in Pennsylvania. According to a "Voices" article by the Governing Institute, Foxconn's planned Pennsylvania plant will require only a few dozen employees, compared to the many thousands of employees its non-robotic plant needed in China. The article further notes that this is indicative of a jobless recovery of the U.S. manufacturing sector, in which returning and already established companies are utilizing automation to replace low-cost foreign workers.

Perhaps this all means that Gen Y and demographics in general are not much of a factor with regard to manufacturing and employment, but do demographics suggest anything else about manufacturing? Given the fading out of the Baby Boomers and the rise of Generation Y, what needs to be manufactured? What assembly lines need to be ramped up and which ones need to be idled? Are we looking at potential upside or downside?

On a bare-bones level, you can take everything you've learned in the previous chapters and apply that knowledge to try to determine which manufacturing streams will need to ramp up production or which ones might need to ramp down. For example, in Chapter 22 we determined that demographics and all the generations from Z to the Boomers support a bull market for just about everything "tech" going forward. Thus, just about any company that manufactures parts used in technology has a potentially bright future and may need to ramp up the production lines. Of course, please take note of *potentially* and *may*, as the business of technology is fast-paced and cutthroat. New widgets are constantly coming online and manufacturers are often in price wars with each other to get tech companies to use their particular widgets. No sooner has one widget been adopted as being perfect for a new cell phone technology, than a newer one is introduced and quickly adopted.

How about healthcare? We saw how demographics will influence that sector going forward, so you can apply that knowledge to manufacturers of healthcare supplies. Right?

Consider this recent headline: "Medical Textiles Market Is Expected to Witness Lucrative Growth by 2022 Due to the Rising Health Consciousness and Technological Advances."

What's missing from this headline?

You got it—any mention of the significant growth of the elderly population, which is probably more of a factor in the expected growth than the two listed factors. At least the article itself acknowledges the demographic component first when talking about what is "fueling the growth of the global medical textiles market." Oh, and according to the article, the growth is expected to rise to more than $20 billion by 2022 compared to the roughly $14 billion value of the market recorded in 2014. So, do you think manufacturers of medical textiles are looking at boom times ahead?

Now consider the many other components of the healthcare field, all the various supplies that need to be produced to support the healthcare needs of the elderly and infirm. Given the massive population of the Baby Boomers, especially compared with the current crop of elderly Silent Generation members, do you think we're going to need a few more wheelchairs, walkers, and home-care beds? Do you think manufacturers of these products, as well as all the other numerous medical products and devices, are going to need to ramp up their production lines?

I believe you get my point and can apply your knowledge of demographics to manufacturing on your own now. So with that, I'll leave you with some manufacturing companies to consider with regard to demographics. You can think about the products these companies make and try to figure out whether the demographics support their various production lines going forward or call for idling. Oh, and if you are thinking about investing in any of these companies, you know the mantra regarding "due diligence." So make sure you follow it.

- o General Electric (GE)
- o Boeing (BA)
- o Procter & Gamble (PG)
- o Cisco Systems (CSCO)
- o Lockheed Martin Corp. (LMT)
- o 3M (MMM)
- o Sony Corp. (SNE)
- o Honeywell International (HON)
- o Johnson & Johnson (JNJ)
- o Boston Scientific Corp. (BSX)
- o Invacare Corporation (IVC)

25

Out with the Old, In with the New— Labor Force Dynamics[1]

I WRITE A LOT—BOOKS, reports, blog entries, tweets, articles, and emails. I like writing because when I feel inspired I can really rip and get my ideas into type form. On one particularly fine day I was one with the keyboard. My fingers were dancing and the ideas were flowing like snowmelt down a mountain stream. My keyboard and I had gotten into a perfect Zen-like rhythm.

Then it happened. Suddenly everything I had written morphed into hieroglyphic symbols—everything.

I stared at the screen, totally befuddled.

What was this?

I could feel the panic coming on, so I paused and breathed deeply.

Let's take a look in the "Documents" folder, I thought. *Maybe this is just a localized issue.*

Nope. Every document I opened displayed the unreadable hieroglyphics. Not a "localized" problem.

I started to perspire. I had not backed up anything because I do not do things "real men" should, you know, like ask for directions when lost.

I envisioned the days, weeks, and months of work that was now lost.

My life felt like it was over. The perspiration started to stream. Strange, cough-like grunts pushed up from my chest as I struggled to breathe. . . .

At some point I heard my as-of-then teenage Generation Y daughter Libby walking up the steps to our home office, where she often works on her schoolwork. I heard the tinny sound of music coming from her earbuds and the rapid-fire tap of her fingers texting on her iPhone, her fingers moving so fast that it was hard to believe the tiny keyboard could keep up with the keystrokes.

We do not make eye contact. She walks behind me and stops. With a free hand she reaches over my shoulder and manipulates the keys on my computer. All of the odd symbols disappear and order is restored. Problem solved. No words exchanged. She slides into her desk chair while still texting and listening to music. Within seconds she has Facebook and Twitter up on the monitor of her desktop computer and begins interacting with other friends and colleagues while still managing her text conversation. At some quick instant, perhaps with a fourth arm that I am not aware of, she gets a hold of the remote control and starts channel surfing the office's flat-screen TV.

I view her silently. I have raised an alien. I want this alien to work for me.

Baby Boomers speak cyber with what sounds like a slow, thick foreign accent—lots of hesitation, grunts, and exasperated wheezes. For the most part we are immigrants in the cyber world. We get by, but we are not comfortable.

Generation X is bilingual and much more comfortable in the cyber realm than Boomers, but Generation Y dreams in cyber terms— it is second nature to them. Boomers and many Gen Xers have to think when making cyber decisions. Generation Y does not. It is part of who they are. Is this a big deal? More than you can imagine.

Generation Y is flooding the U.S. workforce at the rate of about 4 million potential workers a year. The leading edge of Generation Y had their careers put on hold for several years after Boomer retirement was held hostage due to the bursting of the housing bubble and subsequent Great Recession. Boomers couldn't sell their homes and access the remaining home equity, and they suffered a huge collective hit on their stock portfolios, so millions didn't retire as they reached the first of their golden years. In essence, Generation Y couldn't check into the hotel because Boomers were extending their stay. That seems to be over now. Boomers have finally started checking out of the workforce hotel in large numbers, allowing Gen Y to start checking in.

For businesses heavily reliant on computer systems, the Internet, and data processing, the fun is about to start. Gen Y entry-level new hires will run cyber circles around older Generation X and Boomer employees.

My Generation Y daughters are always pointing out features on my phone and computer that I never knew existed. How do they know these things? I don't know. They just do. I think it's in their DNA. I warn my clients about Generation Y's innate cyber abilities and caution them about squeezing another year out of older IT systems. "If it ain't broke don't fix it" is an outdated axiom that does not apply to cyberspace. In fact, I wonder if that colloquial rule ever really applied to advancing organizations. Imagine if Edison had been really happy with candles. Would we have lightbulbs today?

Generation Y will move into the work space and be very amused and then frustrated by outdated systems. Some businesses might even find their anachronistic accounting systems have been hacked and that their new Gen Y employees are driving expensive cars.

Organizations that understand the capabilities of these young workers will not have to worry about what new systems to embrace, as they have just hired the experts on the latest and greatest. Some business leaders may want to remove themselves from the decision-making process and let those who understand advancing technology make the decisions.

Control the money but be prepared to invest in technology on a continuing and ongoing basis. You will never catch up—don't expect to. Just when you think you have spent enough, the IT department will need something new. Buy it. Because if you don't, you run the risk of having your company or organization fall behind, and you can't be leading edge if you have fallen behind.

All indications suggest that Gen Y will make the biggest labor impact through their cyber skills. Consider an article I read several years ago about how Best Buy wanted to create a new employee portal and contacted an outside tech firm that came back with a multimillion-dollar quote. The bid was denied and outside help was not needed. Gen Y Best Buy employees surprised their management bosses by accomplishing the task internally for about $250,000.

Little doubt that staffing and employment services companies are going to be busy in the coming years. Should you want to apply your demographic acumen on this specialized sector for investment purposes, you could check out these companies as a starting base (pssst: "DD"[2]).

- o ManpowerGroup Inc. (MAN)
- o Kelly Services, Inc. (KELYA)
- o BG Staffing (BGSF)

PART**THREE**

THE REST OF THE WORLD (ROW)

26

It's a Mighty Big World Out There

WE HAVE SPENT the previous twenty-five chapters picking apart the roughly 320 million people who call America home, but guess what? It's a mighty big world out there demographically speaking, with roughly 7 billion (and rising) more people we could examine to see what kind of impact they might have on the world of supply and demand. Space in this book doesn't allow for a detailed examination of the rest of the world (ROW), but I think we can touch upon the demographics of various regions and countries enough to spark your interest and give you some things to ponder.

I think you'll find some of this information fascinating and trust that your mind will be spinning while I provide population facts and numbers. And perhaps, as a budding demographer, you'll be able to come up with your own theories about what these numbers might mean and portend for supply and demand, prior to, and/or absent, commentary from me.

With the exception of a few countries that roughly mirror our generational structure, there is no way that I can really parse down the various country and regional demographics on a generational basis, but I can break down the demographics in other ways.[1] I should also note that numerous different organizations count the world's people, so when throwing out population figures I'll try to tell you who has done the counting.

So, without further ado, let's consider the world as a whole before distilling the numbers down at the regional and country level. Of the 7.4 (give-or-take-quite-a-few-million) billion people in the world:[2]

- 50.4 percent are female/49.6 percent male
- 26 percent are under the age of 14
- 16.3 percent are between the ages of 15 and 24
- 49.5 percent are between the ages of 25 and 64
- 8.2 percent are 65 and older
- Just over 52 percent of the world's population lives in urban areas
- Almost 60 percent of the world's population lives in Asia
- The world's median age is a month or two shy of 30
- By 2050 the world's median age is expected to be 36
- 244 million people do not live in the country of their birth (a 41 percent increase from the 2000 world migrant population percentage)
- Roughly 84 percent of the world's population over the age of 15 is considered literate[3]
- Almost 2.2 billion (31 percent) are Christian
- Almost 1.6 billion (23 percent) are Muslim
- Just over 1.1 billion (16 percent) are considered without religious affiliation
- 1 billion (15 percent) are Hindus
- 487 million (7 percent) are Buddhists
- 405 million (6 percent) are "Folk" religionist (faiths associated with particular groups, tribes, or ethnicities)
- 58 million (1 percent) are any number of other religions, such as Taoism, Jainism, Shintoism, Wicca, Baha'i, etc.
- 13.8 million (0.2 percent) are Jewish, of whom four-fifths are equally distributed between Israel and the United States.

The people of the world are dispersed among about[4] 195 countries located in six United Nations–recognized regions, with Asia having the largest landmass and by far both the largest population by number and greatest population density. Oceania, which consists of Australia, New Zealand, Papua New Guinea, and dozens of Southeast Pacific Island chains, has the smallest landmass, population by number, and population density.

The world's population has essentially doubled since 1970, but because of declining growth rates it is estimated that it would take over 200 years to double again. Current United Nations' projections estimate that the world's population will be at about 8.1 billion by 2025, 8.8 billion by 2035, and 9.7 billion by 2050. As of 2016 the world population growth rate was at 1.13 percent, a figure that is expected to drop below 1 percent by 2025, and down to at least 0.57 percent by 2050. While Asia has been the primary driver of world population growth for the past fifty years, its growth rate has fallen below 1 percent, and Africa, with a current growth rate of more than 2.5 percent, is expected to be the primary driver of world population going forward.

People are living longer and the world is getting older; however, there can be wide variations depending upon region and country. In 1955 the world's median age was only 23, but it has risen to almost 30 today and is expected to reach almost 36 by 2050 . . . at which point I'll be so old it won't matter (but wouldn't you still like to see me playing Led Zeppelin air guitar on whatever YouTube equivalent has then become the latest noteworthy video platform?).

With all you have learned about demographics in the preceding chapters, what might you say about this rise in median age? This is not a trick question, and there are dozens of pertinent observations and conclusions that can be drawn from it.

One of the first things that comes to my mind is that aging populations represent both challenges and opportunities. The second thing that comes to my mind is that younger populations (though perhaps not too young) offer more opportunities than do older ones. Thus, I believe that Japan's projected 2050 median age of 53[5] presents far more challenges than opportunities, while Botswana's 2050 projected median age of 34 presents more opportunities than challenges. And then you've got Niger, one of the poorest countries in the world, with a current median age below 15 and a 2050 projected median age of 18. I question whether an already poor country with that many disaffected youth presents much opportunity, and I don't see how its exceptionally youthful and slow aging demographics can help pull it out of poverty in the near term.

In short, while there's not a distinct correlation between the median age of a country's population and its economic success, I believe that countries with younger and more balanced median ages tend to have faster-growing economies than countries that are exceptionally old or young.[6] Furthermore, I believe that faster-aging countries face more potential challenges than do slower ones because policy makers and businesses have less *relative* time to address and respond to ensuing aging-related change.

And with that, let me add a few economic numbers to the mix. First off, the world's ten largest economies are dispersed among Europe, Asia, North America, and South America; however, the 2015 GDP of North America (United States and Canada) is almost as big as that of the GDPs of the eight—China, Japan, Germany, United Kingdom, France, India, Brazil, and Italy—other top countries combined.[7]

Interestingly, many of the fastest-growing economies in the world,[8] as of 2015, were located in Asia and Africa. Almost all the Asian countries and close to two dozen African countries were experiencing GDP growth in excess of 3 percent, while North America, most of Europe, and a good portion of South America's countries were experiencing GDP growth below 3 percent, with several countries, such as Brazil, Russia, Ukraine, and Belarus, experiencing negative growth. Going forward to 2020, the International Monetary Fund (IMF) is forecasting continued strong growth in all of Asia, and expanding growth in African countries.

So, is there a correlation between the economic growth, or lack thereof, and a country's population growth?

Many economists would say yes, a few would say no, and some might point out that population growth can be a double-edged sword. That is, either a positive factor or an obstacle in economic development depending upon numerous other variables. For just one simple example, while high rates of population growth in the last century led to high rates of increase in total product and per capita product in Europe, rapid population growth in many under-developed countries led to an overuse of resources, which stymied economic development.[9]

And I'll leave you with that thought while we take a cursory look at some specific regions and a few select countries.

27

Economic Dynamo— North America

NORTH AMERICA[1]

○ Population: 360.5 million (4.9 percent of world total)

○ Projected 2050 Population: 433.1 million (20.1 percent increase)

○ Number of Countries: Two, plus three "dependencies"[2] (Bermuda, Greenland, Saint Pierre/Miquelon)

○ Largest Population: United States (322 million)

○ Smallest Population: Saint Pierre and Miquelon (6,300)

○ Largest Economy: United States (#1 GDP)

○ Smallest Economy: Saint Pierre and Miquelon (#191 GDP)[3]

○ Landmass: 7.2 million square miles

○ Density: 50 people per square mile

○ Growth Rate: 0.98 percent

○ Projected 2050 Annual Rate of Growth: 0.38 percent

○ Median Age: 38.4

○ Projected 2050 Median Age: 42

Despite having less than 5 percent of the world's population, North America is an economic powerhouse unmatched by any other region, barring Europe. Sure, Asia has been playing a good game of catch-up, and China's economy is larger than that of the United States when considered under the purchasing parity GDP measure, but Asia has needed an oversized cheap labor force to achieve its economic gains. Going forward, Asia's population is rapidly aging and its labor costs quickly rising.

North America's population is also aging, but not nearly as rapidly as that of Asia or Europe. And for the most part, North American countries already have a fairly strong social assistance network infrastructure in place to help it address this challenge. Furthermore, its countries will undoubtedly look to continued immigration, as well as technological innovation, to help them maintain economic success.

As we are already familiar with U.S. demographics, let's look at the region's other country for further consideration.

CANADA

- ○ Population: 36.3 million (0.49 percent of world total)
- ○ Landmass: 3.5 million square miles
- ○ Density: 10 people per square mile
- ○ Growth Rate: 0.96 percent
- ○ Projected 2050 Annual Rate of Growth: 0.36 percent
- ○ Median Age: 40.8
- ○ Projected 2050 Median Age: 46
- ○ 2015 Annual GDP Growth: 1.2 percent
- ○ Projected 2020 Annual GDP Growth: 2 percent[4]
- ○ GDP Rank:[5] 10th

While some Americans like to think of Canada as a "Mini-Me," such a concept is considered highly insulting to the vast majority of Canadians . . . even though the vast majority live within 100 miles of the U.S. border. The 36 million Canadians roughly equal the population of California, and while America considers itself a "melting pot," Canada, with more than ten distinct ethnic groups with populations greater than 1 million (and another twenty-four with populations exceeding 100,000), is one of the most culturally and ethnically diverse countries in the world.

Both Canada and America had a similar Baby Boom, but due to declining fertility, Canada did not experience a Gen Y birth boom, and the combined native-born populations of its Gen X and Y populations exceeded the population of the Baby Boomers and Silent Generation by only a bit more than 1 million. And with that factoid the first thought that should be popping into your head is?

You got it! Canada is older than the United States.

But not by all that much, with Canada's median age of 40.8 being only a couple of years greater than the U.S. median age of 38. This is likely due to immigration, which has been bringing in about 250,000 new residents per year,[6] the majority of whom have been between the ages of 15 and 34. Absent this healthy inflow of immigrants, Canada's population would be more than 6 million smaller and its population would be in a relative steep decline.

As with the world's other older countries, Canada's aging population, with an expected 2050 median age of 46, is going to present challenges going forward, especially with regard to healthcare, social services, and retirement-related gaps in the labor market. While these challenges will be alleviated to some extent by the country's strong immigration policy, policy makers are still sounding the alarm and federal and provincial governments are scrambling to come up with fixes.

28

The Old Country—Europe

EUROPE

- Population: 738.8 million (9.9 percent of world total)
- Projected 2050 Population: 706.8 million (4.5 percent decline)
- Number of Countries: Forty-four countries and four dependencies
- Largest Population: Russia (143.4 million)
- Smallest Population: Vatican City (801)
- Largest Economy: Germany (#4 by GDP)
- Smallest Economy: San Marino (#168 by GDP)
- Landmass: 8.5 million square miles
- Density: 87 people per square mile
- Growth Rate: 0.06 percent
- Projected 2050 Annual Rate of Growth: -0.21 percent
- Median Age: 41.9
- Projected 2050 Median Age: 46

Of all the regions in the word, none appear to be as demographically challenged as Europe. Based on the data above, can you tell me why?

If you focused on "growth rate," you get a gold star. The population of the region as a whole is basically not growing at all, and many European countries are already experiencing population declines. For some of these countries, that decline might be in temporary suspension depending upon how many Syrian refuges might be coming in, but once the Syrian crisis ends, any such declines will likely resume. Absent the immigration crisis, the countries of Russia, Germany, Spain, Ukraine, Poland, Romania, Greece, Portugal, Hungary, Belarus, and Serbia have all been in population decline. Or to put it another way, the populations of 11 of the region's top 20 most populated countries are falling.

Low and declining birthrates are the primary cause of the decline, though Russia also has an exceptionally high death rate, and many Eastern European countries are also losing population due to emigration. Other than during the First and Second World Wars, I don't believe that Europe has suffered population declines since the Great Plague. And some governments are taking measures to stem the slide, from encouraging immigration to offering bonuses, tax breaks, and subsidies to families having children.

OK, so do you notice anything else with the numbers at the beginning of the chapter?

You must have seen the median age? Perhaps a little old? And yes, that could compound the potential problems caused by a declining population. Who's going to pay for all of those old folks as they continue to age, and how are the fewer numbered younger folks going to afford to pay off all the accumulated public debt?

While many European countries have been economically stagnant since the end of the Great Recession, I cannot conclusively point to demographics as being part of the cause, but I do wonder if they might be having a bit of impact. My guess, though, is that any potential negative impacts from declining populations haven't come home to roost yet, especially given that the declines, for the most part, are thus far gradual. And the rise of the median age has not been especially rapid, which I believe helps countries better weather the potential impacts from that. Europe may be old, but, unlike some other regions and countries, it's not aging especially fast.

Europe's most demographically challenged country would be Russia, which has among the highest death rates in the world.

RUSSIA
- Population: 143.4 million (1.93 percent of world total)
- Projected 2050 Population: 128.6 million (14.8 percent decline)
- Landmass: 6.3 million square miles
- Density: 23 people per square mile
- Growth Rate: -0.01 percent
- Projected 2050 Annual Rate of Growth: -0.31 percent
- Median Age: 38.9
- Projected 2050 Median Age: 41
- 2015 Annual GDP Growth: -3.7 percent
- Projected 2020 Annual GDP Growth: 1.5 percent
- GDP Rank: 12th

The country's population has fallen by almost 5 million in the past twenty years and is projected to lose at least another 14 million people by 2050. While many economists had forecast that Russia's population decline would erode its economic output, it hasn't happened to any great degree yet. In part the country's economy is being sustained by being resource driven, and while the population has been declining, its labor productivity has been rising.

Going forward, Russia's demographic transition, and impact on its economy, will undoubtedly be about the most closely watched of any country by economists and demographers.

29

More Than Half the World—Asia

ASIA

- Population: 4.43 billion (59.7 percent of world total)
- Projected 2050 Population: 5.26 billion (18.7 percent increase)
- Number of Countries: Forty-eight countries and three dependencies
- Largest Population: China (1.4 billion)
- Smallest Population: Maldives (369,812)
- Largest Economy: China (#2 by GDP)
- Smallest Economy: Bhutan (#162 by GDP)
- Landmass: 12 million square miles
- Density: 370 people per square mile
- Growth Rate: 0.98 percent
- Projected 2050 Annual Rate of Growth: 0.19 percent
- Median Age: 30.7
- Projected 2050 Median Age: 40

With almost 60 percent of the world's population, forty-eight different and very distinct countries, and varied demographic profiles that run the gamut, this chapter warrants its own book. Asia, as delineated by the U.N., is a monster. Little doubt that the demographics of these fifty-one countries and dependencies is as fascinating as the hundreds (or is it thousands?) of ethnic groups who live in the broad stretch of lands that range from the western edge of Turkey to the Japanese-owned Marcus Island. But for the purposes of this book, let's just look at China and India. And for the bottom line, China is facing a downside sinkhole while India is looking at an upside tsunami.

Those who've heard me speak, read my blog, or read my first book know that I've got an issue with China. It's been the economic miracle of the past thirty years, but I believe that its one-child policy is going to derail the miracle like a bullet train running out of track. And bear with me here, because I always need a lot of air time when discussing China. But that should figure, as by demographic standards it's the biggest country in the world.

China has proved, in a way, that you can get a lot done economically if you don't have to be concerned about kids. It is called a demographic dividend. It is short-termed and incredibly short-sighted, but it is nonetheless a definite dividend resulting from cutting fertility by 75 percent. China is like a DINK (dual income, no kids) couple on mega steroids. A couple without children can enjoy dual incomes, freedom to travel, opportunity to amass wealth, and the luxury of discretionary time. In the last thirty-six years China's one-child policy has been credited with "preventing" 450 million live births. This is roughly the combined equivalent population of the United States and Mexico. Short term, China's economy has benefited accordingly. The country did not have to house, feed, care for, or educate the missing kids. It freed up the parents to spend more time working. For the long term, though, China has decimated its future workforce, tax base, consumer base, and leadership. Furthermore, in twenty years China will have a half billion elderly people who can no longer work. China has no formal social security network and no way of caring for or feeding what is going to be a record-breaking immense elderly population.

CHINA

- Population: 1.38 billion (18.6 percent of world total)
- Projected 2050 Population: 1.35 billion (2.2 percent decline)
- Landmass: 3.6 million square miles
- Density: 381 people per square mile
- Growth Rate: 0.46 percent
- Projected 2050 Annual Rate of Growth: -0.39 percent
- Median Age: 37.3
- Projected 2050 Median Age: 50
- 2015 Annual GDP Growth: 6.9 percent
- Projected 2020 Annual GDP Growth: 6 percent
- GDP Rank: 2nd

A couple of years ago I saw the headline, "China Eases One-Child Policy; Concession Comes as Labor Shortage Looms." I read it several times, thinking I had misread it. Maybe it was a misprint? Did anyone in China really think that a *looming* labor shortage would be remedied by a sudden increase in fertility? China's labor issues were acute at that moment now.

It was the equivalent of saying, *"We were all starving, so we planted corn."*

How's that going to work out? Think the corn is going to grow fast enough to feed the starving?

The worst thing that China could do right now is start having more children. China has a hole in its population that is thirty-six long years in the making and represents a half-billion missing people. When it comes time for this diminutive cohort with missing members to pay the taxes, support the elderly, feed the young, and do all the heavy lifting, they won't be able to because they don't have the critical mass. Having more children now simply means that there will be more kids to starve later. The damage is done and it cannot be remedied!

Another issue that needs to be considered with regard to this thirty-six-year-old[1] "Missing" generation is that it is top-heavy with males. According to the Chinese media, there are about 30 million young Chinese men of marrying age that cannot find wives. This came about because under the one-child policy males were significantly favored by Chinese parents because they were more likely to care for the parents in their old age according to Chinese tradition. Having a girl baby was bad luck because she was likely to eventually marry and end up caring for her husband's parents.

So, ultimately, this means China's labor force includes about 30 million inherently unhappy workers. That can't be good for productivity!

Anyhow, China's economy is still chugging along, though the clickety-clack sound from its wheels is no longer rhythmically smooth and the ride is feeling uncharacteristically bumpy. The economic locomotive "that could" will be sustained for quite some time longer with the assistance of its own fast-growing consumer base and rise of a middle class. At some point though, due to demographics, the train is going to jump the rails.

In the meantime, China's status as the world's most populous country will likely be overtaken by India, which is expected to benefit from both a big increase in its own labor force and from China's rising labor costs. In fact, because of these factors, many economists believe that India will also overtake China economically by 2050. I may not be an economist, but I'd have to say that the demographics seem to support such a supposition.

INDIA
- o Population: 1.32 billion (17.8 percent of world total)
- o Projected 2050 Population: 1.70 billion (28.8 percent growth)
- o Landmass: 1.1 million square miles
- o Density: 1,156 people per square mile
- o Growth Rate: 1.2 percent
- o Projected 2050 Annual Rate of Growth: 0.38 percent

- Median Age: 26.9
- Projected 2050 Median Age: 37
- 2015 Annual GDP Growth: 7.3 percent
- Projected 2020 Annual GDP Growth: 7.7 percent
- GDP Rank: 7th

30

Cradle of Civilization— Africa

AFRICA

- ◯ Population: 1.2 billion (16.4 percent of world total)
- ◯ Projected 2050 population: 2.47 billion (51 percent growth)
- ◯ Number of Countries: Fifty-four countries and four dependencies
- ◯ Largest Population: Nigeria (186.9 million)
- ◯ Smallest Population: Seychelles (97,000)
- ◯ Largest Economy: Nigeria (#24 by GDP)
- ◯ Smallest Economy: Seychelles (#170 by GDP)
- ◯ Landmass: 11.5 million square miles
- ◯ Density: 106 people per square mile
- ◯ Growth Rate: 2.53 percent
- ◯ Projected 2050 Annual Rate of Growth: 1.78 percent
- ◯ Median Age: 19.5
- ◯ Projected 2050 Median Age: 25

To say that Africa is complicated is an understatement, and the demographic information above doesn't really tell anyone a whole lot, as every African country is so different. But it does tell you that Africa is young and growing, two attributes conducive to economic growth.

In fact, youth and population growth combined have been recognized as key to the continent's economic future, with economists forecasting that Africa's labor force will exceed 1.1 billion by 2040, a number that will be greater than that of either China or India.

Africa's recent and relatively newfound economic growth is largely the result of a worldwide commodity boom and various African governments' efforts to stabilize their countries by ending conflicts and improving micro- and macro-economic conditions. In fact, while most people believe that Africa has been primarily propped up by the resource boom, natural resource extraction and related activities contributed to less than 32 percent of Africa's GDP growth in the first ten years of this century

This suggests that the continent's resources provided the ignition and accelerant to get the economy started, and that now the GDP is being propelled more by numerous other sectors and a fast-growing labor force—a labor force that is helping Africans join the ranks of the world's consumers and creating a middle class that is already bigger than India's.

There are economic naysayers who argue that Africa is still too backward, that it won't be able to industrialize fast enough to keep its labor competitively productive, and that it will wither should commodity prices fall. But I would posit that its growing population of youth might be its greatest commodity. In fact, this youth has already proved to be especially innovative in the rise of the continent's digital economy, which is helping boost the rest of the economy. The booming economies of Kenya, Ivory Coast, Nigeria, Ghana, and South Africa—referred to as the "KINGS" countries—lead the rest of Africa economically in part because of the development of their strong broadband networks and government policies that encourage innovation. The KINGS countries have mobile penetration rates exceeding 90 percent, with broadband available on most of the population's phones. All indications point to swarms of youthful entrepreneurs using the technologies to create new businesses. Enough new businesses that the *Harvard Business Review* recently named Kenya, Nigeria, and South Africa as having the fastest-growing digital economies in the world.

31

Latin American Flavors and Down Under

o Population: 641 million (8.6 percent of world total)
o Projected 2050 population: 784 million (22.3 percent growth)
o Number of Countries: Thirty-three, plus fifteen dependencies
o Largest Population: Brazil (210 million)
o Smallest Population: Falkland Islands (2,915)
o Largest Economy: Brazil (#9 by GDP)
o Smallest Economy: Falkland Islands (#192 by GDP)[1]
o Landmass: 7.8 million square miles
o Density: 82 people per square mile
o Growth Rate: 1.05 percent
o Projected 2050 Annual Rate of Growth: 0.26 percent
o Median Age: 29.6
o Projected 2050 Median Age: 41

On the whole Latin America and the Caribbean experienced extensive economic growth in the 1990s and the first decade of this century that lifted millions of people out of poverty and swelled the ranks of its middle class. In fact, the World Bank determined that between 2002 and 2012 10 million people were joining the ranks of the middle class per year, and that the middle class was on the verge of becoming the region's majority economic population group. Unfortunately, growth has stalled in many of the region's countries, especially those highly dependent upon commodity exports, and some countries are projected to face continued economic stagnation in the years ahead. Brazil, Venezuela, and Ecuador have suffered the most during the region's recent downturn, and while Brazil is expected to see modest recovery, the economies of both Ecuador and Venezuela are projected to remain stalled, at best. According to the IMF, among the bright spots for future five-year economic growth in the region will be most of Central America, Mexico, Colombia, Bolivia, Peru, and Chile.

In looking at the demographics of the region as a whole or by individual country, I find myself loathe to make any pronouncements. The countries in many ways have demographic profiles distinctly different from each other, with some having high rates of growth and others slowing, and with some populations being relatively young and others aging quickly. The region in general has had a long history of economic and political turmoil, and the region's ascent toward developed world status has been especially fast.

For all those reasons I am going to withhold comment other than to note that I would be most concerned about the challenges facing those countries projected to experience especially fast—and old—aging. In particular, Chile, which is expected to see its median age rise 12.3 years to 47 by 2050; Cuba, a 10.3-year rise to age 52; and Brazil, a 13.3-year rise to 45.

OCEANIA
- Population: 39.9 million (0.5 percent of world total)
- Projected 2050 population: 56.6 million (42.7 percent increase)
- Number of Countries: Fourteen countries and nine dependencies

- Largest Population: Australia (24.3 million)
- Smallest Population: Tokelau (1,276)
- Largest Economy: Australia (#13 by GDP)
- Smallest Economy: Tuvalu (#194 by GDP)[2]
- Landmass: 3.3 million square miles
- Density: 12 people per square mile
- Growth Rate: 1.45 percent
- Projected 2050 Annual Rate of Growth: 0.79 percent
- Median Age: 33
- Projected 2050 Median Age: 37

I don't quite know what to say here. I mean, I don't count Kangaroos....

Well, I didn't, but after I wrote that I got curious and Googled it. Thus, I can report that there are an estimated 50 million to 60 million kangaroos in Australia, which gives them, by far, a larger population than that of Oceania's humans.

My quick, two-cent demographic assessment of the world's smallest region by population is as follows: overall, fairly healthy-looking profile, especially when measured against the rest of the developed world. Healthy growth in population heading toward 2050. Median age seems to be getting a bit up in years but certainly not at great speed. As with much of the world, population growth is slowing, but Oceania's seems to be a slow deceleration that will hardly cause a demographic ripple on any policy-making or business decisions.

There certainly doesn't appear to be any downside, but the projected population increase could definitely serve up some potential upside. The question is whether that would be region wide or isolated to a country or two.

And I'll leave that for you to figure out, mate!

SOURCES

Sources are listed once in the order they were used, but many—especially those from the U.S. Census Bureau—were utilized in numerous chapters during the development of this book.

INTRODUCTION
N/A

CHAPTER 1
Worldometers. "World Population Clock." Retrieved from http://www.worldometers. info/world-population/#region.

U.S. Department of Health and Human Services Centers for Disease Control and Prevention. (December 23, 2015). "National Vital Statistics Reports—Births: Final Data for 2014." Volume 64, Number 12.

Mattel Inc. (February 1, 2016). "2015 Annual Report." Retrieved from http://files.shareholder.com/downloads/MAT/2216899387x0x884386/BB030C82-FB73-48B8-AFF7-42D39E9E66C6/Mattel_2015_AR_Bookmarked_PDF.PDF.

Urbain, Thomas. (January 28, 2016). "Reality Check: Barbie Now Tall, Curvy and Petite Too." Yahoo! News. Retrieved from https://www.yahoo.com/news/reality-check-barbie-now-tall-curvy-petite-162027073.html?ref=gs.

CHAPTER 2
N/A

CHAPTER 3
N/A

CHAPTER 4
U.S. Census Bureau. "American FactFinder" Retrieved from http://factfinder.census.gov/faces/nav/jsf/pages/searchresults.xhtml?refresh=t.

U.S. Census Bureau, Population Division. (June 2015). "Annual Estimates of the Resident Population by Single Year of Age and Sex for the United States: April 1, 2010 to July 1, 2014."

U.S. Census Bureau, Population Division. (June 2015). "Annual Estimates of the Resident Population for Selected Age Groups by Sex for the United States, States, Counties, and Puerto Rico Commonwealth and Municipios: April 1, 2010 to July 1, 2014."

U.S. Census Bureau, Population Division. (December 2014). "Projections of the Population by Sex, Hispanic Origin, and Race for the United States: 2015 to 2060."

U.S. Census Bureau. (July 2015). "2014 American Community Survey 1-Year Estimates."

Humes, Karen R, Nicholas A. Jones, and Roberto R. Ramirez (March 2011). "Overview of Race and Hispanic Origin: 2010." U.S. Census Bureau.

Office of Immigration Statistics. (August 2014). "2013 Yearbook of Immigration Statistics." U.S. Department of Homeland Security.

U.S. Census Bureau. (2015). "Detailed Occupation for the Full-Time, Year-Round Civilian Employed Population 16 Years and Older: 2010–2014 American Community Survey 5-Year Estimates."

CHAPTER 5
N/A

CHAPTER 6
Camarota, Steven A. (August 2012). "Immigrants in the United States, 2010: A Profile of America's Foreign-Born Population." Center for Immigration Studies.

Easterlin, Richard. (1980). *Birth and Fortune*. Chicago and London. University of Chicago Press.

Howe, Neil. (August 13, 2014). "The Silent Generation, 'The Lucky Few'" (Part 3 of series, "Generations in Pursuit of the American Dream"). Forbes.com.

Retrieved from: http://www.forbes.com/sites/neilhowe/2014/08/13/the-silent-generation-the-lucky-few-part-3-of-7/#2571c1751e54.

U.S. Census Bureau, Population Division. (June 2015). "Annual Estimates of the Resident Population by Single Year of Age and Sex for the United States: April 1, 2010 to July 1, 2014."

CHAPTER 7
N/A

CHAPTER 8
N/A

CHAPTER 9
N/A

CHAPTER 10
Benhamou, Laurence. (February 2015). "Generation Z: Born in the Digital Age." Yahoo! News. Retrieved from: https://www.yahoo.com/news/generation-z-born-digital-age-160347762.html?ref=gs.

U.S. Department of Health and Human Services Centers for Disease Control and Prevention. (December 23, 2015). "National Vital Statistics Reports—Births: Final Data for 2014." Volume 64, Number 12.

CHAPTER 11
U.S. Census Bureau, Application Services Division. (last revised March 2013). "1990 Census." Retrieved from: www.census.gov/main/www/cen1990.html.

U.S. Census Bureau, Application Services Division. (last revised July 2013). "2000 Census." Retrieved from: www.census.gov/main/www/cen2000.html.

U.S. Census Bureau, Population Division. (December 2015). "Estimates of the Components of Resident Population Change: April 1, 2010 to July 1, 2015." Retrieved from: http://factfinder.census.gov/faces/tableservices/jsf/pages/productview.xhtml?pid=-PEP_2014_PEPTCOMP&prodType=table.

U.S. Census Bureau. "American FactFinder." Retrieved from: http://factfinder.census.gov/faces/nav/jsf/pages/searchresults.xhtml?refresh=t.

CHAPTER 12

U.S. Census Bureau, Population Division. (December 2015). "Estimates of the Components of Resident Population Change: April 1, 2010 to July 1, 2015." Retrieved from: http://factfinder.census.gov/faces/tableservices/jsf/pages/productview.xhtml?pid=-PEP_2014_PEPTCOMP&prodType=table.

U.S. Census Bureau. "American FactFinder" Retrieved from: http://factfinder.census.gov/faces/nav/jsf/pages/searchresults.xhtml?refresh=t.

U.S. Census Bureau. (July 2015). "2014 American Community Survey 1-Year Estimates."

U.S. Census Bureau, Population Projections. (last revised March 2015). "Population Projections: Summary Tables." Retrieved from: http://www.census.gov/population/projections/data/national/2014/summarytables.html.

Laffer, Arthur B., Moore, Stephen, and Jonathan Williams. (January 2016). "Rich States, Poor States: ALEC-Laffer State Economic Competitiveness Index." American Legislative Exchange Council.

Atkinson, Robert. (March 14, 2013). "Why the 2000s Were a Lost Decade for American Manufacturing." *Industry Week*. Retrieved from: http://www.industryweek.com/the-2000s.

Atkinson, Robert D., and B. Nager Adams. (June 2014). "The 2014 State New Economy Index." Information Technology & Innovation Foundation.

CHAPTER 13

Everson, Darren. (September 3, 2009). "The Big Ten: Down and Out? Bowl Losses and Population Shifts Sink a Revered Conference; 'Graceless in Defeat.'" *Wall Street Journal*.

U.S. Department of Health and Human Services Centers for Disease Control and Prevention. (December 23, 2015). "National Vital Statistics Reports—Births: Final Data for 2014." Volume 64, Number 12.

Helper, Susan, Timothy Krueger, and Howard Wial. (April 2012). "Locating American Manufacturing: Trends in the Geography of Production." Metropolitan Policy Program at Brookings.

Laffer, Arthur B., Stephen Moore, and Jonathan Williams. (January 2016). "Rich States, Poor States: ALEC-Laffer State Economic Competitiveness Index." American Legislative Exchange Council.

Sangster, Johnathan L. (First posited in 2008). "Are Southern States Better Positioned for Technology Projects?" Area Development: Site and Facility Planning.

CHAPTER 14

Hicks, Michael J. (May 9, 2016). "Other Views: Bring factory jobs back to the Midwest? It's the great lie of 2016." *GazetteXtra*. Retrieved from: http://www.gazettextra.com/20160508/other_views_bring_factory_jobs_back_to_the_midwest_its_the_great_lie_of_2016.

Swezey, Devon, and Ryan McConaghy. (October 2011). "Manufacturing Growth: Advanced Manufacturing and the Future of the American Economy." The Schwartz Initiative on American Economic Policy.

Atkinson, Robert D., and Adams B. Nager (June 2014). "The 2014 State New Economy Index." Information Technology & Innovation Foundation.

Laffer, Arthur B., Stephen Moore, and Jonathan Williams. (January 2016). "Rich States, Poor States: ALEC-Laffer State Economic Competitiveness Index." American Legislative Exchange Council.

CHAPTER 15

Quigley, Winthrop. (January 28, 2016). "New Mexico's Population Struggle." *Albuquerque Journal*. Retrieved from: http://www.abqjournal.com/713533/nms-population-struggle.html.

Walch, Tad. (May 11, 2015). "Mormon families Are America's Largest, New Study Finds." *Deseret News*. Retrieved from: http://www.deseretnews.com/article/865628480/Mormon-families-are-Americas-largest-new-study-finds.html?pg=all.

Pew Research Center. "Mormons in America—Certain in Their Beliefs, Uncertain of Their Place in Society." Pew Research Center—Religion & Public Life. Retrieved from: http://www.pewforum.org/2012/01/12/mormons-in-america-executive-summary/.

U.S. Census Bureau, Population Division. (December 2015). "Annual Estimates of the Residential Population for Selected Age Groups by Sex for the United States, States, Counties, and Puerto Rico Commonwealth and Municipios: April 1, 2010 to July 1, 2015."

Taylor, Paul, Rich Morin, and D'Vera Cohn and Wendy Wang. (December 29, 2008). "American Mobility: Who Moves? Who Stays Put? Where's Home?" Pew Research Center.

CHAPTER 16

N/A

CHAPTER 17

National Funeral Directors Association. "Media Center: Statistics." NFDA.org. Retrieved from: http://www.nfda.org/news/statistics.

U.S. Department of Health and Human Services Centers for Disease Control and Prevention. (October 7, 2015). "National Center for Health Statistics FastStats—Deaths and Mortality." cdc.gov. Retrieved from: http://www.cdc.gov/nchs/fastats/deaths.htm.

CHAPTER 18

Vital and Health Statistics. (February 2016). "Long-Term Care Providers and Services Users in the United States: Data from the National Study of Long-Term Care Providers, 2013–2014." U.S. Department of Health and Human Services Centers for Disease Control and Prevention.

Newman, Elizabeth Leis. (October 3, 2014). "Assisted living continues to grow rapidly in expanded markets." McKnights.com. Retrieved from: http://www.mcknights.com/news/assisted-living-continues-to-grow-rapidly-in-expanded-markets/article/375189/.

Congressional Budget Office. (January 2016). "The Budget and Economic Outlook: 2016 to 2026." Retrieved from: https://www.cbo.gov/sites/default/files/114th-congress-2015-2016/reports/51129-2016Outlook_OneCol-2.pdf.

CHAPTER 19

U.S. Department of Health and Human Services Centers for Disease Control and Prevention. (June 19, 2015). "Overweight & Obesity." cdc.gov. Retrieved from: http://www.cdc.gov/obesity/index.html.

CHAPTER 20

Cassells, Logie, Kenneth Gronbach, and M.J. Moye, (May 2009). "Gens. X and Y to Spur Housing Recovery." The Age Curve Report.

U.S. Census Bureau and U.S. Department of Housing and Urban Development. (May 2015). "2013 Housing Profile: United States—American Housing Survey Factsheets." U.S. Census Bureau. Retrieved from: http://www2.census.gov/programs-surveys/ahs/2013/factsheets/ahs13-1_UnitedStates.pdf.

Peralta, Katherine. (September 17, 2014). "How Millennials Could Be Housing Heroes."

U.S. News & World Report. Retrieved from: http://www.usnews.com/news/articles/2014/09/17/how-millennials-could-be-housing-market-heroes.

Smoke, Jonathan. (November 14, 2014). "3 Reasons Millennials Are Driving the Housing Market." Realtor.com. Retrieved from: http://www.realtor.com/news/3-reasons-millennials-driving-housing-market/.

Canales, Alicia. (January 26, 2014). "Millennial generation key to housing market future." *Phoenix Business Journal*. Retrieved from: http://www.bizjournals.com/phoenix/news/2014/01/26/millennial-generation-key-to-housing.html.

Brody, Ben. (June 27, 2014). "Millennial-driven housing boom coming." CNN Money. Retrieved from: http://money.cnn.com/2014/06/26/real_estate/harvard-millennials-housing/.

National Association of REALTORS. "Home Buyer and Seller Generational Trends Report 2016." Retrieved from: https://www.scribd.com/document/303413452/2016-Home-Buyer-and-Seller-Generational-Trends#fullscreen.

Burbank, Jeremy, and Louise Keely. (September 16, 2014). "Millennials and Their Homes: Still Seeking the American Dream." Demand Institute. Retrieved from: http://demandinstitute.org/millennials-and-their-homes/.

National Association of REALTORS. (March 2014). "Home Buyer and Seller Generational Trends." Retrieved from: http://www.realtor.org/sites/default/files/reports/2014/2014-home-buyer-and-seller-generational-trends-report-full.pdf.

Joint Center for Housing Studies of Harvard University. (June 2015). "The State of the Nation's Housing 2015." Harvard University. Retrieved from: http://www.jchs.harvard.edu/research/publications/state-nations-housing-2015.

CHAPTER 21

Beck, Christina. (January 20, 2016). "Why Are Millennials forgoing driving?" *Christian Science Monitor*. Retrieved from: http://www.csmonitor.com/USA/USA-Update/2016/0120/Why-are-Millennials-forgoing-driving.

McDonald, Noreen C. (July 9, 2015). "Are Millennials Really the 'Go-Nowhere' Generation?" *Journal of American Planning Association*. Retrieved from: http://www.tandfonline.com/doi/full/10.1080/01944363.2015.1057196.

Davis, Benjamin, Tony Dutzik, and Phineas Baxandall. (April 2012). "Transportation and the New Generation: Why Young People Are Driving Less and What It Means for Transportation Policy." Frontier Group and U.S. PIRG Education Fund. Retrieved from: http://www.frontiergroup.org/sites/default/files/reports/Transportation%20&%20the%20New%20Generation%20vUS.pdf.

LeBeau, Phil. (November 18, 2014). "Wave Goodbye to the Two-Car Family." CNBC. Retrieved from: http://www.cnbc.com/2014/11/18/two-car-homes-will-become-less-common-kpmg.html.

Autotrader; Kelley Blue Book. (March 2016). "What's Driving Gen Z" Autotrader_Kelley Blue Book Gen Z Research. Retrieved from: https://coxautoinc.app.box.com/v/autotrader-kbb-gen-z-research/1/6949857826/56691606014/1.

Federal Aviation Administration. (March 13, 2014). "Fact Sheet—FAA Forecast-Fiscal Years 2014–34." FAA. Retrieved from: http://www.faa.gov/news/fact_sheets/news_story.cfm?newsId=15934.

Machado, Amanda. (June 18, 2014). "How Millennials Are Changing Travel." *The Atlantic*. Retrieved from: http://www.theatlantic.com/international/archive/2014/06/how-millennials-are-changing-international-travel/373007/.

Barton, Christine, Julia Haywood, and Pranay Jhunjhunwala. (March 18, 2013). "Traveling with Millennials." Boston Consulting Group. Retrieved from: https://www.bcgperspectives.com/content/articles/transportation_travel_tourism_consumer_insight_travel-ing_with_millennials/.

Kulwicki, Allison. (November 2014). "Travel Research: 2015 Boomer Travel Trends." American Association of Retired Persons. November 2014. Retrieved from: http://www.aarp.org/content/dam/aarp/research/surveys_statistics/general/2014/AARP-2015-Boomer-Travel-Trends-AARP-res-gen.pdf.

Spano, Kirk. (May 18, 2015). "Opinion: Cruise for Fun, Not for Investment." Market Watch. Retrieved from: http://www.marketwatch.com/story/cruise-for-fun-not-for-in-vestment-2015-05-18.

CHAPTER 22

Wadhwa, Vivek. (October 31, 2014). "Why baby boomers are an important part of technology's future." *Washington Post*. October 31, 2014. Retrieved from: https://www.washingtonpost.com/postlive/why-baby-boomers-will-rule-the-future-of-technolo-gy/2014/10/30/6d26f9c8-5f19-11e4-8b9e-2ccdac31a031_story.html.

Rogers, Michael. (October 2009). "Boomers and Technology: An Extended Conversa-tion." American Association of Retired Persons and Microsoft Corp. Retrieved from: http://assets.aarp.org/www.aarp.org_/articles/computers/2009_boomers_and_technol-ogy_final_report.pdf.

O'Connor, Fred. (May 8, 2014). "Baby boomers embrace technology as much as young-er users." *PC World*. Retrieved from: http://www.pcworld.com/article/2153080/ba-by-boomers-embrace-technology-as-much-as-younger-users.html.

O'Neill, Jen. (December 28, 2008). "More and More Baby Boomers Embrace Technol-ogy." Finding Dulcinea: Librarian of the Internet. Retrieved from: http://www.finding-dulcinea.com/news/technology/2008/December/More-and-More-Baby-Boomers-Em-brace-Technology.html.

CHAPTER 23

Cassells, Logie, Kenneth Gronbach, and M.J. Moye, (January 2009). "Beer Sales Set to Rise with Emergent Generation Y." The Age Curve Report.

Tierney, John. (April 15, 2014). "The State of American Beer: What's rising, what's fad-ing, and what people are really drinking." *The Atlantic*. Retrieved from: http://www.theatlantic.com/business/archive/2014/04/the-state-of-american-beer/360583/.

Cassells, Logie, Kenneth Gronbach, and M.J. Moye, (March 2010). "Sector Overview: Boomers to Go Nuts!" The Age Curve Report.

IBISWorld. (December 2015). "Florists in the U.S.: Market Research Report." IBISWorld. Retrieved from: http://www.ibisworld.com/industry/default.aspx?indid=1096.

CHAPTER 24

LeBeau, Phil. (April 18, 2013). "New Study Finds China Manufacturing Costs Rising to US Level." CNBC. Retrieved from: http://www.cnbc.com/id/100651692.

Cheng, Andria. (May 1, 2015). "Record number of manufacturing jobs returning to Amer-ica." MarketWatch. Retrieved from: http://www.marketwatch.com/story/us-flips-the-script-on-jobs-reshoring-finally-outpaced-offshoring-in-2014-2015-05-01.

Zhang, Simon. (July 1, 2012). "China's Rising Costs." *China Business Review*. Retrieved from: http://www.chinabusinessreview.com/chinas-rising-costs/.

U.S. Census Bureau. (March 2016). "2014 Annual Survey of Manufacturers." U.S. Census Bureau. Retrieved from: http://www.census.gov/newsroom/press-releases/2015/cb15-tps108.html.

Bureau of Labor Statistics. (December 2015). "Employment Projections: 2014–24." Unit-ed States Department of Labor—BLS. Retrieved from: http://www.bls.gov/news.release/ecopro.toc.htm.

Hinderstein, Chase B. (June 26, 2014). "Manufacturing Is Coming Back. Factory Jobs Aren't." Voices, as curated by "Governing." Retrieved from: http://www.governing.com/gov-institute/voices/col-u-s-manufacturing-apple-foxconn-tesla-jobless-recovery.html.

Grand View Research. (May 30, 2016). "Medical Textiles Market Is Expected to Witness Lucrative Growth by 2022 Due to the Rising Health Consciousness and Technological Advancements." Grand View Research, Inc. Retrieved from: https://globenewswire.com/news-release/2016/05/30/844265/0/en/Medical-Textiles-Market-Is-Expected-To-Witness-Lucrative-Growth-By-2022-Due-To-The-Rising-Health-Consciousness-And-Technological-Advancements-Grand-View-Research-Inc.html.

CHAPTER 25
N/A

CHAPTER 26
United Nations. "Population Trends." United Nations Department of Economic and Social Affairs, Population Division. Various dates. Retrieved from: http://www.un.org/en/development/desa/population/theme/trends/index.shtml.

Worldometers. "World" and "World Population Sections." Worldometers. Various dates. Retrieved from: http://www.worldometers.info/world-population/#region.

Pew Research Center. (December 2012). "The Global Religious Landscape." Pew Research Center Religious & Public Life. Retrieved from: http://www.pewforum.org/2012/12/18/global-religious-landscape-exec/.

Central Intelligence Agency. The World Factbook. CIA. 2016. Retrieved from: https://www.cia.gov/library/publications/resources/the-world-factbook/index.html.

International Monetary Fund. "World Economic Outlook. IMF. April 2016. Retrieved from: http://www.imf.org/external/datamapper/index.php.

CHAPTER 27
N/A

CHAPTER 28
N/A

CHAPTER 29
Burkitt, Laurie. (November 15, 2013). "China Eases One-Child Policy—Concession Comes as Labor Shortage Looms." *Wall Street Journal.* Retrieved from: http://www.wsj.com/articles/SB10001424052702303289904579199431427590394.

CHAPTER 30
Leke, Acha, Susan Lund, Charles Roxburgh, Arend van Wamelen. (June 2010). "What's driving Africa's growth?" McKinsey & Company. Retrieved from: http://www.mckinsey.com/global-themes/middle-east-and-africa/whats-driving-africas-growth.

Osiakwan, Eric. (January 20, 2016). "Think Africa's economic boom is over? The tech space is about to prove you wrong." Memeburn. Retrieved from: http://memeburn.com/2016/01/think-africas-economic-boom-tech-space-prove-wrong/.

Bhaskar Chakravorti, Christopher Tunnard, and Ravi Shankar Chaturvedi. (February 19, 2015). "Where the Digital Economy Is Moving the Fastest." *Harvard Business Review.* Retrieved from: https://hbr.org/2015/02/where-the-digital-economy-is-moving-the-fastest.

CHAPTER 31
Calvo-González, Oscar. (April 7, 2016). "Economic slowdown puts the brakes on middle class growth in Latin America." The World Bank. Retrieved from: http://blogs.worldbank.org/opendata/economic-slowdown-puts-brakes-middle-class-growth-latin-america.

UPSIDE SOURCES

NOTES

INTRODUCTION

1. Or to look at it another way, and not malign poor Gen X, one could say that the Boomers create tsunamis when they age into a market and then leave sinkholes in their wake.

CHAPTER 1

1. I'll be more specific about the "give or take" in a future chapter, but official U.S. counts are generally subject to debate due to disagreement about exactly how many illegal immigrants are in the country.
2. This count was conducted using birth numbers, and I believe that the addition of any young immigrants would make only a marginal difference.

CHAPTER 4

1. The Census Bureau uses "Black" and "African American" interchangeably and refers to a person having origins in any of the Black racial groups of Africa.
2. Hispanic (or Latino) is not considered a "race" by the Census Bureau, and to be considered Hispanic, census takers must self-identify as such by reasons of heritage, lineage, nationality group, and/or country of birth of the person or his/her parents or ancestors. Hispanics can be of any race.
3. The year 2014 marks the latest year of vital statistic official birth numbers for the country.
4. I am not sure why the Census Bureau estimates are almost a half-million shy of the CDC's birth numbers, as infant mortality certainly isn't that bad. It seems that someone has made a mistake in their counting somewhere and somehow.

CHAPTER 6

1. Also of interest is that the Silent Generation is the only generation that never put one of its own in the White House.

CHAPTER 9

1. Assuming that all generations are being delineated by the standard twenty-year time frames, a one-year shift of those time frames in either direction still gives Generation Y the numerical edge over Boomers.

CHAPTER 10

1. The U.S. Centers for Disease Control and Prevention National Center for Health Statistics, which is responsible for the nation's official birth numbers, had not yet released birth numbers for 2015.

CHAPTER 11

1. While I've primarily been using the Census Bureau's 2014 American Community Survey counts as the latest numbers to guide population figures, the Bureau released its latest estimates of population change numbers in December 2015, allowing me to compare the official 2010 Census numbers with the Bureau's latest population estimates. These latest figures are applicable only on the country-wide, regional, and state basis and do not break down into any parameters beyond the "components of change," which are births, deaths, and migration (thus they cannot be used to compare generations).

2. For some reason I could not find Census Bureau data relating to "Estimates of the Components of Resident Population Change" for any time frame other than 2010–2015. In fact, the 2000 to 2008 data is no longer available on its "American FactFinder" website, but I still had those figures from a project I did back in 2009.

3. The U.S. Census Bureau defines "international migrants" as both foreign-born immigrants moving to the United States and native-born Americans migrating back home from other countries, the latter of which is inclusive of members of the U.S. military returning from overseas duty.

CHAPTER 12

1. At this juncture I have to revert back to 2014 American Community Survey numbers, as the 2015 estimates do not include parameters such as race and ethnicity.

2. Perhaps the Census Bureau was getting flack for making inaccurate projections in the past, but I took a look at its 1995 projections based on the 1990 Census and think the Bureau did a pretty good job coming up with the projected state populations for 2015. In fact, by my count it looks like it pegged the projections of more than thirty states by a factor under 100,000 each (and came within 20,000 for several), and came within 300,000 of another sixteen. The Bureau totally underestimated projections by more than 1 million on nine states, all of which happened to be among the largest and/or fastest growing. As I've noted, counting large populations is difficult, but making projections about what those populations might be in twenty-five years is exceptionally difficult. That said, population projections should never be considered as fait accompli but are certainly useful as guidelines to consider as to what a potential given population might look like in the future.

3. Even though both New York and Pennsylvania exceeded Census Bureau projections as of 2015, the actual growth and projection numbers remain underwhelming.

CHAPTER 13

1. I use "equivalent" here because over the years the determining factor for each year's college football "national champion" has changed and, with the former lack of a play-off system, has always been considered highly subjective. Thus equivalent would be "national champion" as picked by the nation's sportswriters, coaches, computer system, sports foundation, or other method, and as officially recognized by the NCAA.

CHAPTER 14

1. http://www.freep.com/story/money/real-estate/2015/07/12/detroit-home-values-rising/29169949/.

CHAPTER 15

1. As mentioned in previous chapters, the Census Bureau "does not have a current set of state [or regional] population projections and currently has no plans to produce them."

CHAPTER 17

1. The 2014 numbers are from the Census Bureau's American Community Survey, which does not break down numbers by the age 65–74 and 75–84 brackets.

CHAPTER 19

1. There are a few well-established successful biotech companies that never market their own products, and instead sell the rights to their approved drugs and/or devices to other healthcare companies.

CHAPTER 20

1. And yes, some of these Generation Y children do have Gen X parents, but for the most part the parentage of Gen Y is Boomer based.
2. Results from the Bureau's 2015 survey was scheduled for release in October 2016.
3. The purveyors of the above-mentioned surveys share delineations of Gen Y roughly similar to my own, with all giving the generation twenty-year age spans and all a birth range within five years of the one I use.
4. Unfortunately, the sources for this information failed to delineate the generation, so such pronouncements may be suspect.
5. Hurrah! One of the few researchers that gives Gen X twenty years and marks them as being born between 1965 and 1984.

CHAPTER 21

1. While the researchers divided the groups by generations, they delineated with eleven-year generational spans and what I consider to be wonky birth-year ranges. However, the findings do line up roughly with younger members of Gen X and the first years of Gen Y.
2. As with so much generational research, folks just don't want to delineate the generations in a logical fashion. The researchers for this project delineated Gen Z as being born between 1999 and 2016; thus their reference to Gen Z means the last six years of Gen Y and first couple (only "couple" because I doubt they interviewed anyone under 10) of years of Gen Z. Perhaps needless to say, but it should also be pointed out that the researchers have a vested interest in promoting a healthy car-buying public.
3. In the United States, the "high-speed" of high-speed rail is defined as 110 m.p.h., or more; while in Europe "high-speed" is defined as speeds greater than 155 m.p.h.
4. BCG delineates Gen Y as being born between 1980 and 1999, and Boomers as being born between 1946 and 1964. Gen X receives the fourteen-year span in between and is barely acknowledged in the report.
5. Wonder what delineation the analyst is using—likely a fourteen- to fifteen-year age span.

CHAPTER 22

1. And no, Al Gore did not actually invent the Internet. A comment he made in 1999 about taking congressional "initiative" that helped foster the Internet's growth was taken out of context, and Al has been the butt of the "inventor of the Internet" joke ever since.

CHAPTER 23

1. In short, bureaucratic hurdles kept delaying the fund's inception, and the investment firm called a halt to the efforts in mid-2010.
2. Question: Which holiday brings in the most florist business by number of transactions and dollar volume? Nope, not Valentine's Day. Christmas.

CHAPTER 24

1. The fastest-growing occupation is listed as "wind turbine service technicians," employment of which is expected to grow by 108 percent by 2024.

CHAPTER 25

1. And yes, "labor" is not a "business sector" per se, but it is a crucial component of the economy, as well as highly dependent upon demographics, thus worthy of a little examination.
2. Really? Do I have to remind you? "Due Diligence!"

CHAPTER 26

1. Though not necessarily by race or ethnicity, as none of the major organizations that track demographics break down world, regional, and country populations by these factors in a uniform manner.
2. All figures from United Nations Population Division, *CIA World Factbook*, Pew Research Center, and Worldometers.
3. I personally find this data heartening and had mistakenly believed the number was much lower.
4. The number varies depending upon official recognition of statehood by other countries; i.e., the United States and China do not recognize Taiwan as an official country.
5. From *CIA World Factbook*.
6. And there seems to be a thin demarcation line between what might count as too young, as the apparent differing potential for success between a median age of 15 and 18 appears to be immense. I plan on looking into this further, as I find it fascinating.
7. This would be GDP based on current U.S. pricing; using GDP based on "purchasing power parity," China has the world's largest economy, overtaking the United States by about 1.3 billion "international dollars."
8. As measured by annual and projected growth in gross domestic product by the International Monetary Fund.
9. In short, economists have been studying and debating the impact of population growth on the economy for decades with no clear-cut answer . . . probably because there are just too many variables to consider in examining the issue, variables that make each country's economic situation unique and subject to differing influences from their specific demographics.

CHAPTER 27

1. While Mexico is generally considered part of "North America," some organizations group it with the rest of "Latin America," so for the ease of compiling ROW statistics I am doing so also.
2. Autonomous or dependent territories and areas.
3. According to *CIA Factbook*, as dependencies not ranked by IMF.
4. International Monetary Fund "World Economic Outlook," April 2016.
5. Using current U.S. pricing.
6. One of the highest per capita immigration rates in the world.

CHAPTER 29

1. And, yes, I have uncharacteristically given this generation an exceptionally long birth-year span; however, I am delineating it based on generation-specific commonality rather than for the purposes of comparison.

CHAPTER 31

1. *CIA World Factbook*.
2. *CIA World Factbook*.

INDEX